AF522222

ACTION PLAN AND PRIORITIES IN TOURISM DEVELOPMENT

Action Plan and Priorities in Tourism Development

A.K. SARKAR

KANISHKA PUBLISHERS, DISTRIBUTORS
NEW DELHI-110 002

KANISHKA PUBLISHERS, DISTRIBUTORS
4697/5-21 A, Ansari Road, Daryaganj
New Delhi-110 002
Phones : 2327 0497, 2328 8285
Fax : 011-2328 8285
E-mail: kanishka_publishing@yahoo.co.in

ISBN 978-81-7391-256-4

PRINTED IN INDIA

Published by Madan Sachdeva for Kanishka Publishers, Distributors, 4697/5-21A, Ansari Road, Daryaganj, New Delhi-110 002, Typeset by Sunshine Graphics, Delhi, and Printed at Rajdhani Printers, Delhi.

Preface

The Book *"Action Plan and Priorities in Tourism Development"* is a critical analysis of the nature, motivation and changes in development of Indian Tourism. Tourism industry has rapidly for considerable opportunity for generating a number of socio-economic benefits like promotion of national integration and international understanding, creation of employment opportunities, removal of regional imbalances, and main source of foreign exchange earning for redressing the balance of payment.

The development of tourism may entail a more complete utilisation of the system of infrastructure and of services and in turn improve the productivity of related investment. The building up touristic infrastructure is aimed at extending inter-regional economic ties which promote and accelerate the formation of domestic market. Expansion of transport system increases the ties of the country-side with the tourist resort and promotes the disintegration of natural economy. India, however, faces a lot of problems in building the necessary touristic infrastructure which plays crucial role in accelerating economic development. The development of tourism requires financial resources technical personnel for a large scale exploration and evaluation of the tourist areas which determines the possibility of modern tourism.

The National Tourist Organisation (NTO) is the body responsible for the formulation of national tourist policy. It is the proper agency and instrument for the execution of the central government's responsibilities for the control, direction and promotion of tourism. The objects and functions of the NTO are, therefore, to ensure that the maximum possible value from international tourism accrues to the country for its economic and social benefit. Another important area of the work of a NTO is its role as a spokesman for private tourism industries, to communicate their needs to the government and to strive for a most satisfactory solution. Thus NTO has to mobiles all potential forces and resources available for stimulating the growth and development of tourism.

Marketing and tourism is to be understood as a systematic and co-ordinated execution of business policy by tourist undertakings whether private or state owned, at local, regional, national or International levels to achieve the optimum satisfaction of the needs of identifiable consumer groups and in doing so to achieve an appropriate return. Marketing helps to create new customers by way of first identifying their needs and then trying to satisfying these. Customer satisfaction becomes a crucial part of tourism marketing. The first task of marketer is to identify the customer needs in order to guide the development of the suitable product and services and the second task is to motivate all the potential customers to purchase those products and services.

The tourism industry has to be structured upon several vital segments which need to be related and coordinated with each other. Tourist attraction, accommodation facilities and transport services are, no doubt, the essential of tourism, but these factors, by itself, are independent. Hence an intermediary agency is required to combine test individual elements. If India wants to increase the number of foreign tourists, it needs well connected air services to handle mass arrival tourists and improve internal transport system by road, rail, air, water.

Tourists are generally attracted by measures such as provision of adequate and cheap accommodation, availability of cheaper travel facilities, effective advertisement, well connected transport services from airports and railway stations to tourist centres, building up of a new image abroad and above all making the tourists feel at home in the country of their travel. The air transport has facilitated the entry of more foreigners to India. Several ancillary industries like tourist guide, taxi services, Hoteling etc. thrive on the tourist budgets. The network of well developed air services to Khajuraho have attracted more than lakh of foreign tourists to this spot every year. In term of annual turnover Khajuraho crossed more than 15 million in 1996. The tourist centre has generated a lot of employment potential and income by providing new job opportunities to guides, clay modelers, photographers, hotelkeepers, shopkeepers and other varities of artisans.

A close look at Indian tourism in the last 50 years show that the pattern has not changed very much. In fact it was remained almost static compared to substantial changes that have taken place in the demand pattern in several other part of the world. So far as foreign tourists are concerned, there is no good reason to suppose that the pattern of behaviour of those tourists visiting India will be very different from those visiting other countries.

This title contains seven comprehensive chapter including six appendices and index. First chapter deals with the policy, promotion and practice in the process of development in Indian tourism. Product development and demand pattern has been described in second chapter. Third chapter throws light on the finance development and marketing. Fourth chapter gives a critical analysis of nature and changes in tourism transport and accommodation. Civil Aviation and tourism is discussed in fifth chapter. Chapter sixth describes an air transport services and road transport services has been described in the last chapter of the book. Besides these studies, it includes six appendices.

In completing this study, we have come across a number of books, journal, reports and reviews, etc. which help us to make it perfect. We are thankful to all those scholars who works have been utilised in its compilation. We are also thankful to our friends for their valuable advice.

EDITOR

Contents

1

Tourism Marketing: Policy, Promotion and Practice

Tourism marketing includes all direct and indirect promotional activities to sell travel destination. Realistic establishment of goal is the first step in any intelligent marketing programme. Planning a marketing programme should not be the exclusive responsibility of an official organisation. Various segments of travel industry must extend their support and co-operation. To achieve the maximum impact, all marketing activities should be closely knit.

Marketing and Tourism

Marketing affects all the operations of tourism. The investment in modern tourism are particularly very heavy and the establishment of an adequate infrastructure requires many years. To develop the tourist potentials of a country, there is a need of well planned tourist marketing policy.

According to the Krippendorf "Marketing and Tourism is to be understood as a systematic and co-ordinated execution of business policy by tourist undertakings whether private or state owned, at local, regional, national or international level to achieve the optimum satisfaction of the needs of unidentifiable consumer groups and in doing so to achieve an appropriate return."[1]

This definition stresses that Marketing and Tourism involved co-ordination of policies of several organisations at several levels and it also lays stress on this point that marketing in tourism is concerned with the needs of identifiable consumer groups. Thus Krippendorf defines marketing in tourism in terms very nearly the same as given by British Institute of Marketing.

According to British Institute of Marketing "Marketing is the Management function which organises and directs all those business activities involved in assessing and converting customer purchasing power into effective demand for a specific product or service and in moving the product or service to the final customer or user so as to achieve the profit target or other objectives set by the Company."

Tourism Marketing Policy

There are three factors in working out a tourism marketing policy:

(A) Tourism Product

The product plays an important role in the marketing. As far as the tourist is concerned, the product he buys covers the complete experience from time he leaves home to the time he returns home. A tourist product is not airline seat or a hotel bed or relaxation on a sunny beach but rather a 'package.' The tourist product is a composite product, as an amalgam of attraction, transport, accommodation and of entertainment. All tourists buy either separately, or as an inclusive to the various components of tourist product. An airline seat or a hotel bed is an individual product in the eyes of their producer, but they are merely components of a composite-product. The tourist products is what the country has to offer, viz.:

- *(a)* Architectural Resources;
- *(b)* Natural Resources;
- *(c)* Museums and Monuments; and
- *(d)* Culture.

All these things are to be designed and presented according to the requirements of the tourist. There is a need to determine the sector of the tourism market, it is intended to capture. The size of the sector will depend upon the characteristic of the tourist product. For example, a sea-side resort should not attempt to capture the same market as safari or a tour of historic castles.

The tourist product can be analysed in terms of: (a) Attraction, (b) Facilities. (c) Accessibility.

The attractions are those elements in the tourist product which determine the choice of tourist to visit one destination rather than another. They are the factors which generate a flow of tourists to their location. They may be site attractions or those where the place itself is the major inducement to the tourist to visit it e.g. Niagara Falls, The Swiss Alps, The Grand Canyon, or built attractions such as Disneyland. The event attractions are those where the event staged is a large factor in the tourists choice than the site or e.g. the Olympic Games, the Oberaminergau Passion Play or a Congress or Exhibition.

The tourist facilities are those elements in tourist product which do not normally themselves provide the motivation for tourist flows. The absence of these facilities may deter the tourists from travelling to enjoy the attractions. These facilities complement the attractions. They comprise, accommodation facilities, restaurants, ski-lifts, picnic-sites etc. Absence of accommodation facilities would be an obvious deterrent to tourism.

Accessibility is a last component of the tourist product. It relates to the mode of transportation to the destination chosen by the tourist. It is determined by the proximity of a destination to the tourist place of residence and is best interpreted in terms of time and the cost to reach the destination i.e. as economic distance.

The concept of the product is central to marketing strategy and this applies equally to the marketing of international tourism. From a marketing point of view, the tourism product is defined as an experience of the following components taken together:

1. Accommodation: It is defined as establishments which on a regular or on an occasional basis provides over night facilities for visitors. They may also provide other services as meals which are either ancillary to the accommodation as its main business. It includes all hotels and other traditional form of accommodation, such as boarding houses, motels, inns, holiday villages, tourist complexes, camping sites, youth hostel, spas and other places where the construction is of permanent or semi-permanent nature. Private apartments and furnished rooms in private homes are also included under accommodation.

2. *Natural and Other Resources* : Natural resources refer to such amenities and situation such as waterfalls, mountains, sand, beaches and good climate. Natural scenery, springs, beaches, spas and similar resources are also included. Other resources refer to social, cultural, historical and religious attractions, and economic and technological achievements. It also includes man made attractions such as Taj Mahal etc.

3. *Entertainment* : The entertainment component runs the gamut of all non-sport audience-oriented activity composed of people.

4. *Services* : Services include all operations, designed and performed for the foreign visitor to facilitate his entry, stay and exit. Host attitude towards the foreign visitors are included.

5. *Transportation* : It covers all forms of getting people from one place to another. For example, air transport, rail transport, road transport, water transport etc.

6. *Food and Beverage* : This includes different types of food and beverages.

7. *Recreation* : Recreation includes all non-entertainment activities for relaxation and diversion.

8. *Other Attractions* : It includes items such as shopping opportunities etc.

The truth is that the tourist destination as a product is a very complex one. When we try to promote a destination, it is not just beauty, the antiquity, the charm of destination that alone counts, there are many other factors which go to make up the product as a whole.

Let us take for example the Juhu Beach in Bombay. The Juhu Beach has one of finest sands in the world. As a beach it has few peers. The water is warm all the year around. The bathing is safe, but to sell this destination we need many more things than just the intrinsic qualities of the beach itself. First thing we need is hotels. At present, we have only one hotel and it is always full. We do not need just more hotels but hotels of a good standard, otherwise the primary product becomes unsaleable. Hotels are very essential part of the story. Tourists are also concerned with the transport facilities, coaches and taxis. For every tourist destination, we have to have first class coaches. The tourist is not concerned merely with living in the hotel or with using transport for sightseeing, but while he is in the country, he is to take part of every aspect of the country's life. He is perforce, for the duration, concerned with all the civic amenities available in a destination. If the public transport system is bad, it can affect his enjoyment of the destination. If the street lighting is poor that affects him.

The entire environment he is to spend his time has a bearing on his enjoyment and consequently on the quality of the product. If he finds that he is surrounded by a lot of poverty, filth, squalor etc. he cannot remain unaffected especially if he is unused to such condition and his sensibilities have not been dulled by years of exposure to such things. What is true, say of Juhu Beach and its environment, is true of other destinations. Agra—Delhi—Lahore or Kabul—are all very enchanting places full of tourist reaches, but all in varying degree marred by features which tend to detract from the intrinsic value of the excellence of the product.

While talking of tourist destination, we in the region sometimes tend to think that great mountains, fine beaches and historical monuments alone can make great tourist destinations. There is no doubt that if we have these features, we have an advantage over the areas which do not have such features, but a tourist destination can be developed almost everywhere in the world. A classical example of this is Las Vegas. Las Vegas situated in the middle of desert hundred of miles from any centre of big population or a large city with no history, no great natural attraction to boast of, is one of the most flourishing tourist destinations in the world. Today it has some of the finest hotels, finest night clubs, golf courses, and of course casinos. As in agriculture, what really counts is the output. The output is directly in proportion to input. The only difference between the development of agriculture and the development of a tourist destination is that the tourist destination requires far greater inputs than agriculture. A capital investment required to develop a destination like Las Vegas or Miami or Jamaica or Mexico City is really astronomical. Even in India, it has been estimated that to add amenities for one additional tourist for 15 days, we need a capital investment of Rs. 5,000. To provide the kind and standard of amenities that we are currently providing which by no means compare with we have in Las Vegas or Miami or Mexico City. In order to get one million additional tourists, we in India would require an investment of 500 crores of rupees for providing just the tourism infrastructure and this does not take us into account the national and municipal infrastructure without which no tourist plant can ever function at its optimum efficiency.

What is true to India in this respect is true of all the countries in the region. We all need large investments before we can think it in terms of hosting a large number of tourists which other countries are receiving at present. In other words, even though we have potentially a great product and its intrinsic worth cannot be challenged, in its present state of development, it would be deluding ourselves if we were to say it has an unchallenged sales appeal. The sales appeal of our product will increase in proportion to the investment that we are ready to make in the infrastructure. Greater the output, higher the sales appeal. Some neighbouring countries have already done a fabulous job in this respect. Bangkok immediately comes to one's mind. Iran is also doing a noteworthy job. Hong Kong and Tokyo and Taipei are other such examples.

(B) Tourism Promotion

The second important element in the sale of a product is the promotional efforts that are put in. It is relevant that the promotional efforts made by our other neighbours in this region are somewhat more modest than ours and that is one of the reasons why in the Ministerial Conference of SATC held in New Delhi, it was decided that we should enter into joint promotional efforts in the principal markets of the world. We should have a permanent secretariat charged with the responsibility of joint promotion and sales efforts throughout the world. This is obviously a crying need of the hour. Even after we have all decided to do joint promotion, it is obvious that there are going to be serious limitations to the size of our efforts because the funds available for promotion will be limited and they necessarily have to be limited because they have to bear relation to the total earnings of foreign exchange that the country in this region have. There is widespread realization in all the countries of the region that far larger and concerted promotional efforts is required. If the resolutions adopted by the inter-ministerial conferences are ratified by all the countries concerned, we may well have a promotional programme worthy of the product in the selling of which we all are engaged.

(C) The Price of the Product

The third factor that determines the size of the market is the price. No matter how good our product or how skillful our promotion, if the price of our product is uncompetitive, the volume of the turnover will be small. Unfortunately, our region though no fault of any, suffers from a handicap which is that the price of our product is very high. This is purely due to a geographical position. This factor is more important than the other two factors in so far as the size of the tourist market for this region is concerned. There may be some blemishes in our product but they are not really so important. Our promotion may be small in size and not highly skilled in its execution, but that again is not the reason for our market being so small. The reason why our market is so small is that the price of our product becomes uncompetitive because the air fares or sea fares for getting to our region from the principal markets of USA or Europe are very high. So long as this is so, our respective tourist traffic will remain small as compared to countries in Americas and Europe. Following are the main factors in working out a tourism marketing policy:

1. *Prices* : Price is an essential element of any marketing policy. The number and type of customers depend on it. In the tourist industry, it is a determining factor. In this field the formation of prices is facilitated by the broad range of products that may be offered. For example in a seaside resort the product (beach) may be sold both in first class hotel and in the adjacent camping site.

2. *Distribution Channels* : Distribution sector is constantly developing. It requires regular information about the development of commercial structures. In the tourist industry, this channel has an important part to play. There are various selling methods which are undergoing drastic changes.

3. *The Sales Force* : The success of a tourism marketing policy depends on the personnel who carry it out. It requires a team of well trained persons. Keeping all this in view the W.T.O. has set up a correspondence course. The course is called marketing training for national tourist organisation and tourist enterprise. The courses will be helpful to those dealing with tourism.

4. *Advertising and Sales Promotion* : Advertising and sales promotion is the last element of marketing policy. There is a need for coordination of advertising, promotional activities and

commercial activities at various levels. The choice of subject matter and of media and the size of advertising budgets will vary according to the characteristic of the product and the tourist image which the national tourist offices or the tourist enterprises wish to project. The principal reason that keeps a country's tourist traffic small is the distance from the principal markets of tourism i.e. Europe and America. Distance means cost and that is the most important predetermining factor in the size of the tourist market. Quality, infrastructure and professionalism in the sale of the product are no doubt very important but really not so important as the factor of the cost. In this respect, the countries in the region have to play the game of tourism with a serious handicap. The future of tourism even for this region is bright. The tourism traffic is increasing throughout the world. More and more people in the world have larger and larger discretionary incomes and after they have attained a certain standard of affluence, the money that they spend on travel keeps on going proportional. The result is that the tourist traffic is increasing faster than the growth of any other item in international trade.

Tourist Markets

The tourist market is used to describe a collective of buyers and potential buyers of each tourist product. The total tourist market may be divided into three major segments:

1. The Holiday Tourist.
2. The Business Tourist.
3. The Common Interest Tourist.

1. The Holiday Tourist

The holiday tourist has proved to be very sensitive to price changes. It has been regarded as highly seasonal. The introduction of winter package to the seasonal peaking of demand for holidays is being improved.

2. The Business Tourist

The demand for business tourist is relatively priced inelastic. Businessmen are frequent but of short stay. This kind of tourism will be attracted by event attractions in the shape of exhibitions, trade fairs and conferences.

3. The Common Interest Tourist

This category comprises of the following:

(a) Visits to friends and relatives;

(b) Visitors for educational purposes; and

(c) Visitors for pilgrimages and the like.

The demand for this type of tourism will be priced elastic and also sensitive to the absolute level of price.

The national, local or regional tourist organisations are engaged in a marketing campaign to persuade the potential tourists to visit the country for which it is responsible. The official tourist organisations will seek to create knowledge of its country in particular markets and to persuade visitors thereby to visit their country. The main function of the marketing campaign conducted by official tourist organisation will be provision of information about its country and the resorts within it.

Mass Production and the Markets

Introduction of mass production during the subsequent years in the post-industrialisation period brought about a change. There was an increase in purchasing power of a large number of people. Also rapid industrial advancement placed at the disposal of the consumer a large variety of goods of improved quality and in abundant quantity from large number of competing manufacturers. Supply started exceeding the demand. The consumer's choice began to be limited as a result of mass production. This fact compelled the manufacturers to give greater consideration to the needs of the consumers.

With the rapid industrial advancement, the growth of communication was also witnessed. The advent of mechanized transport, first the railways, and later road transport made the physical distribution of goods possible over much wider areas. The increasing production came to be disposed of over wider areas by means of railways and the road transport. Subsequently, the mass communication means like telegraphs, telephones and the newspapers greatly helped the manufacturers in disposing of their goods and services. This eventually led to the adoption of a new concept i.e., the marketing concept by the progressive and forward looking manufacturing organisations.

Marketing Concept

Marketing has been variously defined through time, by different people. The definition which reflects the latest nature of marketing most adequately is: "Marketing is a human activity directed at satisfying needs and wants through exchange processes. In essence the marketing concept is a customer orientation backed by integrated marketing aimed at generating customer satisfaction. The important aspects of marketing concept are:

(i) Customer Orientation: The companies practising this concept think in terms of the benefits they are selling rather than the products.

(ii) Dual-core Marketing Job: This implies that the first task of the marketer is to identify the customers needs in order to guide the development of the suitable products and services and the second task is to motivate all the potential customers, through various means, to purchase these products and services.

(iii) Integrated Marketing: The customer orientation alone on the part of the management is not enough. To be effective it must be backed by an appropriate organisational set-up within the company. Integrated marketing represents such a set-up. It signifies the substitution of a single logic for several different logics of the various departments of the company. It implies the responsibility of the marketing department to ensure co-ordination of various company actions affecting the buyers.

Application of the marketing concept has certain important benefits. Firstly, the management using this concept realise that customer needs are more basic than particular products. This provides a more reliable and enduring base to the operations of such managements. Secondly, the focus on the customer needs helps the management to spot new product opportunities more speedily. Thirdly, merchandising becomes more effective under this concept. This is because managements view their tasks as that of supplying want satisfaction rather than creating demand for its products among the customers. The physical product is only a part of the satisfactions sought by the buyer because he wants, in addition, conveniences, service and certain other symbolic values. Fourthly, the managements are able to create more harmony between their own interests and those of the society because the market orientation under this concept means that the managements build their future profits through seeking better ways to satisfy human needs.

Having considered the nature and meaning of the marketing concept in general, we now turn to marketing in tourism. It is a well-known fact that as long as the inherent sense of curiosity and adventure dwells in the hearts of human beings, the desire to travel in order to see new sights and experience new things, and to live under different environments, will always grow. It may be presumed that such being the case, marketing in the tourism industry is greatly simplified as part of the process has already been completed by the desire for travel in people. The best example would be that a person may or may not choose a tangible product which has been introduced by a manufacturer in the market, solely depending on his ability to afford it or his likes and dislikes. On the other hand, without exception, all human beings will always nurture a desire to travel in order to see places. The question then arises that if the desire is ever present in people to travel and experience new things, why then would the tourism industry need marketing efforts at all?

At this point the questions arise: Are the marketing problems in tourism so much different from marketing problems in other industries that it is justified to make marketing in tourism a subject for separate and specialised enquiry? Next, to what extent can the concepts and principles, the techniques and methods of marketing which have been applied effectively in other industries be applied to tourism? Answer to both the above questions can be found by identifying and considering the differences between markets for physical, tangible goods on the one hand and the market for tourism on the other. The marketing concept, as the over-riding philosophy of any business undertaking, contrasts with the production orientation. Here the emphasis is on producing goods or services whereafter, a sales policy has to be devised to sell what has been produced. In tourism, on the other hand, the product, from a destination viewpoint is an amalgam of various elements or components, some of which are tangible and some are intangible (services). The only open path for the organisation in this case would be to inform itself about the consumer needs, expectations, attitudes of mind, likes and dislikes in order to formulate and constantly develop the tourist supply components or product.

The marketing concept should, therefore, be understood as a

re-orientation of the business policy and an overhaul of the organisation's or enterprises' management concepts and practices. It helps the tourist organisation or enterprise to establish a consistent and effective communication system with actual and potential tourists in the selected markets or market, and to get to know their wishes, needs, motivations, likes and dislikes in order to be able to condition the tourist supply accordingly. The marketing concept, therefore, facilitates a breakthrough in the tourist system.

Tourism is a very complex industry because of its multifaceted activities which together produce the tourist 'product' and various sub-sectors that are themselves complete industries, if considered independently (lodging industry, transport industry, etc.). Its complexity furthermore, lies mostly in the fact that tourist promotion in its various forms has to be directed at a large number of people in various lands of different socio-economic structures, having different needs, tastes, attitudes, expectations, and behaviour patterns. Efficient marketing is the one which succeeds in penetrating the people's tastes and preferences. The understanding that people are different in the same market helps in planning an efficient marketing strategy.

Defining Tourism Marketing

There are a number of definitions of tourism marketing. Tourism marketing could be defined as the "Systematic and co-ordinated efforts exerted by the NTOs and/or the tourist enterprises on international, national and local levels to optimise the satisfaction of tourists, groups and individuals, in view of a sustained tourism growth." Krippendorf has defined marketing in tourism as follows:

> 'Marketing in tourism is to be understood as the systematic and co-ordinated execution of business policy by tourist undertakings whether private or state owned at local, regional, national or international level to achieve the optimal satisfaction of the needs of identifiable consumer groups, and in doing so to achieve an appropriate return.'

Availability of a Product

Availability of a 'product' is the prerequisite for any organisation which indulges in the marketing function. Unless there is a certain 'product' be it tangible or intangible or a service, marketing is not possible. A 'product' may be defined as the 'Sum of the physical and psychological satisfactions it provides to the buyer.' 'Marketing' by definition is the development of a product to meet the needs of the consumer and then employing the techniques of direct sales, publicity and advertising to bring this product to the consumer.

In the case of tourism product, the basic raw materials would be the country's natural beauty, climate, history, culture and the people. Other aspects would be the existing facilities necessary for comfortable living such as water supply, electricity, roads, transport, communication and other essentials. In other words the tourist product can be seen as a composite product, as the sum-total of a country's tourist attractions, transport, accommodation and of entertainment which hopefully result in consumer satisfaction. The tourist product can be entirely a man-made one or nature's creation improved upon by man. Each of these components of a tourist product is supplied by individual providers of services like hotel company, airlines or other suppliers, and is offered directly to the tourist by them. A consumer can combine these individual tourist products through a large number of ways. There would be many possible destinations, each with a number of hotels, each to be reached by more than one airline. Thus the potential choice facing the consumer is very large.

The growing number of tourist destinations have placed at the disposal of a tourist a large variety of tourist products in abundant quantity from a large number of competing nations. This eventually has led to the adoption of the new concept i.e., the marketing concept in tourism by various countries promoting tourism. The important point about modern marketing is that it applies to situations where the choice can be limited to a relatively small number of brands giving the consumer a reasonable choice. The process of selection thus becomes easier. In the field of tourism this process is taking place by the increasing use of 'package tours.' A package tour is a travel plan which includes most elements of vacation, such as transportation, accommodation, sightseeing and entertainment. The tourist product is a composite product, whether it is sold as a package or assembled by the individual tourist himself or his travel agent. The tourist product can, therefore, be analysed in terms of its attractions, its facilities, and its accessibility.

Attractions

Of the three basic components of a tourist product, attractions are very important. Unless these are there, the tourists will not be motivated to go to a particular place. Attractions are those elements in the tourist product which determine the choice of a particular tourist to visit one particular destination rather than another. The attractions could be *cultural* like sites and areas of archaeological interest, historical buildings and monuments or *scenic* like flora and fauna, beach resorts, mountains, national parks or *events* like trade fairs, exhibitions, arts and music festivals, games, etc.

Facilities

Facilities are those elements in the tourist product which are a necessary aid to the tourist centre. The facilities complement the attractions. These include accommodation, various types of entertainments, picnic sites, recreation and so on. These are indeed important for every tourist centre.

Accessibility

Accessibility is another important component in the tourist product. It is a means by which a tourist can reach the area where attractions are located. Tourist attractions of whatever type would be of little importance if their locations are inaccessible by the normal means of transport. If the tourist attractions are located at places where no means of transport can reach, or where there are inadequate transport facilities, these become of little value. The tourist attractions which are located near to the tourist generating markets and are linked by a network of efficient transport, receive the maximum number of tourists.

Identification of Markets

Identification of markets like that of the product is crucial for any organisation which adopts the marketing concept. In fact the first step a marketing organisation will have to take is to identify its markets. The term 'market' is used in a number of ways. It may be employed to designate the place where the buyer and seller of a good or service meet and between them the exchange transaction takes place. The buyer of goods or services may be the *actual buyer* or the *potential buyer*. It may be used in connection with a particular geographical area or in connection with a particular type of service or product. In the context of marketing and promotion, all of the above aspects are relevant, but especially those related to actual and potential buyers, to product and/or service and to geographical location. An important additional element to be considered is the time factor. The 'market', therefore, can be defined as "the totality of actual and/or potential buyer of a given product or service in a specified geographical location at a given point in time or during a given period of time."

Market Segmentation

A tourist market may be identified corresponding to each tourist product. The term market may be used to describe the collective of actual or potential customers of tourism service or destination. It may apply to the geographical area, a country, region or city from which a service or destination draws customers. The identification of tourist market, a segment of the total market, is of crucial importance. With a view to avoid waste, it is essential to reach only that fraction of the total market which is most likely to be attracted. Due to financial constraints, it is not possible for an organisation to reach the entire market. Segmentation of the market is, therefore, made in order to achieve the most efficient use of marketing resources.

Market segmentation is the process of identifying groups of buyers of the total market with different buying desires or requirements. Most markets are too large for an organisation to provide all the products and services needed by all the buyers in that market. Some delimitation of the market is, therefore, necessary to ensure efficiency and also to conserve financial resources of the organisations. This leads organisations to select target markets necessitating market segmentation. Market segmentation has certain obvious advantages in that the organisation is: *(i)* better placed to spot and compare marketing opportunities, *(ii)* makes finer adjustments of the product and marketing appeals possible to cater to the needs of the buyers, and *(iii)* can develop marketing programmes and budgets on the basis of a clearer idea of the response characteristics of specific market segments.

The markets are divided on the basis of several factors. The most commonly used bases of market segmentation include: *(i)* geographic segmentation, under this the market is divided into different geographic locations such as cities, provinces, regions or countries, *(ii)* demographic segmentation, this is on the basis of demographic variables such as age, sex, occupation, income, education, social class, religion etc.; *(iii)* psychographic segmentation: This is on the basis of psychographic variables which refer to such aspects of an individual as his life style, personality, buying motives and product knowledge and use.

In tourism, market segmentation is very important. The strategy of market segmentation in tourism recognises that few vacation areas are universally acceptable and desired. Therefore, rather than to waste promotion resources trying to please all travellers, the best market strategy is to isolate those segments of the entire market which are likely prospects and aim at the promotional efforts specifically to the wants and needs of these selected groups. Thus, one of the early steps in marketing tourism is to divide the present and potential market on the basis of meaningful characteristics and then concentrate promotion, supply and pricing efforts on serving these most prominent sections of the market—the target markets. Usually the market segmentation for tourism is in terms of the following criteria: demographic, geographic, psychographic, social and economic.

For example market for particular area might be largely archaeologists in their middle years who have an income of over $ 40,000 per year and who live in mid-eastern United States, or it might be largely businessmen in the age group of say 40-60 years who have an income of over $ 50,000 per year and who live in southern parts of West Germany. In tourism marketing, the total tourism market can be divided into above major segments. A further segmentation however is possible within each of the above major segments for practical marketing purposes and includes:

(i) The Vacation Tourist: The vacation or the holiday tourist is the most common and popular tourist. He is immensely affected by changes in price, and is easily influenced by skilled and aggressive marketing effort. This type of tourist is resort-oriented (Rome, Bombay, New York, London, Paris are resorts as much as Venice, Goa, Pattaya, Miami). The vacation tourist market has been regarded as highly seasonal.

(ii) The Business Tourist: In recent years the market for this type of tourist has increased greatly. The choice of destination of a

business tourist is generally determined by the nature of his business. The marketing efforts will not influence much the choice of the business tourist. As in the case of vacation tourist who has proved to be very sensitive to price changes, the demand for business tourism is relatively price-inelastic. The demand will tend to be big city-oriented. The visits are of shorter duration and relatively frequent. The trade fairs, conventions, exhibitions, conferences and similar other events attract this kind of tourism.

(iii) The Common Interest Tourist: This segment comprises visits to relatives and friends, and visits for the purpose of education, for pilgrimages, etc. Demand for this type of tourism will be relatively price-elastic. The common interest tourist will not be very readily influenced by the promotional efforts. The average length of his stay will be relatively longer. Because of his friends and relatives, he will not be a significant user of hotel and other such type of accommodation. The visits will not be frequent and expenditure relatively little on his stay as compared with the other two groups.

Concept and Role

In every hotel, airline or, for that matter, any other organisation, there are always two existing conditions, moving forward or slipping backward, and it is well-known that economic forces abhor a static situation. While much may be done, still so much more remains undone and the best use has to be made of the dynamism that is inherent in a situation in the wake of future challenges. How to meet the challenge of the future? The answer is both easy and difficult. It is easy in the sense that marketing provides a ready solution but it is not so easy, if a total marketing concept is not the objective of an organisation. It is this latter philosophy of a total concept that must pervade throughout the length and breadth of a hotel or an airline to give it what it needs, to face the future challenges successfully.

Let us now start with defining what "marketing" is. Most of us know something about marketing, but we seem to appreciate only the part we play in an organisation and a part is never the whole. When a sales manager talks about marketing, he is in fact referring to selling only. An advertising executive thinks of marketing as advertising and a public relations officer or consultant, as public relations and a department store manager refers to marketing as retailing or merchandising, while a field salesman assumes it to be personal selling. All these individual and functional approaches are only but part of the total philosophy of marketing. Prof. McNair of Harvard defined marketing "as the creation and delivery of a standard of living to society," as an ultimate objective. We may use another definition which is comparatively more exhaustive and brings out the qualifying conditions clearly. "Marketing is a total system of inter-acting business activities, the design to plan, price, promote and distribute want-satisfying products and services, to present and potential customers." This definition takes into account management concepts inasmuch as it refers to managerial functions like planning, organising, directing and controlling. It refers to a whole system of business activities which are customer-oriented and is directed to the creation and satisfaction of customers. It also envisages dynamic processes of a total system of interacting business activities.

It will thus be noted that this definition starts with a gem of an idea and progresses on to the stage of satisfaction of the customer's wants. It also refers to both present and future customers and incorporates an idea of development with a maximum of effectiveness and a minimum of cost. Briefly, this definition not only sets out the functions but the elements that comprise a whole concept of marketing. It also establishes a healthy relationship between production and consumption and seeks to prevent a decreased level of economic activity. The economy in an under-developed country, in particular, is subject to various internal and external economic forces and, as such, nursing it calls for a lot of courage, revolutionary zeal and considerable amount of farsightedness so as to achieve a stage of self-generation and self-sufficiency.

Similarly for an airline or a hotel, seeking to be successful in meeting future challenges, growth and profitability, marketing must come to the fore and a more scientific assessment and management of the situation is necessary. By adopting the marketing concept as a practical philosophy and then implementing it would meet the requirements of the situation. Before proceeding further, we must clarify another important distinction between a marketing concept and marketing. The marketing concept is a philosophy i.e., an attitude, a course of business *thinking,* while marketing by itself is a course of *action.* Not only must an organisation from top to bottom be guided to adopt this type of thinking but, for effectiveness and achievement of the desired results, correct follow up action is called for. It is not only that the marketing people alone adopt this philosophy for management and concerted action but administrators and managers in-charge of other departments like production, engineering, operations, finance, etc. also fall in line and approach problems in their true perspective. Marketing cannot successfully operate in isolation.

For an airline to realise the full fruits of marketing, a marketing approach must influence activities for better organisation, co-ordination and implementation. The chief executive must try to look at problems not only from the point of view of each individual department, but in the light of the total picture that he places before himself for the success and growth of his organisation in future. The conception, planning and implementation of this policy, under the chief marketing executive, is what is roughly referred to as marketing management. What are the elements that characterise this marketing concept? The focal point is the customer and serving his needs is the basic objective. It is this philosophy that must be recognised and adopted by the organisation. It emphasises that:

(i) The airline/hotel recognises the customer's strategic position as determinant of its fortunes;

(ii) Customer creation and satisfaction of his needs can be planned;

(iii) An integrated system of marketing action, through continuous, long and short range planning, supplemented by strategies, is a key element in the concept;

(iv) The importance of market research as a foundation for planning is recognised; corporate goals and market potential influence management action;

(v) Integrated marketing action and effort throughout the organisation is sought and should prevail;

(vi) A climate for improved services and/or product innovation is accepted as necessary, horizontally and vertically in an organisation; and

(vii) A marketing focus pervades all objectives and goals and

influences modifications to meet changing passenger/ guest demand and opportunities in an airline or a hotel.

An organisation, adopting the marketing concept as outlined above, would not only recognise the sovereignty of the customer, but ensure that all interaction of people and programmes in that organisation be directed towards satisfying his present demand and meeting his future requirements.

Objectives

Before proceeding to discuss the basic elements of marketing management, it has to be assumed that every organisation has certain well-defined objectives. There must be a goal towards which all the efforts of an organisation are directed. These objectives would not only be clearly defined but be known to all the concerned people, and clearly understood at all decision-making levels. Let us see what the general objectives of a transportation organisation, for example, could be:

(*a*) to provide fast, frequent, regular, reliable and efficient transportation services for passengers, cargo and mail at reasonable cost to the public;

(*b*) to establish an integrated transportation system satisfying the needs of the public with well co-ordinated growth and defence potential; and

(*c*) to run the system at a reasonable profit and not as a burden on the general public.

However, caution against confusing "objectives" with "policies", practices or procedures must be exercised. These objectives will obviously change with different industries, organisations, companies and other corporate bodies.

Planning

Having examined the question of objectives, we should now consider how to achieve these and determine the manner in which we would direct our efforts. Obviously, our proposed actions would be co-ordinated and crystallised into a plan of action. This is planning. We would work out short- and long-term plans to cover the various areas of planned activities and goals, departmentally, geographically, or by each particular desired activity. Nothing would be done unless it formed part of a programmed plan directed to achieving the set objectives. Plans again, it may be noted, are clearly distinguishable from 'strategy' or tactics which are but special steps consistent with present conditions to implement the plans. The mediate and immediate plan, covering short and long range objectives in various departments, like engineering, operations, finance, commercial and personnel, would be established not in isolation from one another but in complete co-ordination, and from which would evolve the total plan of action in an organisation. The steps would formulate a systematic approach to planning, set out clear goals, eliminate confusion amongst groups involved and ensure that these are clearly and quickly understood. It would also lay down marketing strategies in the light of the objectives and specific action required of each area of responsibility, together with succinct reasons, budgets, sales goals as well as objectives for advertising, public relations and sales promotion strategies.

The methodology of planning and the process identified to achieve objectives are essential, with a step by step programme for each element clearly marked out. Tentative approaches as to programmes and, in some cases, priorities in the achieving of these objectives may be considered, but it must not be forgotten that appropriate planning envisages a scientific approach to future growth and development after careful examination, consideration and evaluation of various factors rather than a haphazard, casual and slipshod attempt at dealing with the future of an organisation. It may be stressed that the need for formulating a well-defined, well-co-ordinated and well-programmed plan for achieving the aims and objectives of an organisation is imperative for its success.

Organisation

Having prepared a plan of action, we must have a proper organisation for the implementation of the plan with a view to achieving the objectives set out with the best of co-ordination and highest degree of efficiency. The end picture of this process is a marketing organisation. In creating a good organisation, we have to ensure a proper definition, division and location of responsibilities with a professional approach. Factors which determine the type of structure of an organisation would be the size and type of its organisation, market, the distribution channels, specialised functions, sales force, etc., and inter-relations with other departments.

Close co-ordination is a matter of necessity within and outside the marketing organisation. Within the marketing department itself, the special areas of responsibilities cover the marketing research, field sales, sales outlets, distribution channels, advertising, public relations, customer service, etc. but all these need to have a common pervading outlook, conditioned by the overall marketing objectives of an organisation. Setting up of an organisation involves creating a structure and staffing i.e., the assembling of suitable human resources in specific positions with line and staff functions clearly defined to undertake specific responsibilities. Providing suitable executive and non-executive personnel is the key to a successful marketing organisation which should operate in an environment stimulating the people of the organisation to exercise their capabilities to the fullest.

Marketing Functions

It may be useful to tabulate the principal marketing functions of an organisation and signify, in general, the areas of responsibility covered. These functions include:

(a) marketing research, relating to product services/sales distribution, advertising effectiveness, etc. both desk and field work;

(b) stocking and warehousing of product/services. This includes for example for the airlines and hotels, the reservation organisations/space and occupancy controls system;

(c) sales outlets; through points of sale:

  (i) company showrooms e.g., booking offices for airlines or hotel front offices etc.; and

  (ii) distributors/agents, like travel agents for hotels and airlines, supermarkets etc.;

(d) field sales: field sales staff, who cover commercial, educational and official organisations; liaison with agents/distributors, specialise in bulk sales (like tourism/conventions) or products (passenger, cargo, mail for

transportation companies); (room, food/beverage services in hotels) etc.;

(e) Media and merchandising

(i) advertising,

(ii) public relations, and

(iii) sales promotion activities, like merchandising activities; exhibitions, fairs, etc.;

(f) Customer service

To look after complaints of customers and attend to special requirements or problems of customers;

(g) Product development

It includes review of existing offering and proposals for new ones based on market research and technical advice.

The marketing structure would depend on individual factors relating to an organisation as stated earlier, but it should present an accurate picture of each marketing function and its inter-relationship, and be so designed as to secure a clear understanding of the duties, responsibilities and line of authority of various executives. With larger and more diversified organisations, territorial, product, specialist and technical responsibilities may be represented and the organisation would be enlarged accordingly. Some organisations may include the training and relevant administrative functions also in the marketing organisation structure.

Operating and Directing

Having set up an organisation, it now remains to execute the plan decisions. The plan may be excellent, and a suitable staff hierarchy may exist, but if the defined plan is not implemented effectively, everything will come to naught. It is, therefore, not only important to ensure that the field sales forces act in a particular manner, but the advertising and promotional campaign follows a plan; a system of outlets and channels of distribution of goods and services has been created to meet the demand, and that a marketing programme has been chalked out and implemented in complete co-ordination with and understanding of the plan directed by the chief marketing executive. Without directions, no organisation will thrive and direction or control in this sense is intended to give a forward and upward lift to an organisation and guide it through any difficulties that may arise.

However, guidance should not imply interference in the normal functioning of an organisation or in the execution of the responsibility of each individual. The guidance envisaged here normally manifests itself through controls which fall into the following categories:

(i) controls for general supervision;

(ii) controls for a regular and periodical inspection;

(iii) controls to determine that the functions are performed according to schedules;

(iv) controls for corrective action; and

(v) controls for measuring of the general doings of a particular unit.

The above controls are self-evident and do not need any clarification or elucidation. However, the final management process in this behalf may include the following areas:

(a) analysis of net sales volume—total, and by territories;

(b) analysis of costs;

(c) evaluation of performance and productivity of sales outlets and salesmen; and

(d) evaluation of advertising and marketing programmes.

The process of controls envisages a pre- and post-mortem analysis which operates as a management corrective and assists in placing the activities of a marketing organisation in its correct perspective. It may be pertinent to add that an analysis and evaluation of a programme, alone and by itself, will not guide marketing management to arrive at a right decision on marketing problems in the absence of a correct marketing policy. Marketing policies are, therefore, established to cover every phase of a programme.

What is a marketing policy? It is management views and directions on a course of action to be followed in a given set of circumstances and is different from plans, principles and procedures. Policies are rules which help an organisation to achieve marketing goals e.g., cover quality of service, standards of operation, prices, etc. These are policies and not plans. In order that a marketing programme achieves the desired success, marketing policies have to be clearly defined. These have to be flexible as well as reasonably stable; comprehensive and progressive. These have to be known and well understood throughout an organisation and must be complementary to be general management policies and based on careful appraisal of the aims and objectives of an organisation. As stated earlier, policies are guiding lights for a marketing organisation and assist it in decision-making processes and achieving and assessing results.

Having examined in general and in outline marketing and marketing concepts, policies and planning, functions and areas of responsibility, and the creation and control of a relevant organisation, we may now proceed with the study in some detail of the marketing functions.

Market Research

Research means a careful inquiry or investigation: the effort to find such information by experiment or by investigation; diligent inquiry or examination in seeking facts or principles, to search or examine with continued care. No research is worth anything unless it has done these things. Market refers to the place or method of contact between a buyer and seller and it may be relatively simple, direct and personal or it may be a highly organised institution or it may be almost an abstraction, such as the "tourist market" or "airline market." A study and appraisal of market features and factors, with a view to adopting a correct marketing policy, is the basic function of market research.

Market research has been defined as "the systematic, objective and exhaustive search for and study of the facts relevant to any problem in the field of marketing." There is no universally accepted definition on 'market research' but for our purpose we use the definition adopted by the American Marketing Association as follows:

> "Market Research is the inclusive term which embraces all research activities carried on in connection with the management of marketing work. It includes various subsidiary types of research such as:

1. Market analysis which is a study of the size, location, nature and characteristics of markets.
2. Sales analysis (research) which is largely an analysis of sales data.
3. Consumer research, of which motivation research is a type, concerned chiefly with the discovery and analysis of consumer attitudes, reactions and preferences.
4. Advertising research, which is carried on chiefly as an aid to Management."

Market research is, therefore, the discovery and assembling of all useful and pertinent facts about the customer, the prospect, the competition, the product, the sales force, advertising, and the results achieved. Further, it envisages the whole spectrum of activities which establishes a qualitative and quantitative picture of a particular situation. Some of the important aspects are discussed briefly below:

1. *Research on the Customer (the Market):* As regards the customer, we must identify him and know who he is, who is not our customer, where he is, what are his likes and dislikes, what is his capacity to buy, how he spends his money, what is our competition, who is taking away business from us and why. In respect of a market, it is important to analyse whether in respect of travel, e.g., it is a pleasure market or a commercial or an industrial market and so on, but in general, research in respect of markets would consist of:

(*a*) analysis of the size of the market;

(*b*) estimating demand for products and services;

(*c*) sales forecasting;

(*d*) determining the characteristic of the market;

(*e*) analysing sales potential and relative benefits of territories; and

(*f*) studying trends in market size and composition.

So far as *competition* is concerned, we must ascertain who our competitor is, who takes away business from us or *what* could take business away from us, who is not our competitor and why not, who can take away what from us and, lastly, whose business we can profitably take away and how.

2. As regards research on offerings and services, our study and analysis would encompass the following areas:

(*a*) use of present products and services;

(*b*) sources of customer dissatisfaction;

(*c*) reasons for customer acceptance;

(*d*) evaluating new products or services;

(*e*) simplifying sales methods; and

(*f*) what new lines could be introduced and what old unprofitable lines could be dropped.

3. *Research on Sales Methods and Policies:* In appraising the effectiveness and implementation of marketing policies, the under-noted aspects call for attention:

(*a*) usefulness or otherwise of sales offices;

(*b*) setting up of sales territories;

(*c*) evaluating present and proposed sales methods;

(*d*) studying competitive pricing and sales targets;

(*e*) analysing salesman activity and effectiveness; and

(*f*) studying distribution costs.

4. *Research on Advertising:* It is important to make a systematic analysis of usefulness and effectiveness of advertising and the areas noteworthy are:

(*a*) evaluation of advertising in terms of response;

(*b*) analysing competitive advertising and selling practices;

(*c*) selection of advertising media; and

(*d*) making qualitative studies.

5. *Channels of Distribution:* Through market research, one can establish a profile of the market available with clearly defined sectors like industrial, commercial, personal and goods, etc., as in transportation. In reaching these markets, one has to apply appropriate marketing techniques and, where necessary, establish special selling and distribution channels. These channels may either deal with the customer directly or through middlemen i.e. the agents. Here again, an analysis of its existing selling channels and proposed ones could be subject of research and review and would, inter alia, consider the following:

(a) the effectiveness of own offices;

(b) do these help in building up and meeting demand?

(c) do these help in the improvement of a corporate image?

(d) how do we handle bulk markets, like industrial markets?

(e) what techniques are employed in dealing with commercial markets?

(f) are advertising programmes effective?

(g) are promotional strategies directed towards eliminating weaknesses?

(h) an analysis of travel agents, their status, productivity, efficiency, financial stability, and integrity is a continuous process. An airline or a hotel would study what is their revenue from agents, who are most productive, who specialise and in what type of traffic, who are effective, what new agents could produce traffic, who should be eliminated and whether there is appropriate geographical coverage of areas and servicing and promotion from special sectors of business.

Marketing Mix

The areas of research listed above i.e., of customers, competition, product analysis, sales method and policies, distribution channels, and advertising effectiveness are important elements of the market mix. Combined with a study of the impact of these factors, a highly successful marketing plan or programme, with appropriate strategy tailor-made for the organisation, could be built on these elements. It should also take into account the inter-play of the following economic and other forces:

(i) Company's own resources;

(ii) General economic conditions;

(iii) Governmental regulations and thinking; and

(iv) International factors.

The marketing mix would also provide a check-list on areas in which management action may be called for from time to time. The concept of the mix is a valuable one and plays an important part in marketing.

Collecting the Data

An important step in marketing research is collecting the relevant data. Data collection is done in two ways *(a)* by desk research, and *(b)* by field research. Desk research would begin at home i.e., with the organisation's own records, which would indicate trends in the current and historical perspective of the share of the market, sales by territories, by different distribution channels, by products or services and the effectiveness of show-rooms or retail outlets, field sales and advertising, sales promotion activities as well as the costs structure of these services. Desk research would also establish the competitive standing of the organisation in the market and provide a performance audit of the organisation related to its goals. The second aspect of desk research comprises analysis of consumer characteristics like population growth, age groups, sex, migration, education, occupation, economic factors, habits, customs, buying attitudes, standards of living, etc. and also appraisal of commercial intelligence obtained from official publications, public data, information and statistics from trade, business and other sources. An evaluation of government policies and their past impact and possible future interaction on organisation's activities would also come under this head.

Field research would cover external investigation for specific matters and particular issues, either by the organisation's own staff or through outside specialists or agencies. It is accomplished through interviews based on a questionnaire and field surveys. Interviews are carefully arranged, conducted under specified guidelines which are closely followed. The construction of an appropriate questionnaire calls for skill and much would depend on its suitability and clarity. The supervisors would be well advised to keep a check on the process of collecting the data for errors, misinformation and evasion. When a 'yes' or 'no' reply is not forthcoming, the interviewer should not hesitate to summarise the views of the person interviewed in order to ensure accuracy and eliminate infructuous responses. What constitutes a satisfactory sample for purpose of a survey depends on the merits of each case, but its numerical proportion should be wide enough to produce a representational response. In-depth interviews supplement or clarify information obtained through a questionnaire and assist in arriving at behaviour patterns of customers on specific issues.

Tabulate and Analyse Data

The tabulation of the data collected is the next most important step and should be done in a systematic manner. A statistical approach is the guiding principle in tabulation of the data and its analysis.

Interpreting Data and Making Recommendations

Having tabulated and analysed the data, the next process is that of interpreting the same and making recommendations on the basis of a careful appraisal of facts and figures. The researcher draws his conclusions from the data analysed and develops his recommendations on responses to each question. This is a specialised job and has to be done after careful evaluation of all the data available and not on piecemeal information. The recommendations have to be fully backed by historical and up-to-date statistics and supporting facts. There can be no emotion or hunches about making recommendations emerging naturally and definitively from the data collected. It should, however, be appreciated that research has to assume some burden of prediction and there may be no perfect predictions and none to substitute management decisions, within restricted areas of uncertainty.

Prepare a Written Report

Having arrived at definite conclusions and formulated recommendations, it now remains to prepare a written report. This report will also refer to the methods used in its compilation and must be one based objectively on facts and data collected. Justifications and explanations for shortcomings and deficiencies should play no part in such a report.

Follow-up of Report

Having secured a report, it is necessary to have follow-up action on it and if a report is not followed up, it is obvious that it would mean time, opportunity and, no doubt, money lost. It is sometimes said for non-implementation of a report that the market research study has brought out no new facts and, therefore, nothing was done to implement the suggestions. Certain conclusions may only be known to the higher management concerned, but communication of details to the relevant personnel is a must. Again, market research is a dynamic process and conditions are continuously changing and new perspectives may be revealed and offered for action to marketing management.

It must also be recognised that the future growth and prosperity of a living organisation does not depend merely on supplying the present demand but on anticipating, creating and meeting it in the future. In order to create the right kind of demand and plenty of it, it must set its sights upon new methods and new services and only then can it reach new horizons. Without the basic tools of market research and scientific marketing, achieving the organisation's objectives would be difficult. In the future, new scientific disciplines may bring to bear new techniques, new methods which could offer greater promise, both qualitatively and quantitatively.

Both within a individual organisation and the socio-economic system, modern marketing is the key to successful economic expansion. In fact, one of the most significant achievements anticipated over the next several years is the greater public understanding and appreciation of the social and economic values of scientific marketing and it is certain that the quest for a "science of marketing" will be intensified.

2

Product Development and Demand Pattern

The Product Development and Demand Pattern amounts to talking about tourism in terms of demand and supply. It means taking tourism off the pedestal and putting it in the market place. This may offend the susceptibilities of some people, particularly in our country, whose approach to tourism is mainly ideological. But to be professional one should adopt the more realistic market approach and concentrate on the nitty-gritty of tourism. Of course, the ideological approach is not surprising because the initial motivation of a majority of visitors to India seems to be culture, history, architecture, religion and what is generally called the mystique of India.

The Department of Tourism lumps together all such visitors under the category—Cultural Tourism. The last official survey of foreign tourists made by the Indian Institute of Public Opinion (IIPO) in 1972-73 describes the factors responsible for attracting visitors to India as follows: "Curiosity (42 per cent) and Indian art and civilisation (34.1 per cent) were the two most important motivating factors. Another factor that motivated one in six among the tourists interviwed was that he or she had the opportunity to travel in the vicinity due to business or had travelled a lot but not to this region. Knowledge from previous trips prompted about 15 per cent to revisit India."

A later survey of foreign tourists in 1973-74 conducted by the

Indian Market Research Bureau on behalf of the Travel Agents Association of India confirmed that more than 80 per cent tourists interviewed mentioned more or less the same reasons that attracted them to India.

A close look at Indian tourism in the last few years shows that the pattern has not changed very much. In fact it has remained almost static compared to substantial changes that have taken place in the demand pattern in several other parts of the world. Nevertheless the IIPO survey makes a surprising statement in the chapter called "The Changing Structure of Foreign Tourist Demand." It says, "So far as foreign tourists are concerned, there is no good reason to suppose that the pattern of behaviour of those tourists visiting India will be very different from those visiting other countries. The world growth pattern of tourism follows the growth pattern of air travel both for the world area and the Pacific." The survey apparently confuses structure of tourist demand with the growth rate of tourism.

What are the basic features of the pattern which has remained more or less unchanged? First, two-thirds or more visitors come from what are described as high spending areas: North America, Western Europe, Australia, New Zealand and Japan. In fact the Tourist Department's statistics show that the number of visitors from high spending areas increased from 60 per cent in 1960-61 to 68 per cent in 1972-73. Within this pattern a few noticeable changes in the last few years have taken place: while tourists from Japan, the Soviet Union and Eastern Europe have increased, the North American market has remained more or less static with the result that the share of Western Europe, Australia and Japan has considerably increased. However the US market is showing signs of revival in the last few months. Another noticeable change is the spurt in visitors from Gulf area in the last few years. The ethnic traffic consisting of Indians domiciled abroad and holding foreign passports has considerably increased but in percentage it declined from 13.8 in 1968-69 to 11.2 in 1972-73. This puts paid to the view that a substantial number of visitors consist of Indians who are phoney tourists. Even more significant is the relatively small growth rate in group traffic and in visitors from neighbouring countries. Group traffic still accounts for only about ten per cent of the total.

Let us, for a moment, look at the profile of the tourist. The IIPO survey makes the following observations: Between 1968-69 and

1972-73 the number of middle income groups increased from eight to 20 per cent and affluent tourists with incomes above Rs. 100,000 a year increased from 27.5 to 35.7 per cent. While the percentage of visitors above 50 years remained the same, at about 16 per cent, the percentages in the age groups of 17-30 years and 31-50 years substantially altered in favour of the former.

The question we should answer is: On the supply side are we developing the product in keeping with the demand pattern? The official policy seems to be flying in the face of the nature of demand. For instance, it has been announced that no 4- and 5-star hotels will be built in the public sector and as far as possible would not be encouraged in the private sector. The allocations under the Plan are also slanted towards creating facilities for the comparatively small segment of middle income and lower income group tourists. Fortunately the market forces have proved stronger. In 1963 the total number of approved hotel rooms was 7,085 and of these 2,126 or 30 per cent were in 4- and 5-star establishments. On 31st March 1976 the total approved hotel rooms were 14,992 of which nearly 40 per cent were in 4- and 5-star categories. (No formal classification has taken place in the last six or seven years with the result that 88 establishments comprising 6,427 rooms or nearly 36 per cent have been approved but not classified.

Hence the figure of 40 per cent is based on the category which is claimed by the unclassified hotels as likely to be awarded.) According to the IIPO survey, 47 per cent tourists expressed preference for 4- and 5-star hotels but only 39 per cent were able to find accommodation in such establishments. In other words the trend in new hotel construction is that despite official discouragement private enterprise is gradually meeting the unfulfilled demand. Similar developments are noticeable in the transport sector. During the last few years there have been considerable improvements in tourist coaches and buses, in railway facilities and more significantly in aircraft used for domestic services.

A meaningful discussion of product development must take into account the changes of the last few years and the likely changes during the succeeding years. Unfortunately the economic data available to us is three or four years old, compiled before the sudden increase in the costs of fuel and energy in November 1973, and before the serious inflation and recession of 1974 and 1975.

There has hardly been any research done by the Department of Tourism or by the industry to evaluate the current pattern or to forecast the future. The official forecast for 800,000 visitors by the end of 1978 and a million by the end of 1980 are more in the nature of targets or morale boosters than forecasts based on economic indicators and market appraisals.

While the one million figure need not be taken seriously as a forecast it does indicate that we attach great importance to numbers. There is nothing wrong with playing the numbers game—most of the countries are doing the same—but is our planning and marketing strategy geared to this objective? For a country of the size of India, mass tourism would not start until we have reached the figure of four or five million visitors. If the experience of other countries provides any guidance mass tourism cannot originate from distant markets. European countries, Canada, Mexico and the Caribbean receive a majority of tourists from neighbouring countries. Nearer home Thailand, Malaysia, Singapore and now Philippines, the Asian countries in the one million visitor league, are not getting the million from Europe and North America. More than 50 per cent come from other ASEAN countries or from Japan. Secondly, there has been a great upsurge of tourism in the sun, sand and sea. Like India, Spain, Greece and Italy are also countries with a great history. But in keeping with this new trend they have developed sea resorts. The same has been done by Yugoslavia, Bulgaria, Turkey, the Soviet Union and by Mexico, Venezuela and Egypt. In the last few years we have witnessed a similar upsurge in the seaside holiday traffic to Bali, Sri Lanka and to small islands like Mauritius, Seychelles and the Maldives.

All these years we have not done much either in promoting traffic from the neighbouring countries or in developing beach resorts around south India. Of course, there are practical difficulties in attracting visitors from Pakistan, Sri Lanka, Nepal, Burma and Bangladesh. It is also true that India's image in the tourist world is not that of a holiday destination and it is not easy to change the image. But if tourism featured at the national level in major policy decisions I believe that many of the practical difficulties would have been overcome. Unfortunately tourism does not find a place among important economic activities. Secondly, are we emotionally prepared to accept hordes of holiday makers.

We can change the image only if we make ourselves emotionally ready first, and this may involve a shift in our approach to tourism. Of course, it is not for a moment advocated that any country should change its way of life to suit tourists' likes and dislikes. But even as things are we can certainly attract 100,000 may be 200,000 visitors to our sea beaches provided we developed half a dozen seaside resorts fairly quickly. So far the development has been too slow and too little. This could be a new and supplementary segment of the tourist market. A hundred thousand tourists injected into south India which at present is not visited by more than ten per cent visitors would change the tourist picture of that region. But to do this we have to upgrade the airports at Goa and Kovalam to enable larger aircraft to land there and we will have to follow an 'open skies' policy. You can't sell beach holidays if aircraft land at Bombay and the tourists have to find their way to Goa and Kovalam or other resorts in south India. To build up beach holiday traffic of one to two hundred thousand to add to the present overall figure we have to allow a hundred or two hundred charters a year to land in Bombay, Delhi and Calcutta. So far Air India has not allowed even its own charter company to be more than a paper tiger.

Then we will see a radical change in the demand pattern as has taken place elsewhere. For instance, in Sri Lanka until six or seven years ago the tourist pattern was more or less the same as in India: cultural tourism predominated and group traffic was less than ten per cent. Now 60 per cent tourists come in groups, by charters or by scheduled services, but their primary motivation is a seaside holiday. They hardly spend more than a day in Colombo. The average duration of stay in Sri Lanka has increased from six days to eleven and a half days. It is true that there are a variety of promotional fares available from Europe to India. Why not make use of them instead of allowing a large number of TGCs, ITCs and OTCs? However since my main concern is with promoting group traffic, the charters are only one of the means and back-to-back charters generally make it easier to sell a destination. Also the declaration of an open skies policy alone is not enough; there must also be a matching provision of infrastructure, accommodation, transportation and other facilities. Until now our insistence that charters can land nowhere else except at the four main international airports has also acted as a powerful disincentive.

Since we have a favourable trade balance with Sri Lanka why couldn't we allow our people to travel to Sri Lanka and provide a foreign exchange loan to that small country to enable its citizens to visit us? After all we have given a loan of Rs. 50 million to Sri Lanka to buy our exports; why not for tourism also? Since we have been able to open up communications, transport and trade with Pakistan in the last few months; why not also think in terms of opening up the tourist channels?

One could legitimately argue that we don't want cheap holiday traffic, nor a large influx of visitors who are really not tourists from the neighbouring countries. Again judged by the experience of other countries the non-tourist visitors will predominate in the initial phases but gradually genuine tourist traffic will start building up between us and the neighbouring countries. In any case we can't have it both ways: If we consider that it is unfair to compare our visitor arrival figures with those of European countries, or of Singapore and Malaysia because they receive a good part of their traffic from next door, then it is up to us to promote holiday traffic plus uninhibited influx of visitors from countries nearby. We don't have to love every ton of iron ore that we export, nor like the type of visitor we are getting so long as he fulfils the definition of a tourist, which means he spends his own money here.

With our present emphasis on selective markets the number of arrivals has increased from 1,40,000 in 1961 to 465,000 in 1975, an increase of 320 per cent. The foreign exchange earnings have increased from Rs. 190 million to Rs. 1,040 million. But there has been an increase of 300 per cent in the wholesale price index from 1961 to 1975, which means that at the 1961 price the foreign exchange earnings in 1975 were Rs. 345 million, an increase of only 81.5 per cent, or an annual compound increase of 4.45 per cent. It is my hunch that the rate of growth of earnings from tourism was actually higher than that indicated by the official figures. The prestigious research magazine called International Tourism Quarterly published by the Economist Intelligence Unit, in its issue (February 1976) published a new type of series of tourist statistics based on volume and not numbers. The *per diem* expenditure of tourists in India was shown as US $ 18 in 1996 and for our neighbouring countries, Afghanistan, Pakistan and Sri Lanka it was US $ 26 to 28 a day. The consumer price index of India in 1973 was about the same as of the neighbouring countries.

Believe it or not, India's figure was the second lowest of the 73 countries covered by the ITQ which means that either India was the cheapest country in the world in 1997 or that our tourist industry is so inefficient that it didn't provide sufficient opportunities to tourists to spend their money. Both propositions are obviously wrong. What is wrong is our economic data? Small wonder that studies based on these figures have come to the conclusion that tourism's economic impact on India is negligible.

It all boils down to our taking long-term policy decisions regarding our goals and to developing a conceptual framework for planning and marketing in order to achieve the goals. Call it Perspective Planning— to use the Indian planner's idiom—if you like. The argument that tourism is such a rapidly changing phenomenon that at best one can lay down guidelines, is a confession of bankruptcy in policy making. The global price structure of commodities also keeps on changing; nevertheless certain commercial policies have to be formulated. In a larger sense the same would apply to having or not having a foreign policy. Our promotion is mainly focused on affluent but somewhat distant markets and yet our planning strategy is heavily biased in favour of egalitarian concepts. We judge our achievement by numbers but we are not willing to take bold initiatives required for building up mass tourism. And no country has yet built up mass tourism without permitting its own people to travel abroad. After all tourism, like trade, is a two-way street. You can go on getting more visitors from affluent societies but the rate of growth would be inevitably slow, as has been the case so far. First, unlike the Caribbean or countries like Egypt and Greece the affluent societies happen to be located rather far away; secondly, it is important to remember that more than 80 per cent of tourism generated by affluent societies is either domestic or intra-regional i.e. among themselves.

In the last few years India has taken bold initiatives in order to boost its exports. We have entered into large scale barter deals with other countries, and allowed substantial imports in order to step up industrial production and improve its quality. As a result our exports have achieved considerable diversification and their share of the National Income has risen from 4.2 to six per cent. Tourism's share of the National Income has remained static and its relationship to total exports had declined from 2.8 per cent in

1962 to 2.2 per cent in 1975, however, it increased 2.7 per cent in 1995. For many years tourism was the fourth largest foreign exchange earner; now it is the eleventh. It is no longer the most important single item among Invisible Receipts. Again because of a bold initiative the largest single item among the Invisibles is the remittances of Indians domiciled abroad, running at Rs. 1200 million per month.

If tourism is not to remain a negligible element in the Indian economy, it too needs bold initiatives. In addition to other incentives, exports are receiving cash subsidies. In Singapore, S$ 2 million a year are being given as cash subsidies to the local tourist industry to make it competitive in price with neighbouring countries. All the Caribbean governments give override bonuses to tour operators and wholesalers on the basis of dollar-volume of business produced for the concerned destination. These are examples of bold initiatives in the field of tourism. Tourism is an exchange of human beings and in some ways differs from physical exports, but the basic concept that it is a two-way traffic is the same. We shall move into the area of mass tourism only when we accept this concept.

Resource Management

Tourism in India has now reached a stage where the management of resources has assumed relatively greater importance than the size of investment or resources. We thought that good management of resources so as to derive optimum level of satisfaction would be an area of primary concern to an organisation such as the National Productivity Council.

In the context of tourism the phrase 'resources' may be used in two different ways. First, resources in the form of attractions which bring visitors to a destination. The destination may be a country or at the micro-level, an area or a resort. The resources would also consists of investments that have been made to create tourist facilities and services. Second, the management capability to ensure optimum utilisation of these resources for the satisfaction of immediate and long-term needs of visitors.

Historically, in industrialised countries with free market economy the development of resources was left mainly to private enterprise. But in the last few years the large scale social, cultural and environmental impact of the tourism phenomenon created an awareness among the governments of their responsibility in regard to tourism. By now all governments of developed countries including the USA, which had consistently declined to set up an official agency for tourism, have become fully involved in tourism.

In the case of developing countries the first initiative usually came from the government, generally the Central Government and then filtered down to provincial and local levels. The process of development was, therefore, reversed. India is a classic example of this process. The first initiative came in 1955 when a five year plan for tourism development was submitted to the Planning Commission for inclusion in the Second Plan, starting with April 1956. At a later stage there was a conscious attempt to involve the state governments. By 1965, most of the state governments had set up some sort of an official tourist organisation and by now 15 major state governments have also established public sector enterprises called State Tourist Development Corporations.

At the same time it needs to be stated that tourism is not easily susceptible to planning. It deals with movements of human beings and, therefore, the tourist market is volatile and unpredictable. It is not easy to reconcile the market forces of tourism with the rigid realities of a centralised, bureaucratic planning process. Tourism demands personalised and motivated services which the public sector is not always able to provide. This is seen in socialist societies where the standard of personal service is generally considered inadequate by visitors. The usual complaint of tourists visiting East European countries is that the human relationship between them and their hosts is lacking in spontaneity and warmth.

The process of planning would inevitably involve identifying certain areas or locations with a long-term tourist potential. It would entail social and cultural macro-development and integration of tourism planning with overall economic development as well as micro-development of individual locations.

One has to assume that in developing countries there are constraints on financial resources that can be made available for tourism which doesn't, and in fact can't, enjoy the same priority as the more obvious needs of the community such as education, health, agriculture, basic industries and so on. For instance, in the case of India the allocation for tourism in successive Five Year Plans has never exceeded one quarter of one per cent of the total size of the Plan. The actual funds released year after year are generally less than the Plan allocation. For instance, from 1955-56 to March 1982 the total Plan outlay for the Central and state sectors (including the State Tourist Development Corporations) and ITDC was Rs. 2,338.6 million, which was considerably less than original allocations. The actual expenditure was Rs. 2,250.8 million which gives an average of Rs. 83 million a year. (In the Central sector it was Rs. 394.6 million, in the state sector it was Rs. 1,269 million and for ITDC it was Rs. 587 million). What is important is to note that the Plan expenditure by the ITDC and the state public sector Tourist Corporations was Rs. 1,200 million.

In other words the expenditure on projects specifically related to tourism was only Rs. 1,050 million in 27 years. The public sector has played a useful role but even if no accommodation and other tourist projects were financed by the public sector alternatives in the private sector would have been available. If ITDC had not built hotels in Delhi, Bangalore, Kovalam etc. in all probability they would have been built by the private sector. It would have been more prudent to utilise all the funds available on the infrastructure such as approach roads, transportation and public utilities etc. in new resorts rather than invest half the funds on the construction of hotels, guest houses and cafeterias.

The most important aspect of tourism planning in developing countries is a selective approach. We would recommend the following steps in the planning process. First, setting the objectives—what sort of tourism should we promote at the macro-level and for individual destinations; second, research. As Professor Medlik and Burkart of Surrey University have rightly emphasised, "Market Research is the first essential step both in marketing and in development of both new and existing provisions of tourist facilities. Only when the market has been assessed can a meaningful and rational expression be given to the size and shape of the physical development." Because so much of tourism depends on physical characteristics of different regions, it is essential for the planner to understand their special qualities as either exploitable assets or limitations. Among the several physical factors important to tourism planning are: natural resources, cultural resources such as historical monuments and arts and crafts, existing facilities such as availability of water and power supply, communications and transportation.

Twenty-seven years ago when the First Plan for tourism was formulated a selective approach was adopted. Roughly 25 centres spread over the country were selected for product development for foreign tourists. These centres also happened to be popular with domestic tourists, but it was realised that there would be many other centres in which domestic tourists would be interested for religious and cultural reasons but they would have no particular appeal for foreign tourists. The policy decision then was that the Central Government would finance the development of 25 centres for foreign tourists and the state governments would be responsible for facilities for domestic tourists in these 25 centres and other selected locations. The distribution of Plan allocations were made accordingly.

Planning in any developing country is susceptible to political and, what may be described as, non-touristic pressures. Tourism is, however, not like education and health that every village should have a school and a dispensary. Product orientation will not lead to practical results. The consumer is ultimately king in the competitive travel trade. Furthermore, tourism is not a single industry but essentially a market force. Tourism goals are: satisfaction for the user, reward to the owner, protection of environment and consideration of public good. All these must be translated into policy and programmes for development.

With the passage of time the research-based selective approach has been blurred by extraneous considerations. In the current Plan it is proposed to develop 440 centres with a Plan allocation of Rs. 1,875 million both in the Central and state sectors while the actual release of funds is considerably less. In order to encourage the involvement of state governments in the planning process, no doubt a laudable objective, each state was asked to name the centres it would like to develop. The lists submitted by state governments added up to more than a thousand centres. Obviously these lists were not based on any research or feasibility studies. They reflected the preference of local pressure groups. It was considered an achievement to reduce the number to 440 and then re-arrange them as travel circuits.

There is nothing wrong with the travel circuit concept provided it is based on time-distance scale. Delhi-Agra-Khajuraho-Delhi or Delhi-Jaipur-Udaipur-Delhi are viable circuits because they are inter-connected by jet air services. But to quote two typical examples of these proposed circuits: 'Hyderabad-Nagarjunasagar-Ethipothala-Srisailam-Mahanandi-Cudappah-Tirupati-Kalahasti-Pulicat Lake-Tirupati-Horsley Hills-Lepakshi-Anantapur-Kurnool-Hyderabad or 'Hyderabad-Medak-Hyderabad-Bhongir-Yadagiri Gutta-Warangal-Ramappa-Pakhal Lake and Ethunagaram Wildlife Sanctuary-Warangal-Amaravati (Chirala)-Vijayawada-Suryapet-Hyderabad,' do not indicate a practical approach. We are not sure if it has been ascertained whether all these places are inter-connected with convenient transport services or have any significant tourist attractions. The much publicised travel circuit approach in reality has become a euphemism for planning anarchy.

The second aspect of the management of resources defined at the outset was the management capability to obtain optimum utilisation. Tourism management needs professionalism. Considering that India produces the third largest number of technically qualified personnel, it is regrettable that in the field of tourism management we have lagged behind.

Training in tourism management is an educational process. It is the responsibility of the state to establish facilities for such training. There are four Institutes of Hotel Management, Catering and Nutrition which were established many years ago. Their annual turnout is about 450 graduates. Considering the large size of the Indian tourist industry this number is quite inadequate. These four Institutes have practically no arrangements for practical training and, barring the Bombay Institute, they don't provide any training at the management level. Finally, the government has created a Gilbertian situation by placing these Institutes under the control of the Ministry of Agriculture. The industry has to find alternatives and, therefore, major hotel chains are organising their own training courses. The present situation is that while 4- and 5-star hotels run by major chains are quite well managed, as you go down the scale the quality of management of one, two and three star hotels is not of acceptable standard. Some universities have introduced courses in general tourism training but they are functioning at an extremely low level.

A few years ago on the invitation of the Jammu and Kashmir government we made a survey of tourism in Kashmir. We found that there was appalling misuse of natural resources and the management of all the tourist bungalows, huts and hotels run by the state government was extremely poor.

For instance, the Dal Lake in Srinagar is highly polluted. It is one record that in 1907 its size was 10.5 square miles while the size at present is less than half of it. The pace of deterioration has accelerated in the last few years. Some of us sounded a note of warning that unless drastic measures were taken for the rejuvenation and restoration of the lake, by the turn of the century it would disappear and gradually become a memory of a bygone era. We pursued the matter and as a result the Commonwealth Secretariat was asked to nominate a team of experts to survey the lake and suggest necessary remedial measures. A team of three experts came and submitted a report to the state government. It was estimated that to re-organise the water system, remove the encroachments and rehabilitate the occupants and stop further pollution would cost more than Rs. 200 million. Considering the importance of the lake this is not a large amount compared with the amounts spent on other projects. But it seems to be beyond the capacity of the state government and hence the implementation of the recommendations has been inadequate. The Dal Lake is only one example. There is considerable environmental deterioration of the Valley as a whole.

Of course this is true of many parts of India. Our heritage, whether of natural resources such as mountains, valleys, lakes and beaches, or historical heritage of monuments and temples and so on which are the basic tourist attractions, is being damaged at an alarming rate. The authorities concerned express good intentions which proverbially lead the way to hell. There is not sufficient purposeful action to save the resources.

Jammu and Kashmir has had a much longer experience of tourism than most other states. One would have thought that the public sector management of tourist facilities in Kashmir would set an example for the rest. However this is not true as we found a few years ago when we visited the two hotels and a large variety of tourist bungalows and huts run by the Tourist Development Corporation for the survey mentioned earlier. There may have been a tradition of good management 50 years ago but not much of it has been left by now. A year later we made a survey of tourism in Kerala and found the situation no better. And yet Kashmir and Kerala are not at the end of the line. If you want to get there then visit some of the tourist bungalows in the eastern region in Bihar, Bengal and Orissa. The reason Haryana is quoted as having set an example of operating tourist resorts to be emulated by others is basically a new pattern of good management. Conrad Hilton, the founder of Hilton Hotels, towards the end of his life wrote that one of the profound discoveries he made was that the shower curtain should hang inside the railing. The bathrooms of tourist bungalows all over India are devoid of shower curtains but wherever they have them, they hang outside the railing. The routine system that a room should be made ready for the guest after the departure of the previous one is not followed by most of these supplementary accommodation units. My observation of several states that we have visited in the last few years was that in circuit houses, tourist bungalows and youth hostels, 50 per cent of the plumbing was not functioning, electric bulbs were missing, curtains didn't slide on the rail, air-conditioners and heaters were more often than not out of action, fresh towels or soap were not easily available and furniture and furnishings had no relationship with the size and shape of the rooms.

One of the significant examples of mismanagement of resources is the amateurish way we have gone about developing Gulmarg into a winter resort, for which the blame is to be shared equally by the Central and state governments. It was a few years ago that we got a well-known Austrian winter sports expert Rudi Matt, to survey Gulmarg and Khilanmarg for their potential for winter sports. During the period considerable amounts of money have been spent, and officially it is advertised as a winter resort of international standard. In reality it lacks most of the facilities usually available in an international resort. It has a ropeway only five-eighth of a kilometre in length, a rickety chairlift and no centrally heated hotel. Winter sports have become one of the large segments of the tourist industry. Each resort receives thousands of visitors and, since the season is short, reservations have to be made six months to a year in advance. We believe less than half a dozen groups whose main motivation was winter sports have visited Gulmarg in the last few years. Quite a few Indians and foreigners resident in India visit Gulmarg during the winter months but they are really not winter sporters. In fact Gulmarg at best is a resort for beginners who wish to learn skiing.

Professionalism in Tourism

Tourism, an adaptation from the French word 'tourism' means the theory and practice of travelling for pleasure. Hence it is often regarded as a pastime and consequently a trivial activity. But over the years tourism has become a highly complex phenomenon which has wide-ranging economic, social and environmental effects. In recognition of this, the United Nations General Assembly in 1963 adopted a resolution of which the opening paragraphs read as follows: "Convinced that tourism is a basic and most desirable human activity deserving the praise and encouragement of all peoples and all governments. Recognises the fundamental role played by tourism in national economies through the resultant economic benefits to the participating countries whose foreign exchanges are increased, and whose international trade is stimulated. Fully aware of the social, educational and cultural impact of tourism and of its significant contribution to the promotion of international goodwill and understanding and to the preservation of peace between the peoples."

In the good old days of the Grand Tour only the wealthy and the leisured class could afford to travel for pleasure. Such travellers could afford to make their own travel arrangements. Even so 120 years ago, a man called Thomas Cook in London found it a good idea to start a small travel agency and make travel arrangements for others on a professional basis. Now that about 215 million tourists cross international frontiers every year and presumably 800 million more take one or more vacations within their country, they need professional help to make their travel arrangements. But the ideal persists.

We remember that Nehru who was himself a very well travelled person while inaugurating the Indian Travel Agents Association (TAAI) conference in 1959 said, "Why can't you leave the tourist alone to roam about when he arrives in our country?" In other words he questioned the role of travel agents and tour operators. We are sure that many of you have come across government officials, businessmen and even airline executives and hotel operators who feel that they can do without you and jib at paying you commissions. You must be aware of the continuous battle that has been going on in the United States between ASTA and International Air Transport Association, with the CAB in the middle as arbitrator, on the rate of commission to be paid to travel agents.

Similar battles have been going on in many other countries. Here in India many travel agencies have found it increasingly difficult to handle clients who wish to travel by rail because the commission paid by the Indian Railways is not sufficient to pay for the overheads. It is for you to establish that your role is not peripheral, nor parasitic but essential. Tourism is not only a complex phenomenon because of its wide-ranging effects, its complexity also lies in the extremely complicated arrangements that have to be made for international travellers.

The tourist industry consists of a number of disparate enterprises. After all there is nothing in common between operating a hotel and running an airline. Tourists as human beings need a variety of services. The travel agent is the co-ordinating factor. The second aspect of the complexity arises from the multiplicity of rules and regulations that govern international travel. The paradoxical situation is that until nine decades ago when so many people did not travel, there were hardly any frontier formalities. Many countries did not have the system of issuing passports and visas. There were no vaccination or inoculation certificates required. Many of the present formalities were introduced as war-time measures against aliens during the two world wars. Bureaucracy all over the world suffers from inertia. Once certain restrictions are introduced, it takes time to relax them or dismantle them completely. Facilitation has made a good deal of progress and many formalities have been abolished. Nonetheless a traveller can come to grief if he hasn't armed himself with all the necessary travel documents.

The third aspect of the complexity is the variety of excursion fares and package tours. A few years ago there were 25 types of excursion fares on IATA approved transatlantic scheduled flights. We still have a variety of ITCs, TGCs and Advance Booking fares. The latest are OTCs which have had a phenomenal success. Obviously the international traveller needs the guidance and the counselling of an experienced travel agent. This is what we call professionalism. A professional is one who transforms what is generally regarded as a part-time into an occupation and thereby raises the dignity of his trade. Cricket and tennis may be pastimes but professionals adopt them as a regular occupation and raise the standard of the game. Travel is the name of your game.

How do you assume a pivotal role in the travel industry and how do you develop professionalism? We would like to offer three suggestions.

First, the travel agencies must establish credibility. There has been far too much proliferation in retail outlets, far too many fly-by-night agencies have come into being. As a result, there have been sporadic agency failures or unfulfilled promises. This has led to adverse publicity and tarnished the image of the trade. A licensing system by legislation is one answer to this problem. It separates the sheep from the goats. According to our information, about 35 governments have introduced regulatory measures either by legislation or by executive orders. Among them are Algeria, Argentina, Belgium, Egypt, Spain, France, Israel, Japan, Morocco, Mexico, Tunisia, Turkey and Venezuela. We understand the Singapore parliament has also passed a Travel Agents Bill.

But legislation is only a partial answer. First, it is difficult to regulate a service industry. If the regulations are too comprehensive and drastic they can inhibit growth; if they are not comprehensive then there are too many loopholes and the legislation remains ineffective. Secondly, what is wrong with the existing legislation on travel agencies in many countries is that there is too much stress on financial viability of the agency but not on its competence to render adequate professional services. Of course it is not so easy to frame rules about the competence of an agency. The Travel Agencies Acts of several countries usually lay down that an agency must have been in existence for a certain minimum period and should have produced a prescribed amount of turnover as qualifying clauses. But the mere fact that an agency has been operating for a certain period does not necessarily mean that it has achieved professionalism. Many countries have found that self-regulation by a trade is more effective than legislation. For instance in Britain there is no governmental licensing of travel agencies. Membership of the Association of British Travel Agents (ABTA) is considered a qualification because the agency then becomes subject to the ABTA Code of Conduct. We are glad to note that you have been very selective in admitting members to your Association and have less than 50 ordinary and associate members even though the number of agencies licensed by your Board under old legislation are more than 200. Since you are now in the process of drafting supporting regulations we hope it is not presumptuous on our part to express the hope that you will continue to be selective and that the enforcement machinery would vest in those who understand the nature of your business.

Another aspect of credibility is that travel agents must not promise more to their clients than they can deliver. Travel agents tend to glamourise the product and in the process they build up expectations that may be difficult to fulfil. You work under a handicap because you have to depend on facilities and services in the destination areas over which you have little control. In a sense you are selling an experience, perhaps a dream. We believe that travel agents should be more frank with their customers and prepare them for situations where things could occasionally go wrong. It is not enough to acknowledge that uncertainties are inherent in travel planning by inserting a responsibility clause in the contract which is generally printed in such small type that it is barely legible.

We wish to tell that two important factors are involved in developing professionalism: First, training in the business of tourism and travel agency operation and second, continuity. While there are a number of good institutions in Europe, North America and a few other countries for training in hotel crafts and management, unfortunately institutional training in tourism is almost non-existent. There are faculties in universities or autonomous colleges which are designated for training in hotel management and tourism, but the tourism part of the training is a minor, if not optional, subject of the syllabus. Travel agencies are looking for trained personnel but they are just not available.

A few years ago we saw a statement by a 'head hunting' firm of San Francisco that there are more travel agencies seeking employees on the San Francisco peninsula than there are candidates to fill the available jobs. Some years ago we were asked by United Nations Economic and Social Commission for Asia and the Pacific (ESCAP) to make a survey of the training programmes in the ESCAP region. We found that many countries of this region which includes ASEAN had established or were in the process of setting up training programmes. This is a most welcome development. But the emphasis still was on training in hotel crafts and not in tourism. The situation in our region thus remains pretty unsatisfactory.

We believe that the usual method of finding staff for a travel agency is either to take someone who has had experience of working in another agency or employing young men and women who are reasonably well educated, outgoing by temperament and have an aptitude for PR. We would certainly commend the second procedure. Stealing staff from other agencies in the long run would not lead to a healthy growth of travel agency business. Every major travel agency should have an in-house training programme for the new staff.

The second factor, that of continuity, is even more important. This applies not only to the travel agency business but even more so to the staff of the national tourist organisations. In highly developed countries like the United States, UK, Switzerland, Netherlands, Belgium and so on, NTOs mainly act as a catalyst and if they are granted adequate funds they lead the way in promotion. In the developing countries governments are playing a more decisive role in the development of tourism. It is, therefore, most essential that NTOs should also build up professionalism. Unfortunately in the official hierarchies of most developing countries the head of the national tourist organisation does not enjoy a senior status. He is generally looking for promotion in other sectors of the government; hence the appointments of Director of Tourism and other senior staff are often of short duration and subject to haphazard change.

The main segment of the tourist industry—hotels, travel agencies and ground tour operators—often have to seek the assistance of NTOs. The NTOs cannot render assistance of their staff who do not have an understanding of the problems of the industry. There is lack of continuity in travel agencies because the tourist industry as a whole has still not achieved the status of a major enterprise in the national economies of most countries. The brightest and the best men and women tend to seek employment in government, in manufacturing industries, in banking, or in multinational corporations. Young people in their twenties and thirties are restless and mobile. They are always trying to move upwards and not laterally. It is for you to create such conditions of service that you can attract the brightest and the best and retain them.

Travel agency business all the world over is not highly profitable. Many years ago we were addressing a WATA conference in Geneva and said to them that the Indian travel agents had told us that they were only making two per cent net profit. Some of the WATA members shouted back, "they are lucky, we are making only one and a half per cent." Considering the phenomenal success of Singapore in tourism we hope that you are making more than five per cent. What makes a travel agent love his profession is a question of temperament. It is not easy to define temperament but we are sure you know what we mean. By temperament he is an extrovert, loves to travel, finds the unpredictability of his business exciting, is quick on the uptake but meticulous about details. We are not suggesting that when you are back in the seclusion of your hotel room you should do some heart searching whether you have the right temperament or not. We have brought up this subject because if professionalism is the key to progress then we should mention all the elements that comprise the package called travel agent.

We would like to make a reference to ASEANTA the Federation of ASEAN Travel Agents. We finally believe in regional and sub-regional co-operation in the field of tourism. The first great example of regional co-operation in tourism was set by the West European countries when soon after the War they established the European Travel Commission, for joint promotion in North America as a means of economic reconstruction of devastated Europe. PATA itself is an example of regional co-operation except that the region is so vast that sub-regional organisations have become necessary. The East Asian countries, Japan, South Korea, Hong Kong, Taiwan etc. set up the East Asia Travel Association many years ago. Outside the framework of WTO effective sub-regional organisations have come into being in the Caribbean, the Arab countries, Central and South America. ASEANTA went one step further. You set up not only an ASEAN organisation for tourism as a whole but regional organisation for travel agents *per se*. But we were told that ASEANTA was not doing well. We were happily surprised to see the headlines in a issue of TTG-Asia, "ASEANTA gets 'kiss of life." We think it is a most healthy development.

Sixteen countries of the world produced 81 per cent of international tourism during the year 1966 to 1975. The forecast made in a well-known study recently published by Economist Intelligence Unit, London, is that the same 16 countries were likely to produce 82 per cent of world tourism in the decade 1976 to 1985. All these 16 countries barring Japan and Australia happen to be far from our region. Hence there is a vast scope for intra-regional tourism. To our mind the main function of a regional or a sub-regional tourist organisation is two-fold: Joint promotion in the principal markets outside the region and to further the growth of tourist traffic within the region. We understand that of the 11,83,028 visitors to Malaysia in 1975, more than half came from neighbouring countries, not counting those who came by road over the Strait of Johore. To some extent the same is true of Indonesia and Thailand. In other words you have achieved mobility within the ASEAN. There is a good deal of intra-regional traffic in the Middle East, Latin America, East and West Africa and amongst East European countries. The only area of the world where intra-regional traffic has not developed in the last few years is the region generally called South Asia: Afghanistan, Pakistan, India, Bangladesh, Nepal and Sri Lanka.

Trained Personnel

The need for trained personnel for the tourist industry has been universally recognised. During the last few years many countries of the ESCAP region have had master plans for tourist development prepared by groups of experts engaged through UN Agencies or by direct contracts with market and feasibility research companies. Every major study of this nature has devoted one or two chapters giving an outline of the training programmes; that would meet the requirements of the country concerned. Nevertheless the sub-committee on tourism and facilitation of ESCAP which met in Bangkok in January 1974 noted, "that training facilities for executive and managerial personnel and middle level staff for national tourist organisations, hotels and restaurants, travel agencies and other segments of the tourist industry were virtually non-existent in many countries of the region." Of course, just a few countries of the region have set up hotel management schools; in several others the schools are at the vocational level and impart training in hotel crafts and catering services, and in some others such programmes form apart of the curricula of vocational or technical institutions of the country.

But in almost all countries of the region these programmes have proved inadequate, in one way or another. It is important to examine the reasons of this inadequacy. After all the educational systems of many of these countries have produced highly qualified scientists, engineers, doctors, accountants, economists and specialists in several other disciplines.

There seem to be several reasons for this rather anomalous

situation. First, tourism is relatively a new industry. In fact, many people choose not to define it as an industry. The phrase travel trade was more commonly used until thirty-five years ago. Secondly, tourism consists of a number of unconnected enterprises, and it is not easy to prepare a syllabus for an integrated course of training. The training required for hotel crafts such as cooking, restaurant services, housekeeping etc., is more identifiable and traditional which may explain why there are many hotel schools but hardly any institutions for imparting training in tourism.

However, tourism has become a more specialised activity in the last few years. It has developed a jargon of its own. As tourism grew into a mass market, new methods of selling and buying were introduced. It also became a worldwide phenomenon. In world trade it registered the highest growth rate in the fifties and sixties. Recognising the importance of tourism almost all governments have set up official tourist organisations with an identity of their own, and not as branches of general administration. These official tourist organisations, over the years, have grown in size, not only because of the Parkinson Law, but because they have enlarged their range of activities. Some of the NTO's have a staff of 400-500, as in Cananda, France and India, and Mexico's Department of Tourism has a staff of about 800. Similarly, travel agencies and tour operators, wholesalers and retailers, have grown in number and size. Collectively they have become a multibillion dollar business. There is growing demand for professionalism. In response to this demand several hotel training schools in Europe (including the UK) and North America added tourism to the curriculum. Another development, particularly, in hotel education in the USA, has been that training in hoteliering has become oriented to management training rather than specific instruction in hotel crafts.

If one examined closely the curricula and the day-to-day working of hotel schools of Europe as well as the USA and Cananda, one would notice that there seem to be two opposing schools of thought influencing training in the field of hotel management. One school believes that training should be mainly technical in hotel crafts such as food preparation, restaurant, front desk, waiting and house-keeping services etc; the other school of thought argues that the stress should be on training in the management of an enterprise, with emphasis on subjects like hotel administration, accounting and property management. The well-known traditional Hotel

School of Lausanne is a good example of the first school of thought and the equally renowned School of Hotel Administration of Cornell University may be regarded as a prototype of the second approach. Of course, many schools in Europe, Britain and even the USA and Canada are a blend to these two basic approaches, among them the University of Surrey (UK). Both the content of the programme and the level at which training is offered is to a large extent determined by the approach to which the institution subscribes. Generally speaking, the former approach, the Lausanne model is associated with vocational level programmes while the latter approach is associated with university-based training at undergraduate and post-graduate level i.e. the Cornell and Surrey model. (see Appendix 1)

Considering the present day needs of multifaceted tourism, of which the hospitality industry is a large but more well-defined segment, the present situation in regard to training in tourism is not only unsatisfactory in the ESCAP region but also in the world at large. First, a series of lectures on various aspects of tourism, promotion, marketing, facilities, travel agency operation, package tours etc., comprising about 10-15 hours in a semester, tagged on to the syllabus of a hotel school cannot be regarded as training in tourism. And this is what generally entitles an institution to call itself a school or faculty of hotel management and tourism. A training course in tourism would have to have an identity of its own. It is true that the teaching staff for a School of Tourism would not be readily available. Also reasons of economy may dictate that the two courses may be combined. But the demand for professionalism for the management of tourism enterprises including NTO's is so great that an identifiable tourism course has to be evolved.

The job functions in a travel agency and tour operator's office are not the same as those of an airline office, and they both differ from the job functions in a national tourist office. The training required for guides must involve a sound knowledge of local history, geography, culture, folklore and map reading etc. There are some elements common in the job functions of all these services, but a course of training which would qualify persons for all these job functions would have to be fairly comprehensive and also provide opportunities to the trainees for specialisation. It has also begun to be realised that poor service, whether due to lack of aptitude, insufficient motivation or need for technical training, will create in the visitor's mind an adverse opinion, regardless of the investments in airports, hotels and other physical facilities. The training for tourism should not be merely technical in character; motivation and friendly attitude are equally necessary.

Initiatives have been taken in many countries for evolving a course of tourism *per se.* For instance, more than 15 years ago the Indian Tourism Department started an eight week course of training in tourism repeated twice a year. It was recognised by the ESCAP secretariat and several trainees belonging to ESCAP member states, such as, Thailand, Philippines, Indonesia, Kampuchea, Afghanistan and Iran attended this course. A few successful examples of courses in tourism could be cited: the short courses at advance and junior levels run by the IUOTO (now WTO) in collaboration with ILO and the Italian Government at Turin which are attended year after year by staff members of NTO's of more than 50 developing countries; the courses which have been run for several years under the able leadership of Dr Edward Barnett in Hawaii, and the tourism orientation given to the degree and diploma courses in hotel management and tourism at the new university near Miami, Florida International University. A similar effort was made in framing the syllabus for the Department of Tourism and Hotel Management which was to be established in the University of West Indies in 1973 as a three-year course. After the first year of common instruction, the trainees in the second year were to choose the options of specialised training in tourism or in hotel management. The scheme was approved by the governing council of the university but unfortunately the lack of funds delayed its establishment.

A significant initiative in setting up an institution to provide management training with emphasis on aspects of the travel industry other than hotel crafts, is being taken by the Indian Government's Department of Tourism. A reference was made to this institution at the ESCAP Tourism and Facilitation sub-committee meeting of January 1974. The minutes of the meeting show that the Indian representative indicated that this institute, when established at Bangalore, could be utilised for regional use. The services of Dr. R.W. McIntosh of the University of Michigan were obtained under the Technical Assistance Programme of UNDP in 1973 for preparing the scheme. It is understood that an allocation of Rs. 25 million (approximately US $ 3.25 million) had been made by the Indian Government for the period 1974-78 and input of US $ 2,70,000 were provided under the India-UNDP country programme for 1972-76 for obtaining the services of experts and equipment. The institute had offered a two year post-graduate course for students who had completed three to four years of undergraduate education.

The objectives of the institute are: *(i)* to impart education and information in travel and tourism and management techniques to enable the graduates to occupy executive positions in various segments of the industry and in a few years to reach positions of higher responsibility in the organisation, *(ii)* develop a professional outlook in management of travel enterprises, particularly at the levels concerned with policy making and execution, *(iii)* organise in-service training programmes for the personnel already working in the travel industry, *(iv)* offer consultancy and research facilities, *(v)* establish a library of books and reference material and undertake documentation and publication of technical literature on travel and tourism.

In the foregoing paragraphs an attempt has been made to place the problems of training for hotel management and tourism in proper perspective. The point has been made that training for travel and tourism services cannot be adequately provided by institutions primarily established for teaching hotel crafts. In the long run it would be better to have separate institutions for hotel management and tourism training. This study is intended to deal with schemes for training at sub-regional or regional levels. However, such schemes cannot be divorced from the training schemes at the national level, nor can the sub-regional institutions be a substitute for institutions set up within a country to provide training for its own people. Of course, it is open to any member state to organise management training for high level executive staff. In other words the training at the national level may lead upto senior level management training, which if not available within the country would be available at the sub-regional training centres to be established with the support of ESCAP.

The first step in preparing a training scheme, both at the national and sub-regional level would be to measure the manpower requirements country-wise *(i)* for the official organisations, *(ii)* for the hospitality industry, *(iii)* for the rest of the travel industry including travel agencies, guides, front line staff of airlines and transport operators etc.

Such an assessment has to be based on the conditions of employment obtaining in each country, and on forecasts of growth rates in the next 5-10 years. It would have to take into account the need for training existing employees by means of in-service training as well as the requirements of training new staff. The two types of programmes may have to be quite different in approach and duration of training. For instance, hotels in Europe and the USA employ less staff than hotels in the ESCAP region. A 400-room hotel with public rooms and a modicum of conventional facilities in North America would employ less than 400 staff, but in the ESCAP countries the staff strength may vary from 500 to 800. The same may be true of other operations, partly because of relatively lower wage levels and lack of labour saving devices, and partly this could be attributed to lack of training. For instance, the Checchi and Company manpower estimate for the Bahamas tourism industry was arrived at, after several weeks of investigation, on the assumption that with a ten per cent rate of growth, in five years 15,000 hotel rooms required a staff of 18,000 while the rest of the industry would need manpower strength of 24,000 to serve the need of 1.7 million visitors. The tourism master plan prepared by Arther D. Little Inc. for Tanzania assumed a ratio of 1.6 employees per hotel room and estimated that 5,700 new hotel employees and about 2,500 others would have to be trained in seven years, 1972-79.

The UN-ESCAP covers a very wide area. It would be more practical to establish a number of sub-regional institutions, each one to provide training programmes for a group of five to seven countries. For this purpose the ESCAP region could be divided into four groups. It is for the member states to decide upon the groupings and the location of each sub-regional institution. The following suggestions are for their consideration:

Group I — Iran, Afghanistan, Pakistan, Nepal, Bangladesh, India and Sri Lanka.

Group II — Burma, Thailand, Malaysia, Singapore, Indonesia, Laos, Kampuchea, Vietnam.

Group III — Philippines, Japan, China, Korea plus Hong Kong and Hawaii

Group IV Australia, New Zealand, Fiji, New Guinea and the Islands of the South Pacific such as Tahiti, Western Samoa etc.

If inadvertently any member state does not figure in the above list the commission may rectified.

Only sovereign states are members of ESCAP but in terms of tourism Hong Kong should not be ignored, nor some of the non-dependent islands such as Western Samoa and Tahiti, which are emerging as viable tourist destinations. Taiwan, receives almost a million tourists a year but is no longer a member of United Nations. May be a way could be found to permit it to make a useful contribution to training programmes. Philippines is a member of the sub-group ASEAN and may like to be included in Group II above. Hawaii is a state of the USA but has been mentioned in the above list because it is highly advanced in tourism and already has well-established training programmes both in hotel management and tourism. Hawaii has provided leadership to PATA and it would be a pity if for constitutional reasons advantage cannot be taken of the existing training facilities in Hawaii. It is suggested, therefore, that for technical and training purposes certain territories which have become popular tourist destinations and can make a useful contribution to ESCAPs training programmes may be included.

If the recommendation, that training in tourism and hotel management cannot be combined, is accepted then we need two separate institutions (training centres) in each sub-region. It is not altogether necessary that the two should be located in one city or country, though there may be some political advantage in having them in one location. There will be some common features in management and business administration training in both types of courses, and it may be possible to share some series of lectures and workshop sessions. Keeping in mind the above considerations the following locations are suggested, purely tentatively and without prejudice to other locations.

Group I Bangalore, if the proposed institute gets off the ground in a year or so.

Group II Two of the following locations: Bangkok, Singapore, Djakarta and Kuala Lumpur, depending on the buildings and teaching facilities available.

Group III Hawaii if this is constitutionally possible and if the Hawaii State Administration is able to make the facilities available to other countries.

Group IV Sydney or Melbourne.

The training programme at the sub-regional and regional level would be more management-oriented. One of its functions would be to develop professionalism in the management of travel enterprises, particularly at the level of policy making. It is arguable that since a management-oriented course, whether it develops administrative capacity for hotel management or for a national tourist office or an airline or for wholesale tour operation would have, more or less, the same character, there is no compelling need for organising two special training programmes, one for hotel crafts and the other for training in other tourist enterprises. Considering the dearth of suitable teaching staff it may be more practical, and in any case economical, to establish sub-regional institutes at the post-graduate level which combine both types of training in a two or three year course.

It is further recommended that for training courses at the national level, and more so at the sub-national or provincial level (in case a country finds it necessary to set up more than one training school) the European model of teaching exemplified by schools at Lausanne, Lyons, Grenoble, Salzburg, Heidelberg, Portsmouth and Glasgow, may be followed in the ESCAP region. It would provide more practical training at middle levels and will also fit into the existing educational system of a majority of the ESCAP member states. But for the sub-regional institutes, the North American models of Cornell, New Hampshire, Buffalo, Michigan, Hawaii etc. which emphasise management and business techniques or the University of Surrey model (Appendix 1) may be found more suitable.

It is not possible in this brief report to present a complete training scheme and teaching curriculum of the proposed sub-regional training centres. This is a highly specialised task which should be performed by experts with long experience of teaching in hotel management and tourism schools and it is recommended that the services of one or two such experts are obtained for this purpose. The names of a few outstanding persons are suggested: *(i)* Dr. Edward Barnett, Hawaii University, *(ii)* Dr. Donald P.

Lundburg, formerly Head of the Department of Hotel, Restaurant and Travel Administration, University of Massachusetts, *(iii)* Dr. R. W. McIntosh, University of Michigan, *(iv)* Professor John Fuller, formerly Principal of Glasgow Hotel Training School and Visiting Professor, University of Illinois, *(v)* Director, CIEST (IUOTO-ILO Training Centre) in Turin. Of course, there may be many other equally competent experts and educationists available in Europe and North America.

Perhaps the most difficult problem in establishing training schools for tourism and hotel management in developing countries is of finding qualified and suitable teaching staff, and an almost equally difficult problem is of attracting intelligent and motivated pupils or trainees. It probably took 50 years or more in most of the ESCAP countries to develop indigenous or local teachers at the university level in traditional subjects like natural, mechanical, and social sciences: tourism and hotel management are not only new subjects but in certain respects somewhat nebulous in character not easily susceptible to exact teaching methods. The phrase 'qualified and suitable' has been used advisedly. One may be able to import qualified teachers for hotel and tourism schools by offering attractive terms and yet they may not be 'suitable.' They have to have the right motivation and attitude to be able to work in developing countries. Their main function is not merely to teach but also to train and develop 'native' talent—in short they must aim at gradual self-liquidation, hara kiri, as it were. The problem is further complicated by the fact that most governments of developing countries have tightened up their laws concerning work permits. It has become a matter of national policy, if not pride, not to give work permits to expatriate staff for business enterprises. A medium size one-section hotel school would require a staff of 12-15 teachers. Depending upon the availability of local talent it may be assumed that in ESCAP countries at least four to six members of the staff may have to be expatriates. Some foreign staff, from outside the region, may also be necessary for the training centre in tourism though perhaps, the same ratio may not apply to it. The ESCAP region is rich in native talent and initiative. Its people are also hard working. Many young men and women from ESCAP countries have graduated from some of the best hotel schools of Europe, UK, Canada and the USA during the past 15 years. Quite a few of them are holding senior positions in the hotel and catering establishments in their own countries and in countries outside the ESCAP region.

It may not be easy to utilise the experience and talent of these highly qualified persons. First, the salaries in the academic field are traditionally lower than the emoluments offered by the industry. Secondly, a competent hotel manager may not necessarily prove to be a good teacher. Thirdly, those working in developed countries usually enjoy better prospects and are averse to returning home. It is part of the brain drain that many developing countries of this region have been experiencing for sometime.

It is strongly urged that the proposed sub-regional training centres should offer comparable salaries and prospects to be able to employ suitable and qualified teachers belonging to the region. Secondly there should be no reservations about employing foreign staff in positions which cannot be filled by local talent. Thirdly, for the first five years, the head of each centre should be an outstanding person with qualities of leadership and adaptability. It has been said with considerable truth that there are no expatriates in the hotel field. The phenomenal growth of hotel chains and accommodation facilities has outstripped the availability of highly trained and professionally qualified hotel executives. There are too many jobs chasing too few hotel administrators. Hence you find Swiss, French, Italian, German and Swedish managers in America and you find American and Canadian managers working in Europe and elsewhere.

The problem of attracting trainees in sufficient numbers, particularly trainees of executive material, is further complicated by the prevailing social and cultural patterns in the ESCAP region. The educated young men and women coming from the middle and upper classes, may have the aptitude and sophistication for management positions but they often betray a negative attitude towards menial jobs. Practical on the job training is an essential part of overall hotel management training. But cooking, dish-washing and waiting can be a traumatic experience for boys and girls of upper class Asian societies. These ingrained attitudes become a barrier to their own development. Hotel and tourism jobs in government tourist offices, travel agencies, guide services etc. have to compete with job opportunities in other expanding industries and business enterprises of each country. What we need in each ESCAP country is a public relations programme. First, to create a bias in favour of tourism and a tourist consciousness among the people at large; secondly a campaign among the young people in schools and colleges 'selling' job opportunities in the tourist and hotel industry. In view of large scale unemployment in many ESCAP countries the need or usefulness of such a campaign may be questioned. The answer is that tourism as a new and major enterprise needs for its future success the best or the second best and certainly not the rejected talent of the country. If it remains the last refuge of the unemployed part of the community, no amount of training programmes and well organised training centres will make it competitive and successful.

Investment in Tourism Development

Socrates had the inconvenient habit of not starting a Dialogue before defining the meaning of the questions. So if we may follow the Socratic practice we would like to define the meaning of the phrase 'Tourism Development Projects and Related Infrastructure.' Apparently tourism development projects mean facilities created mainly for tourists such as hotels and restaurants, bus and car-hire services, entertainment, recreation and shopping opportunities. These facilities then have to be supported by 'related infrastructure' consisting of transport and communications network and public utilities such as power and water supply and sewage disposal. Since the related infrastructure is also used by the local people in most countries it is generally considered the responsibility of the government. There are examples of small countries, particularly in the Caribbean, where governments create a tax-free situation and then expect private enterprise to develop the related infrastructure as well. But in the ESCAP region the development of basic infrastructure and public utilities generally has been accepted as the responsibility of the government at the central or local levels.

The governments of the ESCAP region have a responsibility of coping with hindrances to investments for the development of tourism. However a close look at the situation would show that a majority of the governments of this region don't act as if they owe such a responsibility. Indeed, the most identifiable hindrance to channelling investment in tourism projects is the low priority accorded to tourism by almost all governments. For instance, the tourism budgets of the National Tourist Organisations of a majority of countries of this region for the past many years have not exceeded half of one per cent of the national budget of the country. A striking exception is Singapore. After all, the budgetary allocations are indicative of the relative priority a government attaches to various items. We fully appreciate that most governments would inevitably give more importance to agriculture, industrial development, education, health and security. But what seems to be wrong with their thinking is that most of these governments consider tourism a sort of luxury intended to be indulged in by the rich leisure class and not a tool for economic and social change. What has not been recognised is that paid holidays and other social welfare measures have changed the world picture. Increased leisure is now available to both white and blue collar workers. Tourism offers a solution to the present day problem of the use of leisure time. It fulfils the aspirations of almost all classes of people and can be a means for the enrichment of the quality of life. It is also not recognised that tourism can redress regional imbalances within each country. Some of the great historical monuments in this region happen to be located in remote places lacking resources. Tourism can regenerate the development of these backward areas. The flow of tourist traffic has been the answer to the development of some derelict areas like Sardinia and Sicily and can bring prosperity to the beautiful valleys in the Himalayas in India and Pakistan. The example of the development of the remote and waterless village of Khajuraho in central India, with its magnificent temples has already been described.

During the last few years tourism has proved to be a significant means of transfer of wealth from the richer to the poorer countries. The majority of tourists visiting the ESCAP region, or for that matter the entire Third World, come from less than 20 countries with high per capita incomes and they leave a great deal of money behind. It is a mistaken notion that tourism mainly benefits a small segment of the community such as hoteliers, travel agents and carriers. In fact it benefits not only those who are directly employed in tourist enterprises—the tourist industry being labour intensive the number of such employees is very large too—but also benefits a large number of suppliers of goods and retail shopkeepers. For instance, it is not generally recognised that in many developing countries tourism has been responsible for the survival of indigenous handicrafts and folk arts. The traditional artefacts produced by artisans in villages could not withstand the competition of mass produced goods imported from industrialised countries or manufactured locally. They were dying out and it was the interest evinced in them by visitors that helped their revival. The tourist expenditure thus percolates throughout the economy. The question of governments' responsibility to cope with the hindrances to investment in tourism projects would arise if the governments in the first place accepted that tourism can be a tool of economic development and accorded a reasonable measure of priority to it.

On the other hand it was assumed by the newly independent countries in the fifties and sixties that economic growth was the most effective way of eradicating poverty and reducing unemployment. It was believed that the wealth generated by modern, organised, large-scale industrial activity would automatically trickle down to the poor and benefits would spread to all sections of the community. But what has actually happened is different. The growth of modern, urban large-scale industries was accompanied by slow growth or stagnation in other sectors of the economy. Unemployment and poverty have become almost endemic features of most developing countries.

During the last few years we have witnessed confrontation between the rich and the poor countries at almost all international conferences concerned with trade, industry and economic development. A series of UNCTAD and UNIDO conferences have ended in a stalemate, the most recent one being the UNIDO Conference in Delhi which failed even to pass a Resolution. The basic problem at all these conferences has been to find ways and means to improve the bargaining position of the developing countries vis-a-vis the industrialised countries in the matter of trade. It all boils down to transfer of resources, both material and technological, from the haves to the have-nots.

Many years ago the United Nations recommended that the richer countries would contribute one per cent of their GNP to the development of the less developed countries. Since this was not complied with an agreement was reached that the contribution would amount to 0.7 per cent of the GNP. In point of fact the aid given by most of the developed countries has not amounted to even half of one per cent. Two years ago the World Bank appointed an informal but highly prestigious group under the Chairmanship of Willy Brandt, former Chancellor of Germany. The Brandt Commission Report published had called for a more equitable system of managing the world economy. Its major recommendations include large-scale transfer of funds to the Third World, agreement between oil producers and consumers for assured supplies at predictable prices, adjustments in the trade policies of developed countries and key reforms in the world monetary system. The Commission has proposed the creation of a World Development Fund for programmes and purposes for which the existing international institutions are unable or unwilling to provide funds. But what is surprising is that not a word about tourism as a means of transfer of funds to the Third World has ever been mentioned in all these conferences or in the Report of the Brandt Commission even though it enjoys the additional advantage of not being subject to the protectionist policies now being adopted by industrial countries against developing countries. Why?

Presumably there is no simple answer to this question. Tourism is a relatively new phenomenon and its economic benefits have not found general acceptance. The travel industry is a highly fragmented industry consisting of disparate components. There has not been enough research to prove that a million dollars invested in tourism projects would yield comparatively better results for the community than a similar amount invested in other types of industrial enterprises. Consequently the visitor industry as a whole has not been able to establish its case with the policy and decision-makers. The adverse, but not the favourable social, cultural and environmental effects of tourism are too often publicised. It is generally not recognised that most of the environmental damage in the developing countries has been caused by uncontrolled growth of industries, urbanisation and careless management of resources. After all in the vast ESCAP region rivers and lakes have been polluted, forests have been denuded and slums have been created not by 19 million tourists. On the other hand the influx of tourists has often made local authorities more conscious of the value of indigenous arts and crafts.

It is not only the governments but also international financial institutions which have given a low priority to financial tourism development projects. For a long time the view held by the World Bank was that tourism was a fragile and unstable industry; hence investments in tourism would be rather risky. It is true that hotels have a long gestation period and the profits are not as high as in the other industries except in large cities. But tourism as a whole is a fast growing industry and has been able to withstand economic recessions.

In fact tourism has proved to be a more stable industry during the last few years of the energy crisis than many other industries. So it was only a few years ago that the World Bank established a Tourist Wing and started giving favourable consideration to tourism projects. The Asian Development Bank has however been more conservative in its attitude and has hardly financed any tourism projects in the ESCAP region. But now even the World Bank has wound up the Tourist Wing partly because not enough proposals in regard to tourism projects were received from governments to keep the staff of the Tourist Wing occupied, but mainly because it has reverted to its earlier philosophy that the Bank can finance the development of infrastructure which may indirectly help tourism development but need not provide loans for tourism projects such as hotels. The international institutions such as the World Bank, Regional Development Banks, UNDP, Commonwealth Secretariat are usually governed by priorities fixed by governments. To enable these institutions to render financial ad technical assistance to tourism development projects and related infrastructure, the initiative to sponsor such proposals must come from the governments concerned.

Investment, both foreign and indigenous, tends to flow into those sectors of the economy which are comparatively more profitable. If in certain countries investors are shy of putting capital in tourism projects it means that such projects are not considered highly profitable. One of the obvious methods of promoting investment in the tourism sector then would be that the government should provide incentives for investment such as tax exemptions, development rebates or investment allowances, refunds of customs and excise duties, long-term loans on concessional rates of interest, concessions on rates of power supply and so on. The foreign investor also needs a legal framework which provides an assurance for the repatriation of dividends on equity capital and interest on loans. Incentives ultimately amount to loss of revenue.

A government is however, willing to suffer loss of revenue as a means of developing certain industries which it considers highly important. But the value of incentives has to be measured not in absolute terms but in relative terms within the framework of the national economy, which means that certain projects become competitively more profitable. The case studies of several countries of the ESCAP region would illustrate why investment has gone into the tourism sector in some countries like Sri Lanka and the Philippines and not in others like India and Pakistan. For instance, in the last four decades less than three per cent of the portfolio of the Industrial Finance Corporation of India has been claimed by investors in hotel projects as against nearly 40 per cent of the portfolio of the Development Finance Corporation of Ceylon. The obvious reason is that Sri Lanka provides somewhat more incentives for investment in hotel projects than in other industries while India does not. In fact incentives for hotel projects in India are rather small compared to those given to a host of other industries.

A major hindrance to investment in tourism projects in any part of the world could be the political and social environment of the region. If there is political instability in a country or if its people are unfriendly the investors, particularly foreign investors, would shy away. This has happened in many Central and South American republics and also in the Caribbean. By and large the environment for investment in the ESCAP region has been highly favourable. An especially favourable factor in this region is that it offers an extremely hard-working and intelligent work force to the tourist industry which is so largely dependent on good service.

To what extent a government can provide incentives to investors and entrepreneurs would be largely governed by its economic structure and its ideological and political compulsions. For instance, in socialist countries with completely controlled economies there is not much scope for promoting private investment. In highly industrialised countries where tourism has grown from the grass-roots by local initiatives the governments as a rule would like it to be governed by market forces, by the law of demand and supply. They do not feel that it is their responsibility to be closely associated with the operation of the tourist industry even though their involvement with tourist promotion and regulation is far greater today than it was four decades ago. At the first UN Conference on Tourism held in Rome in 1963, we recall that in all the discussions that took place in the Development Committee it was the industrialised countries which consistently opposed the recommendation that governments should provide incentives for stimulating the growth of tourism. In the developing countries the process of development had to be reversed. The majority of countries in the Third World became independent in the post-war era and the initiative to develop tourism had to come from the government. Starting from the government at the centre, the development process then spread to the provincial and local levels.

According to periodic survey published by WTO only about 50 governments provide some sort of incentives to the tourism sector. Excluding a dozen highly industrialised countries and another dozen with a completely socialist system it means that only about half the governments of the remaining 125 member states of United Nations are consciously promoting investment in the tourism sector. Apparently some of the governments do not attach any importance to tourism and others consider that the development of tourism is the direct responsibility of the public sector. Hence in many developing countries instead of promoting private investment in the tourism sector the governments have themselves entered the operational field, either directly or through public sector corporations. In other words they finance the tourist facilities as well as manage and market them.

We consider that this is the wrong approach to tourism development. In the long run it is a self-defeating exercise. First, no government can provide sufficient funds from the public exchequer for investment in hotels and other tourism projects. It is cheaper to give reasonable incentives and let private enterprise find the money than to burden the exchequer. Secondly, since in the long-term the public sector is judged by its performance almost as much as the private sector, the temptation to take advantage of the situation is generally too strong to be resisted, even if a particular government believes in the philosophy of providing equal opportunity to both sectors. My experience over the five decades years, not only in the ESCAP region, but also in other parts of the world is that not many governments exercise the necessary restraint and discipline in competing with private enterprise. As a result private investment is stifled. Thirdly, the private sector is generally more flexible in its approach and receptive to customer demand; as such it plays an invaluable role in the highly service-oriented tourist industry. Fourthly, the public sector should operate tourist enterprises as part of its development strategy, opening up new areas to tourism which may be unprofitable in the initial stages. Private enterprise generally tends to ride on the back of the pubic sector and this need not be grudged in the interest of overall development. In the developing countries the two sectors, therefore, should complement each other, the public sector blazing the trail, as it were, but withdrawing from the operational field after the initial stages.

One of the big question marks in the development strategy, whether in tourism or any other industry, is the extent to which developing countries should encourage foreign investment and management. There is no doubt that foreign investment as well as management have played a major role in the development of tourism in the Third World. In the first place local capital until, say 35 or 40 years ago, was shy of investment in a non-traditional industry like tourism. It was the prestige of the multinational hotel companies which attracted foreign investment in a large measure in many countries of the ESCAP region. They also brought in new management and operational techniques which have raised the standard of hotel-keeping in this region. But at the same time it has resulted in considerable leakage of income derived from tourism. The repatriation of interest on foreign investment and management fees could amount to as much as 20-30 per cent of the tourist expenditure.

We are not advocating a policy of complete self-reliance because it can result in stagnation, as indeed it has in certain countries. The exchange of expertise and technology has helped the economic growth of the developing countries, more so in the tourist industry which is international in character. A closed-door policy in terms of foreign exchange or employment would, therefore, be undesirable, indeed it would be difficult to enforce it in the present day world. We may mention in passing that according to a recent UN survey more than 24 million persons are working in countries other than their own. But what we would like to suggest is that over a period each country of the ESCAP region must develop its own human resources and try to reduce the dominance of foreign management.

Promotion of Hill Tourism

India has made a consistent, though not always meaningful, effort to promote tourism for the last 50 years. The number of visitors increased from 1,23,000 in 1960 to 4,10,000 in 1973, showing an average 12 per cent compounded annual increase as against a nine per cent global increase during the same period. But the rapid growth of international travel has been halted, at any rate temporarily, until the world economy readjusts itself to new price levels. In 1974, there were 4,23,161 visitors to India, an increase of 3.2 per cent over 1973, against a global decline of three per cent. A hopeful aspect of tourism in India is the comparatively long average length of stay of tourists—nearly 28 days. Hence the economic value of 4,23,161 visitors is much greater than a million visitors a year to Singapore or Thailand with an average stay of four and six days. But considering the size of the country, foreign tourism has made a limited economic and social impact on India as a whole.

These figures of course, relate to foreign visitors to India. Foreign visitors are important to the national economy because they bring in foreign exchange of which there is a chronic shortage in most of the developing countries. But the foreign visitors constitute a much smaller market in most countries. For instance, it is estimated that even though the USA has been contributing in the last 45 years the largest number of visitors to the international travel market, the number of Americans who go abroad each year is only six per cent of the total US holiday market. In other words, 94 per cent US residents who take one or more vacation each year do so in the USA.

Domestic Tourism

Tourism in the hill regions of India consists mainly of domestic visitors. Even in Kashmir which has always attracted a large number of foreign investors they constitute only about eight to ten per cent of total visitors. Hence the importance of the home holiday market in the present context. We have talked of the importance of domestic tourism for years but no serious effort on a national scale has been made to promote domestic tourism in India. The reasons given are: our transport system is already over-stretched and promoting travel will impose extra burden; the economic resources are severely limited and should be utilised for priority purposes, not for spending funds on creating facilities for domestic tourists. The answer is that tourism, foreign or domestic, is one of the methods of stimulating production and adding to the GNP. It is a shortsighted policy to consider domestic tourism wasteful of scarce resources.

Unfortunately, we don't know the size of the holiday market for our hill regions. There has been practically no compilation of statistics on domestic tourism, or what may be more aptly described as the home holiday market. The Jammu and Kashmir Government does collect statistics of visitor arrivals. Despite some loopholes in their method of head count, one could regard them as reasonably accurate. In 1973, there were nearly 2,00,000 visitors to Kashmir of which 19,000 were foreigners and about 1,80,000 from the rest of India. According to a survey of tourism in Jammu and Kashmir conducted in 1970-71, by a market research firm on behalf of the Ministry of Tourism and Civil Aviation, the per capita expenditure of the foreign and Indian visitors in Jammu and Kashmir was Rs. 838 and Rs. 481 respectively and the total expenditure by all visitors was Rs. 64 million. This did not include expenditure by pilgrims to Vaishno Devi. The pilgrims, though low spenders, must have contributed a substantial amount because of their larger numbers, nearly 4,50,000. At the present price level, which is about 70 per cent more than that of 1970-71 and with the increase in the number of visitors as well as pilgrims, the input in 1974 to the Jammu and Kashmir economy must have been close to Rs. 120 million. It would be more difficult to make such an estimate for Himachal Pradesh because it is more spread out area and accessible from several entry points. According to the figures we have been given, the number of visitors who called at the tourist centres of Himachal Pradesh in 1974 was 1,78,000. Since only those visitors call at a tourist centre who need some assistance, the total number must be considerably more—may be about 3,00,000. Of those who called at the tourist centres, there were about 9,000 foreigners, but a majority of them presumably were foreigners resident in India. However, no estimate of how much the visitors to Himachal Pradesh spent on board, lodging, transport, shopping etc. is available. No data is available on tourism in respect of hill regions in other states. We would strongly recommend that an economic survey of tourism in all the key hill regions of India should be arranged by the state governments concerned, and administrative machinery for collecting statistics on tourists—their number, length of stay, mode of transport used, places visited and so on should be established for each hill region.

Tradition and History

Mountains have always been a source of fascination to human beings. Perhaps they satisfied a psychological urge to be higher than others and to get closer to heaven.

In India the tradition of going to the Himalayas goes back to antiquity. There are hundreds of ancient stories of men seeking spiritual solace in the Himalayas. We are all familiar with the story that the Pandavas after the pyrrhic victory in the battle of Mahabharata were so distraught that Yudhishthira accompanied by his brothers and their consort, Draupadi, exiled himself to the Himalayas. And, of course, trade caravans traversed mountain passes until recent times. High altitude peaks may not have been climbed by mountaineering expeditions but most of them were identified and named. The first important tourists who made annual journeys to a hill resort for pleasure were the Mughal emperor Jehangir and his empress Nur Jehan. But tourism in the mountains in the modern sense started a little more than a hundred years ago mainly because the British personnel—civil and military— wanted to get away from the plains during the summer. A number of resorts or hill stations were established.

The British then did something unique: instead of going to the hill resorts for a holiday, they started going there for work. The central government moved its offices to Shimla and each provincial government moved to a hill station designated as the summer capital for six months in the year. This inevitably attracted to the hill stations a large number of other people who had some business with the administration or those who wanted to be close to the Rulers. The habit of going for a vacation to hill resorts gradually spread among the richer and upper middle classes. Going to the hills for the summer season became a status symbol with many Indian families. A number of hill resorts that were not summer capitals were also developed. This phase lasted until the Second World War. The development of tourism in the hill resorts, it must be recalled, was a by-product of this exodus of the rich and the elite. At any rate it was not a policy decision of the authorities to promote tourism as a vehicle of economic development of the hill regions.

Post-War Phase

After the war came Independence and the new Indian

Administration, more democratic and popular in character, for obvious reasons, stopped moving to remote hill stations. The hill stations suffered for a few years but a new type of clientele came into being. The number of persons visiting the hill stations was much larger than it was in the heyday of the British period, but they were not high spenders. Expensive hotels and clubs in many hill resorts closed down or were restructured to meet the requirements of the medium income guests. They went to the hills for pleasure, not for business or prestige. A new pattern emerged and the tourist season shrank from six months to three months.

The length of the season is partly determined by the school vacations because families can take vacations when the children have holidays. At present the more popular hill resorts attract the highest number of visitors from May to July, because this is the period of school vacations. September and October still attract a reasonable volume of visitors with a spurt of visitors for a brief period of two to three weeks around Durga Puja holidays, particularly from Bengal. The problem of seasonality is, however, not peculiar to the hill regions of India. It is almost universal.

Throughout Europe and North America, the traditional months for vacations are July and August. Millions of tourists travel during these two months and comparatively much fewer take a vacation in the winter or even in September, October and November. It is obviously most uneconomic to create transport and accommodation facilities which remain unutilised for eight or nine months in the year. Over the years great efforts have been made, particularly in Europe, to expand the holiday season. In certain countries, paid holidays given to workers as part of social benefits have been staggered. Consistent efforts have also been made, with at least partial success, that the school vacation should also be staggered, not only at the national level but even among neighbouring countries. Incentives for cheaper travel are given in the off season and winter sports and other attractions have been promoted to tempt people to take vacations at different times of the year. In fact, the mountain resorts in the Alps and in the Rockies in North America are filled to capacity during the skiing season. The main problem still is the in-between period, usually described in the travel business as the shoulder period. One can see most exciting advertisements which start appearing in the consumer and trade magazines, offering discounts and incentives for holidays in the third season, other than the summer and winter seasons. We have to take similar measures to overcome the problem of seasonality which plagues our hill resorts.

We would like to make some recommendations with a view to expanding the tourist seasons of the hill regions. Their implementation would require concerted action at a high level by the Central and state governments.

(a) The period of summer vacations being eight to nine weeks, a system could be introduced whereby the two months period of vacation in different parts of the country is spread over a period of five months, from the beginning of May to the end of September. The timetables of educational institutions have, of course, to be determined by academic considerations and promoting the economy of the hill regions cannot be an important consideration from their viewpoint. In fact, the educational authorities may consider this suggestion quite unrealistic. However, it may be recalled that until 45 years ago the school and college vacations in the Punjab were in July, August and September for ten to twelve weeks and in Uttar Pradesh in May, June and July for nine weeks as at present. We doubt if the educational system suffered because the two neighbouring states had different periods of school vacations. This suggestion is worth exploring, not only because of the hill regions, but because it would lessen the strain on the transport system of the country if travelling on holiday or for other purposes was spread over five months instead of being concentrated in two months.

(b) Substantial discounts should be granted by railways, road transport undertakings and Indian Airlines for travel to the hill stations during the offseasons, and not in the peak season. At the same time hotels, guest houses and similar tourist establishments in the hill resorts should lower their prices. Such concessions on travel by rail have been in existence for years, but not by road transport undertakings, except on some routes in combination with the railways. Private hotels as a routine sales policy reduce their rates in the offseason and so do, we believe, guest houses and tourist bungalows in Himachal Pradesh. We would strongly recommend a co-ordinated sales promotion policy for each hill region so that package or inclusive holiday tours could be offered to tourists in the offseason based on rebated prices for both travel and accommodation by all public and private sector undertakings.

The railways at present grant a 25 per cent rebate on travel to the nearest railhead from 1st April to 30th September, subject to a minimum mileage which is so high that residents of Delhi going to Kalka or Pathankot are not eligible for the concession. Besides rebate should be granted in the offseasons including the winter and not in May and June.

(c) New attractions should be created particularly in the winter season and the shoulder periods of July and August in Himachal Pradesh; in Naini Tal, Mussoorie and other hill resorts of Uttar Pradesh; in Darjeeling in West Bengal and in Meghalaya; and during October and November in Kashmir in order to extend the brief Durga Puja season. Most of the hill resorts, in particular Kashmir and the Simla region, have been trying to organise winter sports with a modicum of success. It is heartening to note that about 30,000 tourists visited Simla, Kufri and their environs in the 1973 winter season and a few hundred went to Gulmarg even though it is quite a distance from the plains. But winter sports has become a highly specialised international activity. To create winter sports facilities of an international standard at Gulmarg or any mountain slopes in the Simla region would cost millions of rupees. Thousands of people travel between North America and Europe, both ways, or to Japan to ski on their favourite slopes. Many skiers like to try new slopes from year to year for the sake of novelty and a status symbol. Judging from newspaper reports an illusion seems to have been created that our ski resorts in Gulmarg and Kufri would attract a large number of skiers from abroad. This is completely untrue. We think we should be realistic enough to know that this is not likely for many years to come. Our facilities at Gulmarg are at best of the elementary standard even though it has been a high priority project for the 1963-1973 decade. It seems to have been mishandled by too many experts. We are not sure if the money necessary to create winter sports facilities of an international standard is available at present. We suggest that we should give up this objective as beyond our reach, for the present, and instead make many areas in the mountains in Kashmir, Uttar Pradesh, Himachal Pradesh and Meghalaya accessible to domestic visitors in the winter season and develop basic facilities of winter accommodation, small amateur ski slopes and skating rinks.

(d) Winter sports is only one of the attractions. Most of the hill regions are rich in folklore, festivals, fairs, folk dances and music.

Himachal Pradesh, Meghalaya, Manipur, Nagaland and Mizoram are well-known for their folk dances and music. The Dussehra festival in Kulu is, perhaps, the only event which has been promoted and sold nationally and internationally to tourists. We would strongly urge that the tourist organisations of the hill regions should develop folklore attractions on an organised basis but without allowing the genuine tradition to degenerate into a 'folksy' show. Fairs, dances and music concerts, religious festivals, once they are properly organised should then be promoted by incentive travel and publicity. This has been done most successfully in many tourist resorts in other parts of the world. The state governments should set up organising committees to work out the details of such festivals in each hill area.

(e) Trekking in the Himalayas, which is now receiving belated recognition, can be a great attraction. Mountaineering gets more publicity but it is for the few. Trekking is a hobby and recreation which would attract large numbers. Now that the restrictions on entry to certain areas have been lifted, trekking offers a new range of possibilities. We would recommend that clubs to promote trekking should be set up in hill resorts. It would be necessary to compile and collate detailed information on trekking routes and disseminate it in a presentable form all over India through travel trade channels as well as government tourist offices.

(f) Sports: In view of the lack of sophisticated air transport services and accommodation in our hill resorts, except Srinagar, it is not likely that there will be a large influx of foreign tourists. However, we believe that it is still the aim of the authorities responsible for developing the hill resorts to attract foreign visitors. In that case, two added attractions that should be developed are tennis and golf. They are the fastest growing sports of the world today. Like other sports, tennis and golf have also become highly professionalised, but at the same time a very large number of amateurs or ordinary people are increasingly playing these games, particularly when holidaying. It is a pity that even Srinagar which is connected by adequate air services and has several good hotels does not have even one first grade 18 hole golf course or sufficient number of tennis courts for tourists. The one golf course in Gulmarg which was quite famous at one time, now doesn't measure up to present international standards.

(g) Business conventions have become an important segment

of tourist business in industrialised countries. As India is rapidly becoming industrialised many large business houses and professional organisations have started holding annual conventions and seminars. Quite often they want to get away from large metropolitan cities for holding such meetings. We believe that those hill stations which have sufficient hotel accommodation and conference facilities can attract this new segment of business. Convention business is basically an offseason business and, therefore, doubly welcome. To start with hill stations like Simla, Srinagar, Naini Tal, Mussoorie, Darjeeling and Ooty could be the venue of such conventions in months like September, October and November. There are many resorts in other parts of the world which virtually live on convention business. We would suggest that the state governments concerned should seriously consider upgrading the conference facilities in these and other hill stations which are easily accessible.

Investment in Tourism Infrastructure

The total investment by the Central Government including union territories and of the state governments during the last few years for developing tourist facilities, *per se,* is in the region of Rs. 450 million. This covers the period of the Second and Third Plans, the three annual Plans and the Fourth Plan. Considering the size of our national Plans and the magnitude of expenditure an investment of Rs. 450 million in the public sector is pitifully small. The figures of investment in the hill areas of Uttar Pradesh, West Bengal, Meghalaya, Arunachal Pradesh, Mizoram, Manipur and Nagaland are not available but the two states which almost entirely consist of hill areas, Jammu and Kashmir and Himachal Pradesh have made investment of Rs. 21 million and Rs. 10.5 million respectively between 1956-74. Some of the expenditure has also been incurred by the Centre and the India Tourism Development Corporation in these two states. But even these investments, presumably much higher than investment in the hill regions of other states, cannot be regarded as adequate. There is also a tendency to spend the available funds on too many small projects. This may be due to local pressures but it is not a sound tourism policy to spread the butter too thin. Also to look after too many small establishments adds to the management problems.

Transport and Communications

What is equally, or perhaps more important, is the development of transport and communications in the hill regions. After all this has been the biggest obstacle to their development. Transport and communication services to and within hill regions are bound to be far more expensive than in the plains. A number of new roads have been built in most of the hill regions for economic, strategic and touristic purposes. Many areas which were more or less inaccessible have been opened up. This is a most healthy development but from the point of tourist requirements the transport and communication services are still inadequate. The only major hill resort which is connected by air services is Srinagar. Road transport services are available to most of the hill stations but generally speaking not of high quality. The tourists are looking for new places. Ten years ago Kathmandu and other resorts in Nepal were a new sensation in the tourism world. Now it is Bhutan. A tour of Bhutan by an international group of tourists conducted by one of the most adventuresome travel agents, Eric Lindblad of New York, has made headlines in the travel Press of the world. In this context, the major event in the decision that certain areas beyond the Inner Line that were hitherto prohibited would now be open to tourists, Indian and foreign. We are sure that Ladakh, Lahaul, Badrinath and new areas in the north-eastern and eastern borders in Manipur, Arunachal, Meghalaya, now open to foreign visitors, would become great sensation, offering a unique experience to tourists, if properly publicised.

Management and Services

The most important problem of tourism, at all resorts in India, but in particular in the hill regions, is management and services. As mentioned earlier, the change in the visitor profile has made many select hotels and clubs in hill stations unprofitable. One need not feel nostalgic for the old days because the new traffic pattern is in many ways a more healthy and natural development. To meet its requirements, new accommodation has been created by state governments or state financed undertakings. What has gone wrong is that the services provided in the guest houses, tourist huts, youth hostels etc. are by and large unsatisfactory. It is basically a problem of management. During 1972 we have seen quite a few state managed accommodation units and have checked our impressions with other visitors. While there have been marked improvements in roads, transport services and communications, there seems to have been hardly any improvement in services.

Let us identify the problems. First, the furniture and furnishings. Traditionally government accommodation units are furnished by the Public Works Department. An ordinary civil engineer of the PWD is not necessarily qualified to furnish a tourist bungalow or hut. In many of the tourist accommodation units that we have seen, the furniture and furnishings were apparently designed on a standard scale with scant regard for the size and shape of the rooms. They are not functional and in many cases shoddy and in poor taste. The same furniture and furnishings, if suitably designed, could have made the accommodation more comfortable without any extra cost. The next problem is of maintenance. There are more than 1,500 tourist beds spread all over the Jammu and Kashmir state and more than a thousand beds in Himachal Pradesh. On a lesser scale the same may be true of hill areas in other states. It would be a very difficult proposition in any circumstances to maintain a large number of small establishments satisfactorily and to provide good services in all of them. Many of the new tourist bungalows are equipped with electric appliances: heaters (and airconditioners where necessary), geysers, lamps and, of course, plumbing. But the staff in-charge of small units is untrained and in many cases illiterate. The staff structure is also non-functional. In one hill state, of a tourist staff of about 580, more than 300 are watchmen, sweepers, gardeners, labourers and orderlies as against only 15 technical personnel such as electricians and plumbers. It is not surprising that when a guest walks into a tourist hut or guest house he finds that half the gadgets don't seem to work.

It has often been suggested that tourist services being highly personalised, government departments are not geared to provide them. In an official organisation, centralised or remote control is almost inevitable. The man on the spot, in-charge of a tourist establishment, a guest house or a cafeteria, usually has no authority to buy necessary supplies or arrange repairs. Hence the day-to-day requirements of guests are not met. Several state governments have, therefore, set up public sector undertakings and are trying to operate them on a commercial basis. Presumably this is a step in the right direction but what is required is a new management system. We are not the only country which has to run small tourist establishments in out of the way centres, often scattered over a large area. There are a large number of resorts in the Caribbean islands, hill resorts in the Alps etc. with 20 to 40 bed establishments run as commercial ventures.

The manager is often a versatile, all purpose man, sometimes a husband-wife team, with necessary skills for repairs, maintenance, book-keeping etc. In many other countries, as far apart as Mexico and Venezuela in Latin America; Spain and Greece in Europe; Kenya, Tanzania and Zambia in Africa, there are small resorts in the mountains and forests and on the sea beaches. They are generally well-furnished and well-managed and clean. India suffers from a curious dichotomy which baffles foreigners. We have shown capacity for nuclear and space technology, we are producing industrial goods and producing technical manpower for other countries, and yet we can't keep our resorts as clean as Africa and other Asian countries can. It is not often realised that during the last 50 years a great change has come over the lifestyle of our people. The new Indian clientele is more sophisticated and demanding and resents the lack of good management and cleanliness of the resorts and the tourist centres. To bring about a new system may take time but meanwhile we would strongly recommend that each state should establish a massive training programme for the staff at all levels. It is equally important that furnishing, renovation and maintenance should be entrusted to qualified staff with some specialisation in these matters.

The economic value of tourism cannot be judged in absolute terms but in relation to the performance of other sectors of the economy. With the given input, tourism's performance is better and also more benign in relation to ecology than of most other industries. However, many economists have questioned this thesis in the case of developing countries. But it is largely accepted that tourism can redress regional imbalance. We have the classic example of Sicily in Italy and the Caribbean islands, which are poor in natural resources but rich in tourist attractions. Tourism has been the great catalyst for their overall economic development. The economic development of a region is generally determined by the availability of raw materials and sources of energy. The hill regions, almost all over the world, are deficient in natural resources. There may be a potential for developing hydro-electric power but what can be done with it if there are no raw materials and minerals for industrial development. All the resources needed for tourist development however are readily available in the form of mountains, valleys, natural scenery and beautiful weather. Their great virtue is that they cannot be depleted. They can be polluted but, except in the Kashmir Valley, we have not reached anywhere near the danger point which comes with the large influx of tourists. However, well planned development is absolutely necessary as a protection against future environmental pollution. Over the years, people from hill regions have come down to the plains looking for employment opportunities. Tourism is a labour intensive industry and can generate large scale employment in the hill regions. Experience has shown that the promotion of tourism should be integrated with the rest of the economic and social development of the region.

Marketing Hill Tourism

In selling tourism we are selling something intangible and not a product that can be touched or seen beforehand. But the technique of selling tourism is not essentially different from the selling of other products. The product that the hill regions have to offer is highly attractive but the question we wish to pose is: is it being packaged and marketed all over India and overseas. The Jammu and Kashmir government has established a number of tourist information offices, in Pathankot, Delhi, Bombay and Calcutta; the Himachal government has a tourist office in New Delhi; and a few other state governments, Bengal, Orissa and Andhra Pradesh have similar offices. Some of the state governments have also been publishing tourist literature which is available in their tourist offices. All this, however, doesn't constitute an adequate marketing effort. There should be wide dissemination of tourist literature through travel trade channels—travel agencies, carriers, transport operators etc.; promotional campaigns with audio-visual aids should be launched; journalists and travel writers should be encouraged to visit the hill regions and write about them; and even more important, well-designed tours in combination with travel agencies and carriers should be packed and sold. The opening up of new areas beyond the Inner Line offers the hill regions a great marketing opportunity because they now have a unique product to sell. If this opportunity is fully exploited then tourism could really make an impact on the economy of the hill regions and in the course of time redress the imbalance.

3

Finance, Development and Marketing

The tourism organisation in every country looks after the development, promotion and administration which includes training programmes and research. Finance is required for these functions. The formulation and physical development of tourist product requires large capital investment in the infrastructure and in individual facilities. In the developing countries, particularly in new tourist areas, investment in infrastructure must precede investment in individual facilities. It represents a greater proportion of the total investment. For example, in the development of the Kovalam Beach or Gulmarg areas in India almost 70-80 per cent of the total investment requirements was for projects like roads, parks, and clearance services etc. and 20-30 per cent for railways, accommodation and other individual facilities. It all requires a long-term finance. Even in spite of the completion of these individual items, long-term and medium-term finance is required for modernisation and extension schemes. The short-term finance is also required for the maintenance of the infrastructure and for individual facilities.

Tourism promotion also calls for current financing of the media employed. A large part of the budget of most tourist organisations is employed for financing these medias.

The finance is also required for operating expenses of tourist organisation. It includes all costs of the organisational structure.

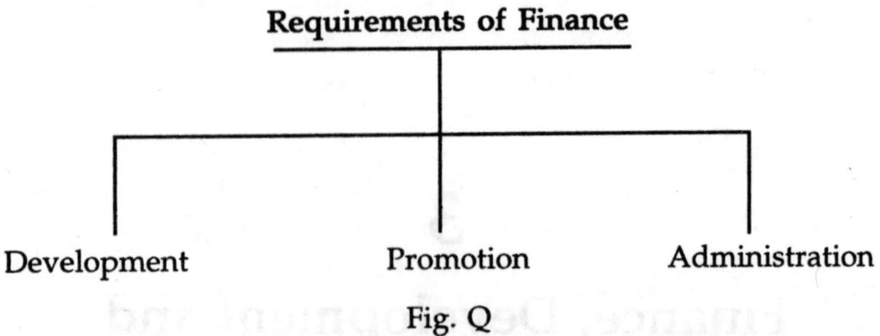

Fig. Q

The financial and technical resources required for successful promotional and development strategies in tourism are beyond the mean of private sector. Tourism is a capital intensive industry where profitability is long-term oriented. Even the most developed countries, where vast travel plan modernisation, expansion and related training programmes are taken up require large investments and are feasible only with state assistance. In developing countries, the state's role is even more vital in paving the way for private sector which is often hesitant, limited and untrained in modern technique.

Sources of Finance

The various sources of finance can be grouped as follows:

1. Government Agencies
2. Leading Institutions
3. Investors
4. Industry
5. Tourists
6. Tourist Organisations.

1. Government Agencies

The state should pay for most of the cost of running tourism development programmes.

Various arguments are put forward in support of the contribution of finance by the government in tourism.

(*a*) International tourism solves problems of direct government concerns and the maximum benefit of tourism goes to the government as compared to any other economic sector of a country. The government is itself a major recipient of revenue from tourism through direct and indirect taxation. The multiplier effect of tourism is 3.2 times a year and the government collects around 10 per cent in tax revenues from this additional business. Compared to the total expenditure required to run tourism development programmes, the tax revenues would give the government a greater return than is earned by any accommodation unit, transport agency or travel agents.

(b) The government of a country has an interest in the healthy balance of payments. Tourism plays a significant role in this aspect.

(c) The economic benefits of tourism often extend directly and indirectly to a whole area and to the whole population. The contribution to tourism by the government can enhance the material well-being of the community.

(d) It is legitimate for the government to intervene financially in circumstances in which private enterprise may not be able to willing to do so adequately.

The government should finance at national, regional and local level. In most of the countries, the tourist organisations are a part of the machinery of the governments. Therefore, it normally plays an active role in tourism and uses the national tourism organisations as its administrative organ for the purpose. In the absence of non-government tourism organisation the government is comparatively less involved in tourism financing. The government should finance tourism development organisation by direct appropriation. Direct taxes on the tourists should be avoided as far as possible. These direct taxes are inadequate to raise the sufficient money, to run an effective tourism programme. It has been observed that direct taxation tend to cut off tourism itself and thus a loss to the government. The government also may utilise local currency funds generated by the sale of imports made available by foreign aid programmes to finance special training programmes, some of the costs of technical assistance, a part of the cost of improving an air terminal, lengthening or building an air strip or building or improving special tourism attractions.

The government assumes a prime responsibility for financing

tourism promotion. The expenditure made by government in this regard enhances the impact of promotion undertaken by individual operators. In some of the countries, the cost of such destination promotion is relatively small in relation to local costs of individual promotion. For example, it is estimated in Spain that individual interest spend at least 10 times as much as the Spanish government does on promotion abroad.[1]

The funds are applied by the government itself or they may be channelled to the tourist organisation by way of grant, loans or fiscal aids. At local level, the local government grant may be raised as a proportion of local taxes. For example, in Britain, local authorities are empowered to raise a given maximum product of rates for tourism promotion purposes. In some cases a given contribution is required from other interests, which determines the size of the government contribution. In Switzerland, the government levies 25 per cent of the cost of the publicity from the beneficiary industries and localities and re-imburses them 25 per cent of the cost of their individual promotion.[2] There is one more method of government contribution by way of incentives. In this case, the tourists are exempted from certain taxes, for example by issue of tax-free petrol coupons.

In order to build up permanent tourism attraction, the government may finance the long-term investments. It is done by directly starting a government operation or by lending the money to the private enterprise. In advanced tourist destination, governments are usually involved in a whole spectrum of activities ranging from investment in transport and accommodation, through various forms of assistance to fiscal arrangements. In the initial stages, a heavy capital is required for the provision of necessary infrastructure. The private enterprise, the banks and the credit institutions also play an important part in this aspect. The government financing serves to stimulate and complement private enterprise rather than doing what private enterprise is able and willing to do. Direct government investment in tourism superstructure is undertaken to stimulate private investment as is being done in countries like Spain, Greece and Portugal. It all is done through sharing in ownership or through providing subsidies to the developers. Thus the government can influence the location, type and quality of development by advancing credit facilities, loan at preferential rates of interest and fiscal arrangements both for investment and subsequent operation of facilities.

The specialist nature of tourism development and the varying scope of the tourist organisation requires a separate government agency for financing physical development in tourism. There are various agencies which provide means of channelling public funds into tourism development. For example, the Caisse centrals de Credit Hotlier in France, the Portuguese Tourist Fund, the Israeli Tourist Industry Development Corporation. In India, we have the India Tourism Development Corporation.

Tourism, in developing countries, however, raises certain problems relating to investment and profitability. Hotel and tourism investment in these countries are extremely heavy both in infrastructure and superstructures. An intensive tourism development policy, therefore, needs considerable capital investments. But the scarcity of capital is precisely one of the principal characteristics of these countries. Hence it becomes necessary to work out a precise and balanced system of planning.[3]

The state should direct foreign capital seeking investment opportunities towards the areas chosen for tourism development. The investments made in the field of tourism should be of benefit to the other sectors of economy. Anything that would reduce the compactness of the amenities should be avoided. Isolated or small sized amenities which may not be put to other uses for a long time should be expressively disallowed, especially in countries suffering from shortage of capital.

An interesting solution which be adopted to the countries is that the state, through a company called the Tourism Development Corporation becomes a minority shareholder in companies wanting to invest. In this way, the corporation can be a constant check on the progress of construction and the observance of deadlines. The success of such a policy, which exclude any state loans or guarantee, seems to depend on several factors:

1. Good profitability of hotel investments based on a regular increase in tourist traffic spread most of the year;
2. Relatively limited size of the construction programmes (6,500 bed over 5 years) to enable a company to follow the administrative, technical and financial developments and to set effectively.

Aid to the tourist industry should be based on the following criteria:

(*a*) need for helping the hotel investor to find loan capital;

(*b*) capital concerned should be long-term capital; and

(*c*) it should be lent at low rates of interest.

On this basis, it is possible to draw up a model of a system of state loans from public funds for the hotel and tourist industries.

The preliminary, but indispensable step before establishing a system of state aid for financing tourism industries for the state is to fix the priority goal to be attained on the basis of an analysis of the potential market. It should work out a tourism policy which necessarily mean planning. It should seems indispensable to link the grant of a loan to an undertaking to train competent personnel at all levels of management executives.

There may be several sources for these funds:

1. Budgetary, where a certain amount is allocated every fiscal year;
2. Proceeds from taxes or other duties levied on tourists and the tourist industries (passport, fees, taxes) on purchase of foreign currency and other taxes etc.;
3. Receipts by state from the earnings of tourist enterprises in which it participates; and
4. Aid from international organisations like the World Bank.

As regards the administration of loans, it seems appropriate to entrust it to a separate body. It should be able to co-ordinate the actions undertaken in respect of infrastructure and superstructure and see that the policy decided upon is carried out and consequently to ensure observance of governmental control. Such a body could be a branch of governmental department or a specialised technical institution. In either case, an effective control should be maintained both before the grant of financial aid and after the execution of the work.

The rate of interest on loan will depend on economic conditions. Such a ratio should be compatible with the anticipated profitability and with the market rate. It may be added that in general, the rate of interest varies from 3.5 to 6 per cent. The application of preferential rate in the field of tourism debars straightway any rate exceeding the maximum of 6 per cent.

The period of the loan should be in consideration of the cost of investments made, anticipated profitability of the enterprises, guarantees offered and the amount of the loan.

The fundamental condition remains that the capital loaned should be on a long-term basis. Under such conditions, it does not seem possible to grant plans to new constructions for period of less than 14 to 25 years. A repayment period of 20 years is often necessary.

The most delicate problem is that of the amount of the loan to be granted. The percentage of the amount loaned ranges between 40 per cent and 60 per cent. Beyond this, difficulties would arise and might seriously affect the profitability of the enterprise and also deminish the responsibility of the investors. Without fixing the amount of the loan as a percentage of the total cost of operations, the system practised in Spain, for example would be quite adaptable in the developing countries. It consists in not exceeding a certain sum per room constructed according to the degree of comfort to be provided. It has the merit of allowing a closer supervision of the progress of the constructions programmes and allowing unnecessary expenses.

Investment and the system established for financing them should not be considered in the abstract. They should always be evaluated on the basis of their direct profitability and their impact on the general economy. The rules must be especially repeated in the field of tourism because of the large size of the investments to be made.

The initial choice to be made regarding the policy to be defined and followed. This is even more important to search for capital funds. Such a choice regarding detailed preliminary studies in the nature, size and direction of tourism investment is absolutely essential.

The state or a public body meets a certain percentage of the investment expenditure in order to reduce the total expenses. This technique is employed in some industrialised countries for the development of less prosperous regions.

The state may offer directly or through the intermediary of a specialised bank, loans which are essentially supplied from the public budget. These loans are added in variable proportions in the capital invested by the private groups themselves. This system is very widely prevalent in many countries. According to the

IUOTO Study referred to earlier, 39 out of 66 countries supply such loans.

The real source of the funds may vary. Some of these loans come from the normal budget of the state, others from multilateral or bilateral foreign aid programme like the Marshall Plan in the recent past.

Without the state having to disburse its funds, one or several specialised banks are authorised to grant loans to investors interested in a particular priority sector like tourism. These funds may come from long-term loans floated by one or several banks inside the country or abroad or issued to international organisations. Such funds may also come from ordinary banks with a guarantee of repayment from the Reserve Bank or from a specialised establishment. Grant of protection guarantees are supplied either by the state or by a financial establishment empowered by it to do so. Other aids and incentives include scheme to provide relief on annual charges.

They concern:

— Reduced rate of interest on loans from public funds;

— Interest rebates paid annually by the state to provide relief on the annual interest payment on ordinary bank loans of or on loans of special kind.

— Exemptions from taxes on profits or corporate taxes or other direct taxes (particularly land taxes, payable by firms).

In any case for choice of types of aid and their application should in every case be subject to a concern for effectiveness as regards employment, foreign exchange earnings and profitability.

In developing countries, investment is not an end in itself but is justified by its direct profitability and general economic usefulness.

There is no other field where this rule is more imperative than in tourism on account of the large size of the investments required, and the high level of capital coefficient which makes it one of the most expensive industries.

A tourism plan, devised in consultation with the tourist industry, acceptable to it and widely understood, is probably the most important step that any country can take to ensure a balanced programme of investment in the development of tourism.

A national programme should state clearly both the objectives and the limit of public investment. Private investors need assurance that public investment in infrastructure will be phased to support their own investment in facilities intended specifically for tourists.

They want to know how far the authorities mean to carry public investment in hotel accommodation and allied tourist facilities. Both Spain and Greece have succeeded in striking a satisfactory balance between public and private investment.

The hotels, motels and wayside restaurants, operated directly by their governments, have been intended to provide accommodation where private facilities did not exist, such as at strategic cross roads remote from urban areas and in some historic towns. They have also been conceived as models for prices, comforts and service which private operation could emulate.

When direct public investment in tourism does take place, operation should be under normal commercial condition, so that private businessman do not feel they are at a disadvantage vis-a-vis the state power. The first essential is that if a public corporation is set up, it should be independent of the national tourist office, and of all other public agencies. Furthermore, the public corporation should be obligated to cover all interest charges and to provide for depreciation. It should also be subject to the same administrative regulation as private hotel business.

Private investment inevitably takes place against a background of various types of government regulation. Government regulation can be of a positive force for creating a suitable investment climate. However, it must not be felt to be cumbersome or arbitrary. It should be established in consultation with the tourist trade, and self-regulation should be encouraged wherever possible.[4]

Experience in successful tourist countries in Europe shows that government regulation of prices has negative effects that are often serious. Official regulated prices are often out of date with current operating costs and as a result price controls are often evaded. This is bad for customer relations and in the long-run discourages tourist potential visitors out to have reliable information about how much their vacation is going to cost. Moreover the experience of price controls—even when they may not be observed in practice—tends to discourage further hotel expansion by creating an additional uncertainty about the return that may be expected on new investment.

Hoteliers should be allowed to fix their own prices from year to year, with different rates for the various reasons if they wish. Once the hotelier establishes his schedule of prices for all the full year, it should be communicated to the official agency and should be published in official guide book well in advance. Hotels should then be compelled to maintain the published rates during the year and should be able to sever sanctions for violating quoted prices.

The abolition of price controls in countries which formerly had them, has not led to an excessive rise in hotel prices. There is too much competition among hotels. Competition has, indeed, been intensified as increasing numbers of hotels have been built, in part as result of the stimulus to new construction that removal of price controls has itself provided. In addition, competition for tourists in other countries includes hotel operation to keep prices in check.

When the demand for tourist facilities in a country is increasing—either spontaneously or as a result of assiduous promotion then there should be room for additional profitable investment. And it should produce quick returns, facilities for tourists can be constructed rapidly and thereafter operating income begins to flow with little delay. The amount of money that comes out to flow into the tourist industry should be determined by comparing the rate of return for projects in this sector with that in other sector.

Expansion of tourist facilities, particularly with respect to hotel accommodation, needs to keep pace with demand. The optimum phasing of investment in tourism is admittedly a delicate task. The desire to meet all potential demand must be balanced against the industry and ability to absorb and use it to provide facilities in sufficient quantity and of appropriate quality in such a way that the long-term demand is maintained. Hasty, get rich—quick investments—with poor standards of construction, inadequate staff and training and without provision for associated amenities and entertainment—can rapidly spoil reputation of a resort and badly damage its prospects for long-term development.

Perhaps the most potent tool for stimulating investment in tourism is the provision of credit. Public credit facilities can augment private capital and act as a catalyst.

Because of the special nature of Indian tourism, a separate tourism credit fund is desirable. It may be operated by an existing credit agency but even then, it should be established as a special section so that, expertise in this particular field is developed. When its activities are extensive enough and experience has been gained, the fund could become an autonomous credit institution. A distinction should be made between hotel financing and mortgage banking. The people responsible for providing credit should be looking at the potential of the business as a growing concern rather than at the collateral represented by the real estate value of the land and buildings.

Devising the development of a country's tourism, concession in credit extension are often necessary. Since cash is usually a limiting factor in mounting a project, an increase in the debt equity ratio can be a useful device; the public credit institution can raise the proportion of the total investment which it is prepared to extend as a loan. In addition, amortisation period can be lengthened, so that the burden on operating income is spread. Furthermore, long-term credit can induce businessmen in underdeveloped countries, to engage in business which show a steady return over a period rather than in the short-term operations of little lasting national value which often seem attractive. In doing this, long-term credit has a very desirable instructional effect.

Whatever credit concessions are offered, it is not desirable to charge interest rates significantly below the prevailing market levels. If a project is economically justified, this sort of incentive is not needed. On the contrary, it leads to a misallocation of resources. The business of a hotel credit institution should not be to make loans below the market rate, but to channel public funds into the industry in order to augment the total volume of hotel investment.

By a judicious use of public funds, the authority can ensure that the expansion of hotel accommodation takes place where it is most needed. Funds for tourist expansion should first be concentrated in existing tourist area where consumer preferences have already been demonstrated and where basic facilities exist. In such areas, relatively small investments will yield immediate and high returns. If such funds were spread around the country, irrespective of established demand patterns, additional accommodation in some areas would not be fully used, while in other more popular areas, the contribution to meeting the hotel storage would be proportionately reduced. This does not mean that, new tourist regions might not be opened up if their potential profitability is reasonably clear. However, public money for tourism, like all public funds, should be first to the areas of greatest return.

Most countries provide a range of incentives for reduction investment in various types of activities and tourist enterprises. A re-examination of such incentive system can ensure that the special needs of tourism are more effectively met. Many countries offer a set of tax incentives for listed investment—rebates, allowances, tax holidays, and the like. Tourism often requires a special 'package, including favourable real estate taxation with incentive used as an instrument of the national programme. Differential treatment may be applied, with zones of high priority receiving the most favourable concessions.

Another way to help tourism and thereby to encourage investment is to liberalise the import of capital goods and equipment required both for starting new tourist facilities and for running successfully those already in existence. Concessions on custom duties are sometimes appropriate and of course no bona fide tourist operators must have access to foreign exchange to purchase the necessary goods.

In underdeveloped countries, where local capital markets are limited the prime source of funds for hotel investment is likely to be found abroad. Foreign capital will be forthcoming only if government takes positive steps to encourage it, including the simplification of regulations, reasonable protection of equity, and assurance that foreign investors will be able to take their profits—or at least a proportion of these that will satisfy them—out of the country.

Investment in tourism is stimulated by the general nature of administrative services offered and the control exercised by the state. Entrepreneurs expect vigorous action in national, regional and international programmes and in the maintenance of places of tourist interest, such as historic sites and national parks. State can be of service through its regulations for land acquisition. Labour laws too, are often important in setting the context within which hotels, restaurants and other tourist facilities must operate. The tourist industry is directed towards an international market, therefore, access to specialised foreign personnel is particularly important.

Thus the government cannot only take direct action itself, but can also create an air of welcome to tourists and to the trade which serves them.

2. Non-Government Agencies

International Bank for Reconstruction and Development (IBRD)

Established after the end of the Second World War by the Bretton Woods Agreements, the IBRD is an international finance organisation associated with the United Nations. Its object is to supply member states who should obligatorily be members of the International Monetary Fund, long-term loan needed by them to finance productive development projects which are of top economic priority in cases where they cannot find funds elsewhere on reasonable conditions.

In the beginning, the bank was especially designed to help countries economically revived by the war. Subsequently, under the impact of the Marshall Plan, it oriented its activities towards helping the developing countries.

IBRD provides loans carrying to 6.5 per cent rate of interest for specific profitable operations to solvent firms and states. These loans are designed to cover only a part of the project costs. Its direct and specific help in the field of tourism has been quite limited. But the part it has played in financing infrastructure, which represents its favourite sector (transport, communication and power) has been in many cases most valuable in promoting the development of tourism (the Adriatic and Central Highway in Yugoslavia).

The International Finance Corporation (IFC)

The IFC was established in 1956 to invest directly, without seeking government guarantees (which IBRD cannot do) in production of private enterprises in the developing countries. As at June 30, 1965, its subscribed share capital was $ 110 million of which $ 99 million was paid by 78 states.

The help given by the IFC may take the form of subscription to share capital, ordinary loans coupled with participation in dividends.

Besides its own help the IFC stimulates investment by bringing together national and foreign investors. It also strives to steer private capital towards productive investments in the member countries.

International Development Association (IDA)

Established in 1960 to fill certain gaps in the activities of two organisations mentioned above, the International Development Association can finance all development projects irrespective of their profitability or productivity. This leads it to undertake investments of a social character. However, the financing of infrastructure (transport, water supply, power) so essential to tourism development represents an important part of its activity.

3. Investors

Financing of Private Investments

Called private because of the builder or investor who undertakes them these investments contain large proportion of private capital, at least for the part which has to be supplied by the builder and often even for a part of the loans also.

Most often, such private capital comes from foreign financial groups for reasons explained earlier, but these groups generally ask for both guarantees and other forms of assistance from the underdeveloped countries in which they are ready to invest:

(a) Transfer Guarantee

The first of the guarantees required is for the free transfer of profits from the business undertaken with the help of foreign capital. It is evidently quite normal for private foreign groups investing funds in developing countries to seek assurance for being able subsequently to transfer back the profits from their capital irrespective of the monetary fluctuations in the country in which the investment may have been made. There is no doubt that foreign financing of investments limited to a large extent to the degree of trust which can be placed in the commitments undertaken by the country concerned.

(b) Forms of Assistance (Incentives and Stimuli)

Besides the transfer guarantee the developing countries may consider that it may help to attract foreign or national private capital investments in the form of assistance and facilities to encourage investors.

Such assistance is designed to maximise final net profitability of the private capital invested either by lowering the costs of investment (land allocation, services in kind, subsidies or investments, bonuses) or by reducing the debt service loan capital (interest, rebates, loan at reduced rate of interest). In other words, the private groups should be able to hope that the returns from their capital investments would be at least equal to what they would obtain—all risks being equal—from investing it in other sections or in other countries and particularly in their own country.

It is immediately noticeable how hazardous and uncertain are such comparisons, and consequently, and fixation of the desirable level of incentives. The result is that the introduction of these incentives within the regulations and as part of general policy or on a piecemeal commitment basis require that the state which intends to introduce them should get detailed preliminary studies carried out by the competent national bodies or technical assistance organs. In particular, to determine the size of incentives of all types, it is necessary to carry out beforehand studies on profitability, from different investments taking into account local characteristics of all kinds.

Two procedures or methodological approaches are possible, at least in theory, for determining the level of such assistance:

(a) Fixation of aids in regulations: The state which wants to develop a particular sector like tourism decrees and publishes the type and amount of aid it will be willing to give in that sector for each kind of investment (hotels, holiday camps, sailing, sporting and recreational facilities). The aid may be adjusted along various lines and according to the geographical position, the technical characteristics of the installations, their capacity, their method of management etc. But, in any case, the determination of the aid should be one beforehand on an objective basis.

(b) The ad hoc approach of piecemeal commitments whereby the state—in fact, one of its specialised departments—decides about the type of and size of the aid to be given to particular

investment projects by taking into consideration all the features of the project (location, size, method of financing, profitability expectations). This technique, should in theory, result in optimising aid. But it implies, in general, longer and closer study by the state. Besides, it is best with uncertainty and hence less stimulating for those who wish to invest. In the case of the developing countries, it has the disadvantage of opening the door to difficult negotiations with private groups who are often quite powerful.

First type of aid includes schemes, designed to reduce the initial cost of investment.

Assistance in kind are designed to reduce the initial cost of investment.

This comprises the supply to a private investor by a public body or the state of certain physical elements belonging to this body. The most frequent case is that of land allocations.

The cost of loan in developing countries is not very high. Assistance in this connection is often accompanied by the state paying for a substantial part of the construction of infrastructure.

4. Industry

The participants at each vertical level of the tourist organisation are the government and the private tourist interests whose geographical areas of operation corresponds to that level of tourist organisation. They also finance the appropriate level of tourist organisation, central, state or local.

Tourist industry is the main financial beneficiary from tourism. The firms and industries participating in tourism contribute to the financing of the tourist organisation in form of subscriptions, and donations. They also take active part in the co-operative research and promotion projects and share the costs of such schemes. The contribution by individual firms and industries is determined by the level at which these firms and industries operate. The local government play a prominent role in a district, resort or town. The hotel and other local operators participate in the local tourist organisation either directly or through the local association or both. Similarly at regional level, the participants in the tourist organisations are the state government. The groups of hotel located in those regions and the transport companies (bus or coach) operating in the area also participate. At the national level, the

Central Government is the sole financier of the tourist organisation. In addition to it, there are a number of contributors such as airline, railways, chains of accommodation providers, travel agencies, bank and financial institutions of national coverage.

5. Tourists

The main objects for the promotion, development and administration of tourism is to extend the maximum benefits to the tourists. They are the main beneficiaries of tourist services. They must make the contribution for financing tourism. A part of the revenue required by the tourist organisation may be raised directly from the tourists. They make the payment for the services they buy and pay taxes while buying the various services. Thus they are the main contributors of finance in tourism. There are special taxes imposed on them in various countries like Switzerland, Austria Germany etc. These taxes are a good source of revenue to the tourist organisation. The taxes thus collected are utilised

(i) to offset the cost which tourists create, and

(ii) to provide a more equitable basis for sharing the cost of providing and maintaining the amenities used by local residents as well as visitors to that region. The foreign tourists have to pay some indirect taxes. They spend much higher rate than the resident population. The contribution by these tourists is greater as compared to the resident. In Ireland, it has been calculated that an increase of £ 10 million in gross tourist receipts generated by multiplication of income, means an increase of £ 5 million in tax revenue.

Hotel Tax and Tourist Tax

The method of imposing taxes on foreign tourists are to levy a tourist tax at points of entry or exit at the destination. This makes a distinction between the foreign and other visitors. Another method of taxing the visitor is confined to those spending at least one night at the destination i.e. hotel. These taxes in Britain and India are known as hotel tax and tourist tax. If the hotel acts as a collector of the tax on behalf of the community, it is known as Tourist tax or Visitors tax. In case this tax is levied on the accommodation unit, and it recovers it from the visitor, it is called as Hotel tax. The proceeds received from the hotel tax or tourist tax may be retained by the authority for general purposes or it may be applied to finance the tourist organisation, for the provision, improvement and maintenance and amenities and facilities for tourists or even for promotion purposes. Thus the tourists are a great contributor for financing tourism as they are required to contribute directly in particular for purposes of improvement of amenity.

Government and local authorities often levy various taxes on tourist and tourist services trades to recoup the costs incurred in financing the construction of tourist amenities and facilities. The idea of users paying for acceptance is almost all the tourist regions. A rational policy for collection of taxes is urgently needed that is not inconvenient to the tourists, avoids any discrimination and channels the money collected to the expansion and improvement of tourist amenities.

Embarkation Tax

An embarkation tax on domestic air travel may be levied. The government levies a tax of certain percentage of the total value of the ticket. It collects through this device a good sum which could be used for improving airports, communication and navigational facilities and providing civil aviation infrastructure for extending air services to un-connected areas in the other parts of the country.

Already international passengers pay foreign travel tax of certain percentage of the value ticket in many countries. Besides, a flat rate is also paid as airport tax for travel abroad.

In India this tax was recommended as a means to finance a subsidiary of Indian Airlines to operate third services and also to meet the requirements for improving the civil aviation infrastructure. The DGCA (Directorate General of Civil Aviation) hopes that an embarkation tax of 10 per cent will enable it to raise about Rs. 143 crores of next seven to 10 years.

The DGCA feels that there is a rationale for recovery from users the cost of services provided by the department. Its cost of maintaining and modernisation facilities has increased considerably over the past few years. Its revenue has not however kept pace with it.

The Tata Commission on Civil Aviation Review in India brought to the notice of the government the inadequacy of communication and navigational services and the need to immediately modernise the civil aviation infrastructure.

The Civil Aviation Department has also been under pressure from the International Civil Aviation Organisation (ICAO) and the International Air Transport Association (IATA) to revamp ground and navigational support to international services. International and domestic airlines have been opposing the increase in landing and en route navigational charges and other unconventional methods for raising funds. By increasing landing and en route charges, it increased its annual revenue. It, therefore, feels that a levy of embarkation tax would make available sufficient funds needed for this purpose.

Indian Airlines is averse to the embarkation tax, it feels that such a tax will limit its manoeuvrability in increasing its fare. For sometime past the airline has been operating under considerable financial constraints due to the steep rise in the cost of fuel, import of spare parts, sales tax, excise duty and wage bill. It maintains that till today its fare structure is perhaps the lowest for any country. Recently, it was subjected to an additional burden following the steep rise in landing and en route navigational charges.

IA have a times hinted at the expected increase in its fares. They feel that the levy of an embarkation tax will certainly circumscribe their ability to increase its fares.

6. The Tourist Organisation

This is one of the most important source of finance. A tourist organisation may generate income for its purposes through income from other levels, as it is often in a position to earn revenue for the provision of particular services. There are three methods of financing:

1. Grants

In most of the countries, the central tourist organisation wishes to stimulate the state organisation and the state organisation to the local organisation. For this purpose, the higher level of body provides finance to the lower body by way of grants for specific or general purposes or some other means of support. This helps to establish a strong influence to carry out the direction of the higher body. In some of the cases, this type of financing continues till the lower level of organisation becomes established and well organised.

2. *Levies*

There is another method of financing also wherein the lower level organisation finances the higher level organisation in order to create a strong higher level organisation. The countries having advance stage of tourism development, have the method of a levy of other contribution by a lower level organisation to higher level organisation in the vertical structure.

3. *Revenue Earnings*

There are various tourist organisations in different countries which earn revenue from its own activities. The following are the important methods of earning revenue:

(a) Sale of information materials to tourists;

(b) Advisory services to individual firms and industries participating in tourism for fee;

(c) Provide research and other material to operators and other interested parties; and

(d) Advertising space in its publications to advertisers.

Public and Private Finance

There is a mixed pattern of financing in tourism—public finance and private finance. The mixed form of financing is considered appropriate provided that the respective constructions of public and private funds is determined rationally as a matter of policy. The tourism programme should be based on close co-operation between government and private business. Contribution from private will help to ensure active participation by private business e.g. hotels, carriers, travel agents, tour operators and reputable business concerns. The political and economic system of the country, the importance of tourism to the national economy, the stage of tourism development reached in the country and the historical and other influence determine the respective rates of public and private finance in tourism.

The public funds are applied to promotion and administration and for development to be financed largely by private enterprise. The private fund, tend to supplement the provision of public funds for promotion and other purposes. Public finance is the prime and exclusive source of finance at the central level of the tourist organisation and the private funds are used at regional or local levels.

Domestic and Foreign Finance

Finance in tourism comes from both within and abroad. Tourism organisation get financial support from another level of organisation or from outside its own area of operation. These organisations may derive income for the purpose of promotion from transport undertakings, which handle traffic to the destination. In a developing country like India, local capital is generally scarce and foreign investment constructed a necessary means of building upon tourism industry. International character of tourism find an expression in the international ownership and operation of tourism industries in individual countries. There is much wider availability of foreign capital for individual facilities particularly when our area has satisfactorily demonstrated its tourist potential. The main sources of foreign finance are private developers, investors, international agencies, and the foreign tour operators representing a growing source of funds for hotel development. The international agencies and the foreign tour operators and the foreign private investors may undertake a hotel project or enter into partnership with local capital both private and public. The glaring examples for the main source of foreign investment in infrastructure is World Bank and its affiliated development banks.

Co-operation and Co-ordination

There should be free and close collaboration at inter-regional and international level, with the sole aim of promoting stable conditions for the economic development of all the sectors of tourism.

The state authorities should work together to draw up the framework of a uniform policy with regard to international aviation.

The state authorities responsible and the consumer defence organisations should adopt the same attitude with regard to the cost of other elements in the travellers journey as the attitude they at present hold about the air transport sector of tourism.

State, industry and the administrations should co-ordinate to stagger holiday period over the year as a whole so that the tourists infrastructure and air transport equipment can be more intensively used. This should enable economies to be effected.

State and official bodies should initiate campaigns encouraging tourism by facilitating policy and customers facilities, as well as other areas in the treatment of travellers. There should be at least a temporary reduction in all the various fields and tasks whose aim is to pay to the authorities the money they have deposited improving airports and tourist infrastructure.

State should clearly define and legislate the role of 'organisers' in the tourist industry to ensure an orderly development of the industry and the protection of the public interest. Qualifications should be awarded to companies and individuals according to pre-determined standards. It might be a good idea to make compulsory for contractual arrangement between organisers and transport to be accompanied by a definite agreement and for the rates charged by organisers to be supervised.

Development of Tourist Resort

With leisure times as well as discretionary incomes becoming increasingly abundant in countries and cultures throughout the world, travel and tourism would manifest itself strongly in the way of life of the people. Not only would there be greater need for the general infrastructure for tourism, like hotels, restaurants, transportation, entertainment, etc., but large-scale resort developments will be necessary to meet the future growing demand for travel and recreation. Further, man's longing for a paradise where he and nature are in harmony can come true through the creation and utilisation of resort facilities. What is a resort?

A resort is more than a hotel set upon a beach or the lee of a mountain and it must offer a wide range of facilities and qualify as a total development. The Pierre Marques resort outside Acupulco, or the Agha Khan's Costa Smeralda resorts are of world renown and have their own stories to tell. Resorts are of different types and are located in characteristic areas of each type, like sea-side resorts near the seas, health spas, sources of special mineral waters, winter and ski resorts for winter sports on mountains and the hill resorts for cool, bracing air away from summer heat, etc.

The trend for resort development is strong in Europe, USA and certain South American countries, but not much has been done in Asia to create, develop and promote resorts. The benefit of resorts would be basically to provide *(a)* a vacation site and accommodation, *(b)* built-in recreation and sports facilities, *(c)* comparatively isolated and quiet complexes, and *(d)* if possible, an opportunity to have financial interest in a privately-developed resort.

While tourism has already entered the realm of big business, resort development has remained an individualistic and relatively unsophisticated pursuit. The success of each project depends on the varying degree of skill and experience that the promoters may bring to bear upon it. What is required is a combination of specialists in the very sophisticated and technical phases of resort development, marketing and management. Many projects in USA, and elsewhere, have showed poor performance and suffered in the past due to miscalculation of market potential and poor economic feasibility, and some had inappropriately designed facilities, poor activity programmes or poor management.

In this connection, reference may be made to the interesting development of holiday villages established after Second World War. A village complex is a self-sufficient centre of accommodation and recreation. Accommodation is in multiple units, simple but practical with furnishings, fittings or other self-catering facilities. Recreation includes sports, swimming, sauna, badminton, golf etc. The atmosphere is kept as informal as possible. Though these villages became popular in Italy and Spain to start with, it was the Club Mediterranee which institutionalised the village concept. Since 1950 in Majorca, and now covering 25 countries, there is an average of about 600 beds in each village providing excellent accommodation and a variety of recreations. Increasing diversification of facilities is taking place now and business conferences and conventions are being promoted in the villages also.

Considerable research and planning by experienced technicians is essential for the profitable developments of each type of a resort project and careful evaluation of all the geographical and topographical, financial, constructional, marketing and management aspects, is important. The creation and development of a resort would normally have three distinct but consecutive phases as follows:

(*a*) feasibility phase;

(*b*) development phase; and

(*c*) operations phase.

Feasibility Phase

To start with the tourism resources and attractions of a proposed area are listed, studied and analysed in terms of variables and appropriate decisions maximising the objectives planned. This phase is concerned with an analysis of the market, an evaluation of the site for the project, a preliminary design of facilities and lay-out and an estimate of costs and revenues. Market potential, both present and future, must be studied and established on the basis of populational and economic growth, demography of age-groups, present and anticipated consumer preferences, levels of income and leisure.

The site would be evaluated in terms of environment, topography, size of land, soil and water conditions, accommodation, location in terms of markets, supplies and transportation facilities. An appraisal is also made of the widest possible programme of activities and attractions that can be conducted on the site. It is essential to develop concepts which are imaginative yet practical so that the project would attract visitors in volume and the resort would have sustained patronage. Financial feasibility is governed by profitability and the rate of return on invested capital. While the resort may be fine by other standards, it has to meet strict economic tests for present health and future growth.

Development Phase

Having established a positive feasibility envisaged in the type of the project, it is essential to evolve a systematic plan and practical programme for its development. Since resort-users are becoming increasingly discriminating in their demand, they want the facilities provided in an atmosphere of uniqueness and good taste. Profitable operations will depend on good project designs to attract people initially and to sustain their interest for repeated visits. It is a combination of physical and economic interest and aesthetic factors that must be reflected in the design of the resort and its facilities. Each type of the resort, e.g., associated with a beach, a spa, a hill or a mountain for sport or health will have special and characteristic requirements and will call for special approach, facilities and services to give it a distinct particularity and quality. The developmental plan requires overall consideration of the services to be offered, their harmony with the natural setting and a happy relationship and affinity between indoor and outdoor activities. A strong theme should be created and it should pervade as a basis for attracting tourists and to facilitate active promotion of the resort.

This phase involves the designing of a master plan which includes the concept, size and capacities of buildings and special facilities, landscaping, roads, parking and other utilities. Upon completion of the design, a step-by-step programme for construction is drawn up, bearing in mind the most productive and most economical completion period and schedule within the budget. Application of the PERT and CPM has, by experience, been found to be most useful and assisted in time and cost savings.

Operations Phase

No matter how well a project is designed and developed, success in its operation will depend on the competency of the operating staff. Specialised training and experience in particular types of resorts, tourism administration, and business management are fundamental qualifications. Professionally competent sea-beach or skiing experts and ones trained in running different types of resorts are important elements. Careful and imaginative marketing programmes, which arouse interests and create customers for the season and off-season, have to be designed and pursued. Special staff selection and training programmes must be established in order to assure long-term and efficient staffing of the resort facilities. Also important are proper accounting and management systems to supervise, control and evaluate operating results and managerial decisions.

The development of successful resort projects requires integrated professional team work, with a blending of practical experience, professional skills, including market and economic evaluations, suitable and satisfactory facilities, design and operating and financial management. With professionally efficient design men and methods governing a resort, its success and future growth could be assured.

Below is appended a model outline of a hypothetical resort project, which would bring out and amplify the background, concept, objectives and national benefits of such projects. The format illustrates the development plan, likely facilities, project phasing programme, job opportunities, possible management structure which could be usefully adopted as a guide by prospective developers of tourist resorts. India is used here as an example, while the elements of the outline could apply to any country, especially in Asia.

A Resort Project

It is known that right from Japan in Asia to Europe, no major resort complex of high international standard has been created and marketed as such. Studies reveal this void in the world tourism infrastructure, which needs urgently to be filled. The Pacific area represents the highest growth potential for travel in the entire world. The Pacific has every thing that a tourist wants and there is no reason why future growth in tourism would not be accentuated.

India is a tourist wonderland. It has beautiful beaches on one hand, delightful landscapes and awe-inspiring mountains on the other. It is a smiling, welcoming land of sunshine, a country of many cultures, variety of scenes—nay, a tourist paradise. Its history, its pastimes, its festivals, its handicrafts, fascinate and enchant all who visit this land. The creation of a world standard resort complex could be the highlight of any programme to give a boost to its tourism. Not only would it help national development and economic advancement, but it would also establish an attraction of great international potential.

Concept

The basic concept is:

(a) to provide the finest in modern recreational facilities, while retaining and improving the natural beauty of the environment,

(b) to control the quality and rate of development in a manner most advantageous to all who visit or live there, and

(c) to protect and enhance national gain.

A resort is more than a hotel. In order to qualify as a resort, it has to offer a wide variety of elements; and, as stated earlier, a truly great resort must qualify as a total development. This cannot be achieved without assistance from internationally recognised experts in the field, who would be directed to ensure all-round development, in keeping with the spirit of the environment and the elan of the nation.

Objectives of the Project

Nearly every project has its origin in the desire of man to utilise the environment for specific purposes. Studies were, therefore, undertaken to investigate the potential of the hypothetical site and the concept and to determine the policy by which a tourist complex could be created with maximum benefit to national interest without abusing the environment.

National Benefits

The national benefits to be derived from the project are expected to be as follows:

(a) The creation of an international resort and tourism centre attracting tourists from all over the world.

(b) The providing of an international standard recreation centre for the people of the state and other states, without damaging the environment.

(c) The promotion of economic development of the State and the neighbouring states.

(d) The regeneration and strengthening of interest in the historical, traditional and cultural affairs of the country.

(e) The maximisation of the social utility of the investment and resource development with an eye towards earning foreign exchange.

(f) Enhancement of national wealth and tax revenues.

(g) The promotion of secondary support industries by the people of the state.

(h) The creation of extensive job opportunities for the residents of the state and other states.

Development Plan

The concept, as stated earlier, is to create an international standard resort complex with wide-ranging and high quality facilities under a fully controlled growth and development.

An inventory of the widest possible programme of activities and attractions that can be conducted on the site is envisaged. Imaginative yet practical concepts would be developed in order that the resort attracts visitors in volume and, in addition, be a matter of national pride. The programme of development would comprise many phases within a total concept.

The attractions would cover tourist accommodation, recreational facilities, entertainment, shopping and commercial areas, art and craft centres and public holiday services.

Facilities

The facilities proposed could be divided into four groups as follows:

Group A

1. A luxury resort hotel with all modern services; size and future expansion to depend on feasibility.
2. An 18-hole championship golf-course to be designed by international experts.
3. Cricket Club, tennis and badminton courts and a bowling alley.
4. Marinas and boating facilities with a yacht club.
5. Sailing, scuba diving, snorkel, waterskiing and fishing.
6. Floating restaurants.
7. Horse riding, polo, bridle paths and breeding studs.

Group B

1. Indigenous Craft Centre,
2. Artists' village.
3. A games centre.

Group C

1. Shopping centre and commercial complex.

2. Dining out facilities and entertainment clubs.
3. Convention and conference centre,
4. Community Hall.
5. Children's Park and Nursery.
6. Public Parks and Swimming Pools.
7. Car Parks.

Group D

1. Private villas with own garden, with or without private swimming pools, with privacy, yet allowing maximum access to recreational facilities. (Ideal for families).
2. Vacation homes for low-income groups.
3. Employee residential centre.

These and other facilities together with the planned development of the resort infrastructure, the water and electrical support system and other public works utilities would create an attractive package to draw international tourists in bulk and, supported by domestic tourism, the resort would assuredly help the country to capitalise on its creation and growth.

Site and Location

On the basis of well-known criteria for resort development and bearing in mind the considerations of proximity to transportation markets, its terrain, environment, potential for public acceptance and possibility of future growth, preliminary studies indicate the initial requirement of 1000 acres of land as a first step for its development in a phased programme at the hypothetical location.

In case of a sea-resort the site should be located at most an hour's drive by car from an airport or rail-head and may have sandy beaches and beautiful landscape and unexploited environment. The site should be evaluated in terms of topography, climate, soil and water conditions and should be suitable.

An imaginative resort complex, in an atmosphere of uniqueness and good taste, could be created at the location as disclosed by the feasibility report. Indigenous materials designs and traditional arts would be used to the maximum extent possible to provide a local flavour and enchanting Indianness.

Project Development Programme

Project development of the resort could be undertaken in phases:

(I) *Preliminary Phase*

- *(a)* Planning phase includes short and long-range master plans.
- *(b)* Creation of public infrastructure, roads, drains and laying of utilities.

(II) *Phase One*

- *(a)* Construction of international standard luxury resort hotel with all modern facilities and capable of future expansion.
- *(b)* Development of sports and other recreational facilities or the sea-beach and sea-sport facilities or hiking, riding and other games facilities in case of mountain resort.
- *(c)* Designing and establishment of a championship golf course to attract international tournaments.
- *(d)* Setting up an indigenous craft centre.

(III) *Phase Two*

Establishment of the following:

- *(a)* A convention centre.
- *(b)* Yacht club, where appropriate water front facilities are available.
- *(c)* Shopping facilities.
- *(d)* Expansion of hotel accommodation.
- *(e)* Artists' village.
- *(f)* A Games Centre.

(IV) *Phase Three*

- *(a)* Development of villas.
- *(b)* Completion of the remaining facilities envisaged.

Management and Operation

The resort to be created and planned with the advice of internationally reputed architects and design developers, ensuring a synthesis of indigenous and international design concepts, leading to quick worldwide acceptance of this resort. The management and operation would be under the guidance of an expert team of internationally reputed and qualified resort managers having experience in hotel, tourism and resort trades, supported by local talent and staff. It would be the avowed policy and intention to utilise local talent and availability to the maximum extent possible and establish training programmes for a systematic Indianisation of the operational and technical management.

Job Opportunities

On the completion of Phase One, it is estimated that the number of persons to receive direct employment would approximately be as follows:

1.	Resort Management	50
2.	Luxury Hotel (e.g. for 200/250 rooms)	300-325
3.	Golf Club/Course	70
4.	Other Facilities	100
	Total	520-525

It is estimated that not more than one per cent of the above could be foreigners. On the completion of all phases of the project, it is expected that total direct employment and jobs offered would have multiplied approximately *five times*.

Several hundred jobs would be created in connection with various government, private and commercial services such as utilities, post and telegraph offices, marine boats, taxis, shop-keepers, artisans and artists and suppliers of goods and services to the resort. In addition, indigenous secondary and tertiary support industries will be able to offer job opportunitiers, hitherto not available in the area.

In pursuance of earlier stated objectives to assist in the development of the concerned state, and India in general, it is important and in public interest that the state be invited to participate in this venture of national importance and, in addition, secure support of leaders of business interests active in hotel, tourism and resort trades. It is also essential to attract foreign investment in accordance with governments' rules and regulations and technical expertise to ensure the development to provide the required foreign exchange and continued economic success of the project. Accordingly, it is proposed to incorporate under the local laws a Resort Corporation, as a joint venture with the participation of *(a)* State Tourism Development Corporation or any other designated body representing the state; *(b)* a well-known Indian tourism business leader and industrialist as promoter; and *(c)* Internationally famous businessman, investor, hotelier or one specialising in resort development.

Financial Structure and Operational Policies

The capital structure would be based on the recommendations of the feasibility and financial reports and additional capital would be inducted progressively in a phased manner.

The Corporation would be run on profit-oriented and sound economic policies and in accordance with the laws of the country. Its management would be governed by well-established principles and disciplines of sound and efficient management. While investors' right would be protected, it is intended to re-invest the profits from the resort in the state and other parts of the country. The feasibility

---

Enclosures: The following additional information or details are necessary:

1. Location of the project proposed.
2. Proposed name of the Company, whether partnership or incorporated.
3. Capital structure and source of finance.
4. Proposed directors and their experience.
5. Feasibility report and other financial statements, including profitability and foreign exchange gains.
6. Documentation regarding site.
7. Legal Adviser.
8. Proposed Bankers.
9. Proposed Auditors.
10. Proposed Secretary.
11. Proposed Registered Office.
12. Project Manager, with details of experience etc.
13. Project Consultants with addresses.

report outlines the foreign exchange gains which are substantial and future prospects in such earning from the resort.

Preliminary studies establish the economic feasibility of a resort complex as envisaged, but examination and details are subject to the terms and conditions of acquisition of the site required and the granting of various industry and special incentives. The tentative revenue/expenditure estimates of the proposed resort and other facilities, however, show a positive profitability, yielding an annual estimated return on investment of over 20 per cent, exclusive of non-operational income.

In conclusion, the preliminary resort development project feasibility being undoubtedly positive and its economic, social, cultural and national benefits definitive and decisive, an early implementation of the project may be successfully pursued.

The above outline of a hypothetical report illustrates the various aspects of resort development and provides guidance for a project and the establishment of a tourist resort. It must, however, be stressed that the financial and technical feasibility of the project must be assured before embarking upon the same. To obtain long-range benefits and continued public and official support, environmental constraints and protection of the special characteristics of the area must be ensured. Last, but not least, the resort must be operated and marketed in a professional and efficient manner to attract sustained customers.

In reviewing the following project and summarising the requisites of a tourist resort, three elements emerge as being essential: *(i)* its attraction was based on special characteristics; *(ii)* its easy accessibility; and *(iii)* its being able to provide the necessary facilities for stay and recreation. Another over-riding consideration for attracting international tourists and the support of domestic visitors is that the resort must be unique and of a highly exclusive nature and be able to create and maintain standards of a high order in all respects of infrastructure, services and operations to achieve continued patronage. If there is the least doubt about meeting the quality of standards required in each category, it would not be correct to proceed with such a project.

The following categories of tourist resorts may be identified and these, as is apparent, are based on the special characteristics of each centre:

1. National attractions:
   - *(a)* Holiday centres—having good scenic and climatic features, summer and winter resorts, etc.;
   - *(b)* Sports centres—winter sports, beach sports, water sports, rowing, etc.;
   - *(c)* Health centres—health farms, spas and mineral springs, for therapeutic purposes. A spa has been defined as "a place in which scientifically approved deposits of therapeutic substances may be used and in which the necessary spa facilities exist" and mere existence of mineral water is, therefore, not enough.
2. Special historical and cultural centres:
   - *(a)* Places known for historical importance, uniqueness of monuments or architecture and other special features;
   - *(b)* Centres with outstanding traditional and cultural attractions e.g., music festivals, folklore events, theatres etc.;
   - *(c)* Places of religious significance, like Lourdes, Jerusalem, Mecca etc.
3. Other centres:
   - *(a)* Man-made attractions of recent origin, the Disneyland, the Disney World and the Mineral King in U.S.A.;
   - *(b)* Centres of education, folk museums, art centres, research centres;
   - *(c)* Centres of economic importance. Places of economic interest and associated institutions like fair-towns, exhibitions and technological centres of interest to business;
   - *(d)* Centres of scientific and technological significance;
   - *(e)* Political centres include capital attraction and administrative centres, as well as national shrines, places of political festivals, celebrations or political conventions etc.;
   - *(f)* Mixed centres, would include recreational attractions with facilities for business, conference and conventions.

From the above list of categories, which is by no means exhaustive, it would be clear that the development of each type of a resort would require special attention to create its particular features and to maintain these at a high degree of efficiency and utility. For example, in a Disneyland project a distribution of visitor activity was programmed and allocated to amusement, rides, entertainment shows and special events, restaurants, shopping, aquariums and marine gardens and revenue projections arrived at from each unit of activity and related to land requirement and considerations such as access, cost, suitability, size, flexibility and future expansion. The overall feasibility must be positive to be a success.

As stated earlier, each country and each entrepreneur interested in resort development must carefully consider the special requirements of each category and decide which of the special attractions it can successfully offer to domestic and international tourism, consistent with the highest standards of the category and with scrupulous regard to the preservation of environment, both short and long-term. We must avoid the mistakes of Miami Beach, Torremolinos, perhaps of Pattaya and other such resorts. Resort development offers great opportunities on a wide front, but it encounters tough challenges as well.

Advertising, Publicity and Public Relations

Advertising, Publicity and Public Relations are often so confused with one another that it becomes necessary to clarify these so as not to take chalk for cheese or vice versa. By advertising is meant "any paid form of non-personal presentation and promotion of ideas, goods or services by an identified sponsor." Against this, "Publicity" is "a form of commercially significant news or comment about a product, an institution, a service or a person, published in space, radio, or TV that is not paid for by the sponsor." The distinction is, therefore, based on sponsorship and direct payment of charges.

Advertising

Why advertise? Advertising, to say briefly, is necessary for both the producer as well as the consumer. For the producer or seller, "good advertising produces a good balancesheet" and for the buyer, "it pays to buy advertised goods." Large sums are allocated and budgeted by producers of products, sellers of services and business houses in general for advertising, to make contact with the public, the customer, informing him who the advertiser is, what he is offering, where he is and what he has to sell. Advertising is the most forceful and can be the most economical method of selling goods and services. However, it can also be the most expensive and non-productive of efforts, if not done properly and systematically.

Before an advertiser commits himself to any advertising programme, he must be reasonably sure that he can get the best return for his money. He will be well advised to enlist the guidance and service of an advertising agency i.e., an expert in the field. In most countries there is a wide choice of efficient and comprehensive advertising services. However, having allocated a certain budget, the advertiser or his agency will plan a campaign in the light of the media selected, frequency of appearance, types of ads, etc. and come to a conclusion as to how to utilise the funds to promote the product. Having designed a co-ordinated campaign, the next step is to produce ads that would be effective and yield favourable results.

What are the requirements of a good advertisement, or negatively, why do ads fail? That is a difficult question to answer and it is doubtful whether any ad fails completely. However, let us indicate some of the reasons which may not create the desired impact and not sell the goods or services advertised.

The first, though not the foremost one, is that an ad does not *attract attention*. The reader's attention, as is well-known, is available for a fraction of a second a turn of the page and the message can be lost forever. It may be an illustration or a caption, or the layout, or a combination of these that may result in arresting attention but it must hold the reader long enough to make him or her pause. Even the most convincing story will not sell if people do not read it. It is often necessary to make the headlines striking and the illustrations attractive so as to stop and hold the reader and make him read on.

It is of benefit to remember that people are interested generally in themselves. Silently, everybody asks "what do we get out of it?" or "how will it benefit me?" If we can provoke the reader's self-interest, then the ad has gained the first step i.e., attention value.

Does it promise the reader something? If so, he will read on. Having succeeded in attracting attention the next step is to *hold the interest* of the reader and lead him on. The copy must be well written with short paragraphs, short sentences and selected words. Such a composition is easily read and easily assimilated. Once the ad is made interesting, it brings out the most powerful selling point early, namely, the greatest benefit from buying—the feature most likely to appeal to the buyer. If an ad does not arouse the reader's interest, it has little chance of succeeding to culminate in a sale.

Having aroused and even briefly sustained, a buyer's interest, the ad must create a desire in him to possess the product or service. If he turns over and ignores the message after the initial favourable response, we must analyse what went wrong. May be, we did not inform the reader enough of the details or we bored him with and the length of the copy resulting in a loss of interest. Copy matter should be only as long as it takes to tell the sales message sharply and briefly and unnecessary words must be dispensed with and the essential, if long, must be presented with copy, sub-headings. The ad must convince the reader about the product by giving him the facts, the advantages *he* gains, the money *he* saves, the better quality *he* gets, and so on.

It must, however, be noted that truth is the best instrument of sale. Do not forget that the public have developed a resistance to high sounding superlatives and such claims as 'the best,' 'the finest,' 'the greatest,' 'the purest' have become worn out and lack conviction. Ads must be written convincingly, using simple words and phrases in everyday use. Testimonials from users should be convincing, but only discreet use must be made of this aid and no customer's name should be published without his formal permission.

Having attracted attention, aroused interest and created a desire by a convincing ad, it must then *stimulate* action, and persuade the reader to act. If the ad fails to stimulate action on the part of a reader, it must be assumed to have failed. How can we get the reader to act? Perhaps we offer further information without obligation, a free sample, perhaps, a free demonstration, free illustrated brochures or some useful giveaway, which he may retain for future use. The chances of translating action on the part of the reader into a buy will then brighten. The customer may retain the information gained for future use or act upon it without delay. Repeat ads will keep the already motivated reader informed and reminded.

Further, the choice of media i.e., in which we are to display our advertising, is equally important as the use of unsuitable media will not yield positive results. Each medium, as is well-known is judged and measured by two yardsticks; *(a)* volume of circulation, and *(b)* its character and influence.

Of these, the volume of circulation is an important consideration to influence judgement, but that is not always the only case. Fortunately, most countries have an Audit Bureau of Circulation, which regsters certified circulation figures of each medium. The various advertising agencies are in a position to indicate the circulation of each paper and outline the usefulness of a medium from its volume of circulation and the type of clientele it caters for. The cost of an ad is also related in general to the circulation of a medium and the entry and readership it is able to offer to advertisers.

The second factor i.e., the character and influence of a paper, is also important. There is danger of waste if, for example, motor launches and sailing craft ads appear in a women's magazine (though women are getting interested increasingly in these sports) and ads relating to cosmetics appear in an engineering journal. It would, therefore, be clear that the nature of the product or service will influence the choice of media. These are just two examples, which highlight the importance of selecting the right medium. Judging suitable media is the job of a specialist and a wrong choice can cost the advertiser considerable amounts of money and bring about the failure of a well designed and well produced ad.

In most countries, advertisers are flooded with guides, journals and other so-called newspapers, but many of these are worthless as advertising media. There is no organisation, in many countries, to protect the interests of the advertisers against unethical, uneconomic and worthless media. There is, always, a compelling need for an association to expose fraudulent, wasteful or obscene advertising propositions. Such an organisation would promote, maintain and uphold sound ethical and economic principles of advertising and protect the interests of advertisers, and help them in excluding wasteful advertising and assist in generally raising the standards of advertising.

Having selected a good medium, there are other important

factors why ads may fail e.g., if you attempt to sell a poor quality product. It has been said that advertising can sell anything. May be it can, initially; but quality or lack of it will determine ultimately whether the public will patronise the product or service. Articles of inferior quality or merit can be promoted by misrepresentation and advertising through unethical, irregular and unscrupulous ads. In many countries, self-regulation by media or laws and rules govern advertising practices, procedures and standards. In other parts of the world, practices and ethics are spelt out which are policed by advertising associations, who prevent the publication of ads containing misleading or false statements. Any service must measure up to a standard of quality that is generally acceptable to the public. Any weaknesses will soon be found out and even the best of advertising will fail to maintain sales of an inferior product.

Another important aspect relates to sales service. Inadequate distribution and difficulty in obtaining the product by the public may kill a very well organised advertising campaign. If a reader is influenced by advertising, he should be able to procure the product without difficulty or delay. So the advertiser must make sure that the potential buyer can obtain the advertised goods easily or else he will ignore the advertisement in future.

Last, but not least, although ads may individually be well conceived and well crafted, these may fail in their results because the whole campaign is not well designed. An individual ad cannot stand on its own and must be part of a programme which must be carefully prepared and well designed. The programme must maintain continuity irrespective of the size and frequency of an ad. If continuity is not sustained, even good ads will be lost in the wilderness. A successful programme is evolved after a market survey and is based on motivational research. Market survey and research would include the study of and conclusions about the following factors, amongst others:

How many people are likely to use the product or service?

Where do they live?

What is their paying capacity?

How much of the product or service will they use and how often?

At what time of the year?

What media reach these prospects?

As regards the motivational research, psycho-analytical factors guide campaigns of persuasions—groping for more effective ways to sell ideas, attitudes, products and services. These "brokers" are looking for the way of our behaviour, so that they can more effectively manipulate our habits and choices in their favour. Prof. Packard said that "Motivation research is the type of research that seeks to learn what motivates people in making choices." As an example, while selling soap the motivation factors in favour of soap might be health, cleanliness, beauty and these factors could be stressed for greater impact on the buyer. A campaign based on an appropriate survey and research and on the recommendation and guidance of experts has every chance of success.

The creation and use of a symbol, an image, a slogan or a distinctive personality in ads gives the necessary impact, and provides the continuity that triggers sale. A loyalty to brands is created as a result of which sales boost. The techniques of research and methods of persuasion have turned professors into merchandisers thereby enriching the advertising industry.

To sum up, for any business to grow it must *(i)* attract new customers, *(ii)* hold old customers, and *(iii)* create the desire to buy. A potential buyer must, therefore, be informed of the product or service available, convinced that it will be pleasant or profitable for him and directed to the most convenient source of supply. If our ads do not meet the above requirements, they are doomed.

Publicity

We referred earlier to publicity as exposure, secured in the Press or with the public by an organisation through non-paid and non-sponsored activities. To illustrate the various ways and means applied to securing this kind of publicity, a sample programme of publicity for a hypothetical airline is given below. The programme should give the scope, the methods, the elements that can form the basis for a successfully conceived and implemented programme for publicity. Naturally, the programme has to be spelt out in broad outline only, and variations, amplifications and modifications can be effected depending upon the special needs and requirement of each organisation. Similarly, the basic programme can be suitably adopted for publicity by hotels and food service facilities and other transportation industries. It would be of advantage to note the various suggestions given in this regard to derive maximum benefit through a comprehensive programme of publicity and public relations:

Programme of Publicity for an Airline

1. Press Relations

Press Office

Staff airline Press Office deals with all enquiries (day and night service).

Contact Work

Through personal contacts with the Press, Radio and TV and other media personnel endeavour to create goodwill for the airline.

2. Press Analysis

Keep a check and make an analysis of all enquiries. These indicate trends of public opinion, consumer demand and criticism.

3. Inaugural Flights, Press Conferences and Receptions

Make necessary arrangements, including:

- *(a)* preparing speeches,
- *(b)* writing and issuing invitations,
- *(c)* staging the event, conference or reception,
- *(d)* producing handouts,
- *(e)* giving radio and TV particularly the necessary facilities, e.g. lighting, etc., to cover the events.

4. Facility Visits

Arrange Press, Radio and TV facility visits e.g., the airline training school for pilots/air hostesses, catering department, etc.

5. Press Propaganda

To protect the airline from receiving bad publicity and presenting the true facts on matters involving the airline in an appropriate manner. To keep the name of the airline *constantly* before the public, through:

News Stories

A. To issue Press releases and pictures whenever the airline makes news, e.g. personalities arrive or depart via the airline.

B. In cases where it seems more appropriate, to "tip-off" the editors, news agencies and picture agencies and seek their co-operation on special occurrences.

C. To supply news releases regarding new services/new routes, new aircrafts, etc.

Feature Stories

A. Suggest features (exclusive) to the Press, and provide all background information and facilities.

B. To issue feature stories and/or pictures. Arrangements for carrying out the necessary photography to be made. Feature stories could cover and highlight innumerble topics, for example:

   (i) Training given to pilots, crew, technical staff and air hostesses. Competence and precision of crew stressed. They may outline advantages of travelling on the airline aircraft e.g., special comfort, good food and general welfare, including care of children and babies. The method of looking after passengers at airports could be highlighted. The type of aircraft used and all the ensuing advantages of passenger comfort should also be put over to the public, e.g., lack of noise, speed, easy landings and take offs, etc.

   (ii) Places of tourist interest on the routes of an airline and what facilities the airline offers the tourists visiting those areas. News of special interest tours and groups handled by the airline.

   (iii) Special stories regarding conventions, conferences and special meetings with which the airline is associated, or may be a designated or officially appointed carrier. The general public should be made aware of the fact that the airlines aircraft maintenance and airmanship are *reliable*.

6. Competitions

Competitions have always proved a most vaulable avenue of publicity. These could be run on an exclusive basis through a group of newspapers, through an editorial announcement. An air trip could be given as a prize, wherever rules permit.

Competitions could also be run through any of the media listed below:

1. Newspapers and magazines.
2. Club journals and magazines.
3. Clubs of all kinds.
4. Exhibitions.
5. Schools, colleges, universities, etc.

Exhibitions

Whenever possible, a special airline exhibition (mobiles included) could be organised or suitable arrangements for the airline to be prominently featured in an exhibition could be made.

Arrangements for this include:

(a) Supply of photographic displays.

(b) Prepare literature, e.g. leaflets, competition entry forms, etc.

(c) Arrange film-shows, lectures, etc.

(d) Script talks to be given at exhibition.

(e) Arrange necessary Press, TV and radio coverage.

Educational Campaigns

(i) These are of the utmost importance and should be put across through the undermentioned means:

(a) Schools—government, non-government.

(b) Social welfare organisations e.g., the Boy Scouts Association, Girl Guides Association, Boys' and Girls' Clubs, etc.

(c) Clubs have a great potential for public relations exploitation.

(d) Universities and other technical colleges.

Arrangements include:

(a) Talks and illustrated lectures.

(b) Film and film-slide showings.

(c) Photographic displays.

(d) Supplying lecturers and teachers with travel material and aids. Providing booklets and leaflets for distribution to aid pupils.

(e) Competitions.

(ii) Community welfare and social organisations programmes: These programmes cover the airline's activity in the community, the co-operation, the help offered for example in discharge of its obligations to society.

The methods used would be the national Press, radio, TV, journals and other media.

9. Public Opinion Research

This is an expensive operation but a continuous measure of public opinion research is vital to the airline because of the high-degree of competition in the airline business today. Survey necessitates:

(a) Draft questionnaires.

(b) Selecting the informants and interviewers.

(c) Recording the answers and selecting, analysing and arriving at results.

(d) Preparing a report.

10. Liaison with Press and Public Relations Officers

To remain in contact with other Press and public relations officers help in gaining maximum publicity. A well-known fashion house may be sending a fashion team overseas on a tour and this information is of great interest to an airline. If the airline supplies transport it could obtain valuable publicity, by collaboration or tie-in.

11. Special Aspects of TV and Radio Coverage

The same activities (described earlier in this report under number 1, 2, 3, 4, 5) as for the Press.

Obtain Publicity for the Airline also by the Following Means:

(*a*) Arranging for the airline distinguished passengers to broadcast or televise interviews. There is a reference by name or inference to the airline.

(*b*) Obtaining newsreel (TV) and radio coverage of important arrivals.

(*c*) Persuading a passenger—with a story to tell—to broadcast or televise, script the programme.

(*d*) Arrange for the airline staff to broadcast or televise, e.g., an airline chef may broadcast recipes; a stewardess may talk about her experiences whilst travelling, etc.

(*e*) Maintain a library of the airline's documentary films to be screened on television and obtain and stock films which can provide a useful tie-in.

12. Maintaining Stature of and Building Up the Airline's Personalities

Whilst keeping the name of the airline before the public, it is necessary to have personalities that are easily identifiable with the airline to be seen. In this way, maximum publicity is ensured. This can be done by exploiting the airline representative in a number of ways:

(*a*) He could give talks and lectures to clubs, schools, social welfare organisations, etc.

(*b*) Whenever he appears at a public function, endeavour to see that he (and as a result his airline) obtains publicity.

(*c*) His comings and goings should be noted by the Press, radio and the TV.

(*d*) Arrange TV and radio talks by representatives.

(*e*) Whenever the representative participates in social or technical programmes, provide adequate publicity.

13. Constant Liaison with Aircraft Manufacturers

Work co-operatively with the public relations department of aircraft suppliers, obtain and stock technical data and photo records for use.

14. Overseas Publicity

Should have frequent contact with the airlines' public relations departments throughout the system, establishing communication channels for active distribution of publicity material, storage and for feedback.

(a) Overseas public relations officers should keep areas informed of their activities and supplied with material suitable for usage.

(b) Areas should feedback useful material for exploitation purposes.

(c) Areas can issue news and feature stories overseas through the news and picture agencies, radio, TV and newsreel services and foreign correspondents.

The above publicity programme is not an all inclusive one but is only illustrative of elements that should be featured, especially the public relations aspects.

Public Relations

Public relations has been defined as "the activities connected with interpreting and improving the relationships of an organisation or an individual with the public." It is a "deliberate, planned and sustained effort," dedicated to the goals of better mutual understanding and co-operation among the diverse individuals, groups, institutions and elements of our modern society. While these and other definitions may differ in terminology or nuances, three basic elements must, however, be recognised as common i.e., the institution or individual on one part, its public on the second and their mutual relations on the third part. Creating, sustaining and updating favourable relations with the spheres of each institution's public, is the essence of public relations.

Who needs public relations? An individual or institution seeking public co-operation, support or mutuality of interest would invoke public relations activity. Such institutions would include a business corporation, a trade association or labour union, a public utility, a non-profit organisation, an educational institution, political parties and the governments. Each such group seeks the favourable attitude and goodwill of the people they have to deal with directly and those they consider as their potential public. Each institution has its public; every industry, every association, every person corporate or otherwise has also its public. Such public includes employees, members, communities, stockholders, customers or consumers, suppliers, competitors, dealers, agents and the government. The interaction of each institution's activity and its public's response aims at an improved corporate image, increased goodwill, better education and informed attitudes. The fostering of good public relations is a necessity of our times and, in the growing complexity of our society, an imperative activity.

The history and growth of public relations is a long and fascinating one. In the fifth century, the Greek poet Simonides sang songs of praise for the sake of publicity. Egypt's Rosetta stone inscriptions informed the public that Ptolemy V, the boy king, was a just and generous ruler. In 60 B.C. Julius Caesar ordered that publicity be given to acts of the Roman senate. In England it was not unusual for authors to be in the pay of political groups. Writers like Swift, Addison and Walpole used and distributed political funds for writers and printers to secure favourable publicity. In France, Moliere and Racine were among the distinguished writers to join others in this activity. Napoleon was a master in public relations as his pronouncements and actions clearly indicate.

Thomas Jefferson used the term public relations in 1807, but in a different sense, namely, that of foreign relations. In 1882, Eaton, referred to public relations, in the context of the legal profession in his lecture at the Yale Law School. The first industry to make use of the term was US Railways in 1913. Leaders of business were, however, until recently, not favourably inclined and there are well-known examples of opposition to the idea of public relations. George Baken said "it is none of the public's business what I do;" J.P. Mergan said, "I owe the public nothing;" W.H. Vanderbilt, the railroad owner said "the public be damned." This negative attitude certainly caused a lot of damage to business. However, the trend began to change from the early 1920s. In 1921 Ivy Lee issued a bulletin on public relations in connection with accidents to railways in USA. Other institutions also started appointing directors of information, to keep the public advised. Bell telephone company notified the public about their reasons for their inability to grant more telephone connections. And so on. During Second World War, Britain appointed public relations directors to various departments. The original thinking about public relations slowly evolved into a professional approach.

After 1948, much greater interest ensued and most of the 2important companies, industries and institutions created departments under the charge of special executives, to handle public relations. Many training institutions and colleges added courses in public relations to their curriculum. In 1947, Boston University started the first School of Public Relations. There are now literally hundreds of such schools all over the world, teaching and training people in public relations which has developed into a full-fledged profession with highly evolved norms and ethics.

What does public relations aim to achieve? Goodwill and favourable attitudes, yes—but more concretely, there are certain other objectives and these depend on the type of each institution. As an example, take a hotel, which achieves the following objectives through expert public relations activity:

1. A good and prestigious image: The reputation and name of a hotel is one of its greatest assets. The prominence of a name is taken as a warranty of success and generates confidence in the mind of the public about the quality and standards of service likely to be available. The prestige or a company's good corporate image helps attract customers and better staff, increase profits and create a climate of receptivity and preference for the hotel. Carefully conceived public relations activities enhance prestige and help sustain the shining image of a hotel.
2. Marketing of goods and services: For a hotel the support offered by public relations activities to other direct selling programmes and promotions (advertising and publicity) results in increased customer creation. Public relations keeps the name of the hotel in the front, thereby influencing the attitude of the public to patronise its services.
3. Public relations not only attracts worthwhile employees to an organisation by their desire to be associated with a good hotel thereby identifying themselves with good organisations and securing job satisfaction and better prospects in the bargain but also gains goodwill of employees by improving communication with them, giving them pride of achievement and recognition of the value of their contribution to the progress of the hotel. Making an organisation known and respected is conducive to

assuring its healthy development. Good public relations in regard to employees can also assist in stabilising labour relations, improving morale and understanding of the employees, thereby eliminating strife. The impact is both preventive and curative of problems.

4. Public relations fosters goodwill of the community, the share-holders and the government. The generation of a friendly attitude towards a hotel and the high regard in which a community holds it, make an invaluable contribution to the success of its operations. The community appreciates the value and importance of a hotel facility and responds by its support and consideration in community and social matters. How an organisation recognises and fulfils its social obligation is of utmost importance within the responsibilities of public relations and a consistent image and awareness of its economic and social obligations creates a very favourable public impact.

   The shareholders understand and appreciate the value of operations and activities of the hotel better and they thereby widen their interest and investment in the facility with greater confidence. A shareholder who receives public relation attention through newsbriefs, annual reports and news of financial evaluation of stocks, etc. has much to be satisfied with.

   In most countries, the gain of goodwill of governments is the *sine qua non* of public relations and determined efforts are directed to ensuring this. While the attitude of government is ordinarily influenced by the reputation acquired and usefulness of an organisation to the community, the soundness of a hotel's public relations generally determines its relations with public officials. If the officials are kept well informed that a hotel operates in the public interest and has a sustained reputation for fair practices, government officials are less likely to make unreasonable demands on hotels or issue unfair restrictions on them, apart from what flows from changes in government policy. A hotel has everything to gain by good public relations with government.

5. Gaining goodwill of suppliers, on the one hand, and dealers and agents, on the other, is a continuous

requirement and calls for unremitting public relations action. The supplying agencies assist in building a reputation for good dealing and reliable customer opinions for a hotel and offer preferred services, particularly in times of difficulty and scarcity. The goodwill of the travel agent, the wholesaler and the airlines that offer business to a hotel is of prime importance to successful marketing of its services. Keeping them well informed and sympathetically influenced by public relations action is more than half the marketing work done, as they become frontline promoters of sales and goodwill for the hotels.

6. While public relations must act to influence the general public and secure its goodwill, it is all the more important to expose its customers to public relations influence and ensure that they not only continue to extend their patronage to the hotel directly or through their organisations, but to retain and enhance their esteem, goodwill and satisfaction for the services offered by the hotel. The manner in which a hotel guest is received, kept informed, served and looked after and the manner any complaints are attended to, reflect the public relations success of a hotel. These elements form part of a full scale public relations programme of a successful hotel.

7. Influencing opinions and overcoming misconceptions about an organisation, which have a tendency to injure its efforts to goodwill, is an important activity for the public relations experts. Unfounded opinions, prejudices and misinformation, likely to prove harmful to a hotel must be countered by appropriate public relation action—through dissemination of correct information and education of the public. Favourable reactions have to be encouraged. In fact, the hotel would be better advised to examine and assess in advance any proposed action for possible effect on opinions and attitudes of its customers and the general public. When a hotel raises its charges or introduces new ancillary services, public relations must envisage and anticipate the public reactions such actions are likely to provoke and the steps that would be necessary to inform and explain the compelling reasons in appropriate perspective for the decisions. The guidance and advice of

expert public relations is also necessary, therefore, to proper policy formulation.

It is well worth noting here that prevention of errors is an important responsibility of good public relations. Public relations thus not only influences the general public externally, but also an organisation internally in the formulation and guidance of policies likely to be misunderstood by the public. It performs a function of not only publicising the organisation's activities but also making these activities conform to public interest. These and many other objectives can be achieved by professionally competent public relations executives but this result will naturally depend to some extent upon the policies and circumstances of each institution. It is also to be noted that public relations is a mangement function and should not be relegated to lower echelons.

A director or special executive or manager (whatever the designation) is in-charge of public relations and he may head an organisation or a department manned by persons with specialised knowledge fulfilling specified functions. The director must have sound judgement, broad knowledge and specialised skills and be well versed in the art of public relations. He must be fully aware of his organisation, its background, objectives and operations. He must have an understanding of each organisation's public and their behaviour. He should be able to assist in sound policy formulation which would result in goodwill and understanding. He would find desirable ways and means to getting his point across effectively.

On the other hand, a public relations consultant heads a specialist organisation which renders professional consultancy services in public relations. Such organisations have grown in numbers, size and in variety of services offered and are well organised. They enter into contracts of service for a fee for specified services. It must, however, be noted that public relations conducted through one's own employees or through outside consultants, in order to be successful in the long-run, has to be supported by satisfactory *performance* by the organisation to claim the goodwill of the public. Public relations is not a substitute for performance. So are fair play, truth and integrity important. Public relations cannot operate in isolation but is well geared to and co-ordinated with other activities of an organisation like publicity, advertising, etc., which are also its tools, and it is this co-ordination that yields the best results.

The basic function of public relations is to establish and maintain goodwill for an organisation. A realistic view of the public relations field "avoids over-idealisation, on the one hand, and a cynical view on the other." Public relations experts should anticipate problems, visualise corrective action and not work merely as professional firemen. They *(i)* advise and counsel management, *(ii)* provide a communication service through which activities of public interest are conveyed to media, *(iii)* undetake public relations research and feedback for an organisation, and *(iv)* undertake promotions and publicity campaigns through the various media available. These activities include releases to the Press, radio stations, trade papers and the news agencies, arranging Press conferences, and public, T.V. and radio appearances, issuing pamphlets on specific issues, preparing and issuing magazines, house journals, films etc.,—in fact, every medium is open to them.

The specific functions, for example, in a company include building a corporate image and undertaking general publicity, product publicity, looking after community and shareholders' relations, devising publicity programmes, supervising guest and government relations. Within an organisation, appropriate internal communication for employees and executives is also a special responsibility. These specific functions may be administered by individual staff in the public relations set-up, depending upon the quantum and responsibilities of work load. The functional division may cover Press relations, community relations and government relations or, with large organisations, the responsibilities could be divided according to media.

It may be of interest to note here that outside public relations consultants or an agency also plays a useful role, whether or not an internal set-up exists. Such services are retained with the predominant object of securing public goodwill and covering various aspects of public relations. The consultants provide satisfactory liaison with the media and represent the organisation at appropriate levels. The consultant or counsel is not an employee and as such he retains a degree of objectivity about an organisation, offers professionally competent and varied services at a cost presumably lower than what individual staffing and organisation would necessitate. He has wider contacts and provides a better feedback. His work is confidential, he avoids conflicts of interests and follows a professional code of ethics, which is an assurance of his conduct. It is for these reasons that public relation consultancies are well patronised and have become a profitable business. Many organisations depend heavily on their services and support, both for day-to-day activity and for trouble shooting.

In public relations work, many media can be made use of. The Press, also called the fourth estate, is the most potent means for conveying a message to a large number of people. The Press can be reached directly through appropriately prepared releases or by giving news to members of the Press. News can be divided into *spot news* i.e., news consisting "of spontaneous outburst of nature or mankind" beyond the publicists' control and *created news*, which he controls or helps to create. Spot-news could be unfavourable to an organisation although its proper handling can to a major degree minimise its harmful impact e.g., an aircraft accident is unfavourable news both for the operator and the industry. Good public relations can, however, secure a sympathetic news coverage by reporting as many facts as available, quickly, accurately and fully. It is not good policy to censor and belittle the scope of the accident and strive to keep newsmen from locating and reaching the scene. We must appreciate that they owe a duty to the public and reporters would do everything to ferret out the news. Any indication of non-co-operation would create an impression that there was something fishy which the airline and its public relations department are trying to hide.

Background facts should not be hidden and what is not certain should not be affirmed. It must be understood that every aircraft accident is subject to an investigation and the cause of an accident can be stated with finality only after full evaluation of evidence. Preliminary inferences could be misleading for the reporter and the public as well and as such shoud be avoided. An aircraft crash in 1954, which created international repercussions, is a case in point. Reporters filed long copies about their views of the causes of the crash, while the Chinese Government hinted at sabotage. The airline representative, when contacted by the Press said, "It is difficult and premature in the circumstances to come to an immediate conclusion on the causes of the accident, but when the formal investigation is conducted later, sabotage would not be excluded from consideration." The third government which investigated the accident under international law came eventually to the conclusion that sabotage in fact was the cause and most of the newsmen who had brushed aside the Chinese view, had been proved wrong.

To create news, there are many ways and experts in public relations always find something new, novel, topical, mysterious, funny, futuristic, or relating to famous persons or of interest to a large segment of the population. For any event to be news, it would contain one or more such ingredients.

News in order to gain publicity can be created by any of the following means:

(i) tie-ins with news events, newspapers, public projects, national events, anniversaries, etc.;

(ii) arrange an interview of a celebrity for a hotel or airline, use celebrity association, special items, special facilities;

(iii) use the chief executive to issue a report, announce an appointment, adopt a programme of work, issue facts and statistics, make an award, hold a contest, announce a community programme from a social obligation's angle, either through a Press conference or otherwise;

(iv) issue a statement on a subject of public interest, take part in a controversy, make analysis of prediction, pass a resolution, appear before public or parliamentary bodies, write or answer letters to the Press or release letters or documents of public interest received;

(v) issue testimonials received, extracts of reports favourable to the organisation, adopt national reports and statistics; and

(vi) organise a tour, inspection of the facilities, inaugurations of new services and products, new or expansion projects, dealers or agents tours and Press tours.

Experts in the public relations field use this armoury from time to time with the best possible effect and devise ways and means to deal with new and potential situations.

Considerable importance is, however, attached to holding Press conferences as a means of good public relations and for securing valuable publicity. We shall briefly delve on the holding of a successful Press conference. A Press conference, to begin with, is a meeting called to inform member of the Press about an important event or subject of public interest and to provide an opportunity to them to seek clarification and amplification of the matter and pursue areas of special interest. A Press conference, in order to be successful, must be embarked upon only after careful preparation, at an appropriate time and place and with facilities for Press, radio and TV coverage, in an atmosphere of mutual courtesy and friendliness and with full understanding of the respective responsibilities and duties of the Press and the giver of a Press conference.

The organisation should be represented by the chief executive, who would be fully briefed on the subject of the conference and would be guided to anticipate questions of likely interest to various types of Press representatives and be prepared with answers. He should consider objectively how those answers may be challenged and how in turn to meet the challenge. He may be accompanied by experts, who may be in a position to assist, and by the public relations executive, generally in touch with the Press. He would exercise tact, frankness, courtesy and not give any impression of unfriendliness or unhelpfulness in his responses. The Press would normally be represented by the regulars who generally cover the organisation or the industry (like aviation correspondents) and those representing national or trade Press. However, depending upon the event and its importance, a Press list may be specially devised on each occasion for its maximum effectiveness. It is usual practice to provide a prepared release, relevant extracts of reports or other supporting data. Refreshments and sometimes food and drinks are also provided at Press conferences, especially when new products or services are introduced.

In regard to holding a Press conference and the exposure an organisation receives, it may be useful also to refer to very important mass media like TV and note a few tips on successful TV appearances. Dress simply and, so far as women are concerned, do not wear things with fussy patterns. Avoid being overdressed, over-jewelled or over-manicured. Do not try to show off or score off the interviewers. The answers should be short and to the point and talk naturally. Your facial expression and gestures should not be animated or exaggerated to give an impression of a public platform. Do not make too many points in the course of a single question. Do not say too much or too little and do not give the impression of a closed mind. Do not forget that everything you say or do before a camera, especially in a live interview, you are forming or unforming an opinion for yourself, your organisation and on a matter of public interest, which will have serious repercussions in view of the very wide coverage available. Incidentally, what has been said above regarding TV appearances also applies squarely to a Press conference.

Internal publications: In order to achieve better communication between management and employees, an internal publication is a must. Basically, such a publication achieves the following main purposes:

(i) It gives information on the organisation's objectives, policies, operations and problems for better understanding;

(ii) It attempts to draw individuals into closer contact with an organisation and makes them feel that they are members of a single organisation;

(iii) It helps employees to understand each other; and

(iv) It provides a forum for employees to communicate their view on matters of mutual interest or those of the public interest.

The size, type and choice of format would depend on the policy of each management and would be governed by expert public relations advice. The circulation of such publications may be limted to employee distribution alone or to other media as well, in which case editorial care is necessary. An external publication is directed mainly to the business, political and economic environment outside the organisation and is a particular public relations responsibility to inform and influence the general public.

Evaluation of Public Relations: While public relations should "advance in standards, stature and acceptance" an organisation or an individual with greater experience and expertise, it should be able "to sift out the ineffective, the misleading and the inadequate" in public relation effort. However, this measurement and evaluation is not an easy matter. Often, criticism is levied against public relations men that they have an inadequate grasp of business in general and of the organisation in particular, have unrelated views to the actual situation and are overtly sensitive to the usefulness of their advice. To be more effective, modern computer methods are now invoked to adjudge their valuation. They must move away from the Press clippings and Press pictures era. They must establish that by their actions, public attitudes are being influenced and tangible goals have been achieved and negative influences limited if not eliminated altogether.

Ethics: In the role public relations plays and the opportunities that become available to it in the various fields, the danger of wastage of resources, malpractices and unethical behaviour become a serious hazard. To overcome these, a code of professional conduct is being enforced for public relations consultants and executives in different countries which *inter alia* covers the following:

> It envisages fair-dealing, public welfare and accepted standards of accuracy, truth and good taste, avoidance of conflict of interest, non-engagement in any practices tending to corrupt the integrity of the media and preventing dissemination of false and misleading information.

A code of ethics, based on the above, would encourage and foster high professional standards and eliminate unethical practices to the advantage of not only individuals, but also of the organisations concerned. Public relations would have fulfilled its role and met its objectives if it were conducted appropriately to establish and maintain mutual understanding between an organisation and its public on a long-term basis, and thus become a 'voice of conscience.'

The functions of advertising, publicity and public relations are links in a chain of customer information, customer creation and customer retention, thereby accentuating the growth and prosperity of an enterprise.

Notes and References

1. OECD, *Tourism Development and Economic Growth,* p. 23, Paris, Dec. 1967.
2. OECD, *Tourism Development and Economic Growth,* p. 23, Paris, 1967.
3. H. Barre, *Financing Tourist Development in Developing Countries,* Indian Hotelier and Caterer, Jan. 1971, p. 43.
4. H. Barre, *Financing Tourist Development in Developing Countries,* Indian Hotel Keeper and Traveller, April 1969, p. 25.
5. H. Barre, *Financing Tourist Development in Developing Countries,* Indian Hotel Keeper and Traveller, March 1969, p. 65.

4

Tourism, Transport and Accommodation

"Tourism is about being elsewhere and a major component of any tourist activity must necessarily be an element of transportation."[1] (Estimates show that a tourist spends about 40 per cent of his total holiday expenditure on travel and transport.) As such transportation forms an integral part of tourism and that an efficient system of transport is very much imperative in the sphere of tourism development. Tourism is travelling for pleasure and for relaxation and so the actual travel must be made very comfortable and congenial. The significance of this aspect could be better appreciated when it is realized that lack of comfortable and proper travelling facilities will make a tourist really frustrated, particularly when he is tired. Then he may go to the extent of saying that travelling "is the ruin of all happiness."[2]

It may be noted that the transport requirements of the tourism industry differ from that of the other sectors of the economy in terms of quality, nature of services and cost. A tourist would require quick, comfortable, safe and fairly cheap transport facilities at the time he wants. Though transport industry provides services for all and sundry, it is not possible to provide exclusive transport facility for the tourists except the provision of special coaches, fare concessions and other incentives. However, with the increasing importance of tourism industry, various state governments and the Central Government have taken special care to develop additional and special transport facilities.

Tourism can be seen as the sum of the relationship resulting from travel and accommodation of non-residents to the extent that the stay does not need a permanent residence and does not come from a paid activity. It clearly shows the relationship of two ideas—travel and stay, within the complexity of tourism and of fixing at the same time, the order of events. Hotels are not essential—they are desirable, but if people can move on their own they can stay with friends; they can even take their own homes with them in the form of tents and caravans etc. or use supplementary accommodation. Every tourist wants to travel to see some of the places of interest, quite apart from the place he lands. He is anxious to see the number of places in the shortest possible time. Transport is the key factor for the development of tourism. The means of transport, and the supply of a service, in making possible the travel to a place rather than the place of residence, are thus not only the *sine qua non* of tourists movement, but also limit the tourist flow quantitatively—the capacity of the means of transport decides the tourist volume—and qualitatively—the quality of the transport service offered decides the type of tourists in the flow.

The tourists travelling abroad spend less than half their total holiday money on transport and travel and rather other half on accommodation and other activities. It is estimated that travel costs are typically about 40 per cent of total holiday expenditure. The travel proportion of total expenditure did not vary much from 40 per cent irrespective of the form of transport which the travellers used, whether travel is by sea, by air or by coach or by private car.

Different Means of Transport vis-a-vis Tourist Preferences

Once a tourist lands in the country he has normally the option to choose more than one mode of transport. The survey of the foreign and domestic tourists reveals the relative preferences of the tourists for internal transport.

It could be seen from Table 4.1 that 87 per cent of the foreign tourists prefer railways, 56 per cent prefer 'buses and coaches,' 20 per cent prefer airways, 15 per cent prefer 'taxis' and 4 per cent prefer waterways. As against this, the corresponding percentages of the domestic tourists are 43, 81, 4, 12 and 1 respectively for different modes of transport. These percentages reveal that the preferences of the tourists are overlapping. If a comparison is to be made between foreign and domestic tourists in this context, it could be seen that relatively larger number of foreign tourists prefer railways whereas majority of domestic tourists prefer buses and coaches. This is mainly so because of certain specific travel habits of domestic tourists. They usually visit all places of importance particularly religious centres en route and for such itineraries buses and coaches are most useful.

Table 4.1

Tourists' Preference for Different Modes of Transport Within India

Mode of transport	*Number of tourists*			
	Foreign (Nos)	*Percentage to total*	*Domestic (Nos)*	*Percentage to total*
Airways	102	20	21	4
Railways	437	87	215	43
Buses and coaches	282	56	404	81
Own car	—	—	14	3
Taxi	75	15	59	12
Waterways	20	4	5	1
Total responses	914		718	

Note: Total respondents 500 for each category tourists.
Source: Primary data.

Factors Influencing the Choice of a Particular Mode of Transport

The relative preferences of the tourists as to the different modes of transport are influenced by the places of travel, availability of the particular mode of transport at the required time, time of travel (day or night), distance to be covered, and so on. The more important specific factors that influence the choice of a particular mode of transport indicated by the number of tourists are given in Table 4.2 (The survey was confined to foreign tourists only.) It could be seen that 'time taken for travel' has influenced the users' choice of airways. Railways are preferred for more than one reason, namely, 'cost considerations,' 'comfort and safety,' 'flexibility' and 'distance' in the order of importance. Similarly 'cost' and 'flexibility' have influenced the tourists to prefer 'buses and coaches' and 'taxi.' It is significant to note that 'cost' is the most important factor that has influenced largest number of tourists to prefer railways and roadways. This signifies that the market is 'price-conscious,' by and large. If this is true with foreign tourists, it will be more so in the case of domestic tourists.

Table 4.2

Factors Influencing the Choice of a Particular Mode of Transport (Foreign Tourists Only)

Factors	*Modes of transport*			
	Air	*Rail*	*Buses*	*Taxis*
	(Distribution of tourists)			
Time taken for travel	213	52	33	14
Flexibility	20	148	133	70
Comfort and safety	65	205	54	16
Cost	3	347	174	77
Distance	45	100	20	15

Source: Primary data.

The above preferences are to be taken into consideration by the government in transport planning with respect to tourism. Pointed discussion of each mode of transport is made here in so far as it relates to promotion of tourism particularly with reference to existing infrastructure, future needs, modernisation schemes, concessions, promotional measures, shortcomings and suggestions.

Means of Transport

The evolution of tourism and its different parts is generally affected by the development of the means of transport. It is simple to recall those three inventories which have turned the individual voyage, which formerly constituted tourism, into the mass phenomenon of today,—*the railway,* and by it the collective organized trips introduced by Thomas Cook, *the motor car* meeting the individual demand and being a "constant temptation to travel" *and the aeroplane* distinguished by its qualities of speed and ever increasing capacity.

Transport is a necessary condition of tourism. Expansion of transport has always preceded the periods of great increase in travel and tourism.

The various forms of transports may be divided into three categories:

1. Air
2. Land— (*a*) Road Transport.
   (*b*) Rail Transport.
3. Water Transport.

Air Transport

Air travel is known as the baby of all the means of transport. Majority of the tourists prefer to travel by air, especially for long distance journeys. The principal method of travelling abroad either for the holiday purposes or on business is by air. In 1920, it took about 120 hours for the fastest steamers from London to New York. The jet plane of today takes 6 hours and the Ango-French SS Concord with a speed of 1,450 miles would reduce the London-New York time to 2 hours and 45 minutes and the USSST having a speed of 2,000 MPH would reduce the distance to 2 hours and 10 minutes. The USSR TUIUU SST, has a speed of 1,560 miles.

Aeroplanes play an important part in the world tourism. The measures taken to increase capacity (Jumbo jets) and speed (supersonics) means that their part will continue to increase in future. For some years the airline companies have sought to increase their traffic by using the most modern aircraft and by a price policy taking into account the purpose of travel and elasticity of demand. The policy is determined by increased capacity coming from new aircraft, on the one hand, and the stiff competition from the chartered air transport companies, on the other hand.

The technical progress towards bigger and faster plane is not only due to competition between regular and chartered air companies, but it is equally due to the need to reduce costs, the need for qualified pilots and the need to stop the overcrowding of air space and airports. The tourist market has been characterised upto now by a very high price elasticity of demand. IUOTO puts the coefficient of elasticity at about 1.5 to 2.0. Therefore, a reduction of 10 per cent in air fares would lead to growth of 17 to 22 per cent in traffic.

Air traffic rights in international sectors are arranged bilaterally between countries. Air services are either scheduled or non-scheduled. On scheduled services, it is possible to travel as an independent passenger, as an inclusive tour passenger (individually or in a group), as an excursion fare paying passenger or as a member of an affinity charter group. Fare structures are calculated, following a chart of normal fares, one way fares, round trip fares, round the world fares, circle trip fares, G.I.P. fares, IT fares, or special distinguished fares. On unscheduled services, it is impossible to travel as a charter inclusive tour passenger, as a member of an affinity charter group or a member of a split charter group.

The IATA (International Air Transport Authority) is the body that fixes international fares of member airlines. The interdependence of tourism and aviation is an indisputable fact. Improved airline services and promotion fares attract an ever increasing number of tourists. Air transport depends on tourist traffic to a great extent for their revenue and, therefore, makes strenuous efforts in promoting tourism.

The air transport helps in the development of foreign tourist traffic in the country, thereby making valuable contribution in the foreign exchange earnings of the country. It helps people in distress by reaching them long distances within a short time. Although from the point of view of volume of traffic, the role of air transport in the country transportation system is insignificant, except in the case of international passenger traffic, its value from the point of the quality of its service and the clientele it serves is very important. It also helps in the supply of essential supplies to hilly and inaccessible areas with no other means of communication. In the international field, air transport has helped in developing trade with other nations. With the faster development of passengers, major cities of the world have come nearer to each other.

In the field of international passenger originating or terminating in a particular destination air transport plays a very important role so far as passenger traffic is concerned. In international passenger traffic, air transport is fast developing and capturing the traffic handled by sea transport. Air transport which handled almost an equal number of passengers as sea transport now accounts for nearly four times the traffic by sea.

The air transport is the modern and efficient components of the transportation system. The expansion of air transport throughout the world has been a post-Second World War phenomena. India did not lag behind in developing air transport. Its progress after the commencement of the First Five Year Plan has been accelerated keeping in view the growing economic activities in the country.

In the field of International Tourism, airport plays a very important role. Tourism is one of the largest single element in international trade for its contributes significantly to the nation's earnings. Developing airline services and offering attractive air-fares have largely contributed to the success of world tourism. It is estimated that 85 per cent of the foreign tourists arrive in India by air. The relative decline of air fares has made international air tourism increasingly attractive and as a result tourists arrival in India have shown remarkable increase.

According to a survey, 80 per cent of those who come to India by air, like to travel within the country also by air. To meet the demands of growing traffic, the fleet of the two national carriers—Indian Airlines and Air India were expanded and equipped with modern jet aircrafts.

Air Transport in India has been nationalized from 1st August, 1953, by the Air Corporation Act, 1953, and two Corporations have been established i.e. the Air India (International) and the Indian Airlines Corporation. Prior to 1953, the air transport services were conducted by various companies such as the Air-India Ltd., The Bharat Airways Ltd., the Deccan Airways Ltd. etc. It was felt necessary in the public interest to nationalise air transport on the ground that communication and transport both play an important role in the defence of a country and are vital for its well-being. The main function of these corporations is to provide safe, efficient, adequate, economical and properly co-ordinated air transport services.

Air India

Formation: Air India became an international operator in June 1948. In 1953, following nationalisation, the air transport industry was designated the national flag carrier for international operations. The Corporation was set up on 15 October, 1953, under the Air Corporation Act, 1953. Its main object was to provide adequate and efficient air transportation service covering international routes, excepting adjacent countries such as Afghanistan, Burma, Sri Lanka and Nepal. Nationalisation opened a new and a more orderly chapter in the history of Indian Air Transport. The scale of operations and the route system of the corporations have expanded continuously since 1953, when it took over the predecessor companies.

In the year 1963, *Ad hoc* Committee on Tourism made the following observations and recommendations for airport facilities:

1. The first and the last, and perhaps the most lasting, impression on a tourist's mind is that of the treatment he receives at the time of his arrival and departure, usually at airports. Much of the criticism against various formation and regulations stems from the fact that our facilities at airports are poor.
2. The terminal building need improvement and in this task, the advice of competent firms abroad who are experienced in this field may be sought. The possibility of new air terminal buildings exclusively for the use of international passengers being financed by international airlines should be explored.
3. Special attention should be paid to the air-conditioning of those areas of the air terminal where tourists have to spend considerable time. The airport building should provide adequate rest room facilities for the customs, police, health staff, who have to be on duty at odd hours. The senior most officials in-charge of customs and of immigration formalities should be given residential quarters at the airport.
4. Postal, banking and exchange facilities should be available at every airports round the clock. Arrangements to make hotel and transport reservation should exist in the terminal building. A few retiring room should also be provided.
5. Catering and shopping facilities at airports should be considerably improved. Duty-free shops should also be provided to enable tourists to purchase articles of day-to-day use such as photographic materials, alcoholic beverages, tobacco products, toilet requirements etc.
6. The most important factor is the human element. Special training should be given to personnel at airports, who should have a reasonably long tenure of service and should possess a reasonable fluency in English so as to avoid misunderstandings in dealing with tourists.
7. The immigration staff at airports should be under the control and direction of the Central Government.

8. The Aerodrome Officer should be fully responsible for the management, upkeep and maintenance of the terminal building and should hold periodical meeting with the heads of the customs, police and health staff to ensure co-ordination of efforts.
9. The Aerodrome Officer should be given financial powers to incur reasonable expenditure on maintenance, petty repairs etc. A readily available source of finance for this could be found by levying a fee per international passenger at the time of departure.

Organisation: As per the Air Corporation Act, 1953, the general superintendent, direction and management of the affairs and the business of the Corporation rests with the Board of Directors, appointed by the Government of India. The Corporation is expected to conduct its operations on business principles. The day-to-day management functions are looked after by a part-time Chairman and the Managing Director who is assisted by the different departmental heads. Air India operates on the international routes and for that purpose maintains 35 on-line and 97 offices in India and abroad. At present the Board of Directors consists of 11 members. Through its offices, the sales activities are conducted. Air India also appoints a number of General Sales Agents and Agents who are approved by IATA through whom it carries out its activities all over the world.

Finance: Air-India has financial march of its growth in the last 30 years from its internal resources. It raises the finance from Ex-Imp. Bank and U.S. Commercial Banks and from the Deutche Bank. Apart from the fact that Air India has helped promote tourism and exports by air, it has made no less significant contribution to the foreign exchange earnings of the country. Air India is playing an important role in increasing and promoting tourism and the results of "Operation Europe," "Operation U.K." and "Operation U.S.A." entrusted to Air-India have proved a success and this programme is proposed to be extended to the Far East and Australia. As a result of this programme, the pattern of tourist traffic has shown a distinctive change. The number of foreign tourists have steadily increased during the last few years. Although India's share in global tourism is negligible, the rise in traffic has been steady.

The introduction of bigger aircrafts and the growth in traffic and the expected increase in tourism call for heavy investment in the development of international airports, in building up domestic air transport capacity, in surface transportation and in accommodation sector.

Air-India conducted a number of cruises to the Indian Ocean, particularly to the Island of Lakshadweep. For this purpose a Greek Shipping Company's luxury liner was chartered. Now Andaman and Nicobar Islands has been opened up to foreign tourists.

Air-India started promoting mountaineering and trekking to the Himalayas. During 1974, Air-India flew 5,000 tourists for trekking in the Himalayas.

The promotion of congresses and conventions have become an important aspect of tourism. Both Air-India and the Department of Tourism have recently established special cells to persuade governmental and non-governmental organisations to provide better facilities for holding of congresses and conventions in India.

In August, 1973, Air-India's offices in Paris promoted a tour of 199 tourists to travel within India by train for 25 days. The train was used as a hotel during their stay with the exception of some places where hotel accommodation was provided. The tour was given excellent publicity abroad. Another group came in 1974 and now more and more tourists use Air-India and trains travelling within the country.

The Centaur Hotel at Bombay Airport, is the first of two hotels built by the Hotel Corporation of India Ltd. a wholly subsidiary of Air-India. The other hotels to be built are at a site near the Juhu beach and Airport Hotel, New Delhi.

With the approval of the Government of India, Air-India set up in 1971, a wholly-owned subsidiary company called 'Air-India Charters Limited.' This is non-IATA charter company and is set up with a capital of Rs. 5 lakhs.

Functions: The principal functions of Air-India are laid down in the Air Corporation Act, 1953. The main object of Air-India is the operation and management of safe, efficient, adequate, economical and properly co-ordinated air transport services of the country on the international routes. The corporation has been empowered to:

1. Operate any air transport service or any flight by aircraft for commercial or other purposes and to carry out all forms of aerial work;
2. Provide for the instructions and training in matters connected with aircraft of persons employed or desirous of being employed, either by the Corporation or by any other person;
3. Acquire, hold or dispose of any property;
4. Repair, overhaul, reconstruct, assemble or recondition aircraft machines, vehicles and parts, accessories and instruments and to manufacture such parts, accessories and instruments;
5. Enter into and perform all such contracts as are calculated to further the efficient performance of duties;
6. Determine and levy fares, freights, rate etc. with the prior approval of the Government of India;
7. Take steps to extend the air transport services;
8. Take steps to improve services which the Corporation may provide.

An important contributing factor for the promotion of tourism is the effect made by Air India to establish promotional fares for individual and group travel. With the decrease in the cost of international travel, a large market with predominantly middle and less than middle income group will become available as a source potential traffic.

A major event is the installation of a "real time-computer" reservation system, that will enable the airline to maintain an instant inventory of space after each flight.

Air-India and Indian Airlines may decide to have a single computer installation, like BOAC and BEA, to enable any Air-India station anywhere on its route network to sell space on domestic flights after querring of computer memory for an instant reply.

The satellite communication channels and micro waves link Air-India's real time-computer facility at Bombay to its booking offices in 28 countries. The airline now operates to 34 cities across the world and draws customers through 95 off-route sales offices.

Domestic Air Transport

Indian Airlines was constituted under the Air Corporation Act, 1953 by nationalising eight of the Airlines engaged in operation of domestic and international air services.

The functions of the Corporation are to provide safe, efficient, adequate, economical and properly co-ordinated air transport services within the country and to the neighbouring countries.

IAC is headed by a full time Chairman-cum-Managing Director who is assisted by two Dy. Managing Directors. The two Managing Directors are assisted by various functional heads dealing with Commercial, Engineering, Finance Operations, Personnel and Stores activities of the Corporation.

The operational activities of the IAC have been divided into four regions i.e. Bombay, Calcutta, Delhi and Madras each one of which is assisted by a Regional Director.

Indian Airlines have a distinguished and enviable record of safety in their services. From the point of view of the foreign tourist, there are certain difficulties and drawbacks. "The major single obstacle in the growth of tourist traffic in India is the difficulty in getting confirmed accommodation on aircraft. It is possible for a potential traveller in New York to get confirmation for around the world travel while in Office. But there has been cases where individuals have waited two to three weeks for Indian Airlines confirmation only to abandon the idea of visiting India after such a wait."[3]

Indian Airlines should get itself better known overseas through Travel Agents and Tourist Offices. Adequate notices should be given for introducing summer and winter schedules. Speedy confirmation of booking is essential for the tourist traffic. The introduction of Central Reservation Agency, made a remarkable improvement in this direction.

Some seats on all routes, normally used by the tourists should be kept in reserve for them to enable tourists to make changes in itineraries. On an enquiry, it was revealed that one of the difficulties experienced by the tourists is that confirmation of bookings from intermediate stations cannot be obtained and confirmed at short notice. The IAC should link up all its stations by Telex to facilitate bookings from intermediate stations.

The IAC personnel have also an important role to play in terms of public relations with the tourists. They may help and guide the tourists. Among the public sector undertakings, Indian Airlines is an important foreign exchange earner and its performance is steadily improving.

In spite of considerable development in the field of civil aviation, the role of air transport in the country is that the domestic transportation system is insignificant so far as volume of traffic is concerned. Its growth in the past has been impressive, but its share in the domestic passenger has remained relatively small.

The domestic airports which are under the control of Civil Aviation Department are being extended and improved to keep pace with the expansion of airline work and introduction of bigger and heavier aircraft for commercial operations.

India's new tourism strategy designed to attract a large number of tourists who cross national boundaries on pleasure or business, assign a key role to air transport. Domestic air transport is an essential component of the tourism infrastructure. According to available statistics, 81.8 per cent of foreign tourists travel by air, 10.8 per cent by sea and 7.4 per cent by land. Those who come to this country by air or otherwise prefer to travel within as well by air. In the context of its new market-oriented drive the Indian Airlines is being geared to meet the demands of the new strategy. As part of effort to market tourism, the airline has announced concessional dollar fares for large group movements. "Travel When You Please Scheme," "Discover India" and "Discount To Children" are some of the good schemes. The Indian Airlines has also made arrangements for quick confirmation of bookings with computerized systems. Advance booking points to a welcome response to the package plan. Tour conductor who bring in 15 or more visitors get a "travel anywhere" ticket free. Itineraries of air connections for more frequented tourist centres have also been planned in co-ordination with the Department of Tourism.

An important contributing factor for the promotion of tourism to Indian is the effort made by Air-India to offer promotional fares at a discount for individual and group travel. As the cost of international travel comes down, a larger market predominantly middle class and less than middle income group will become available as a source of potential traffic.

International Airport Authority of India (IAAI)

The Government of India appointed a committee on international airport under the Chairmanship of Shri J.R.D. Tata, which submitted its report on April 1969. The Committee drew up a three phased plan with an outlay of Rs. 106 crores for the development of big aerodromes at Delhi, Bombay, Calcutta and Madras. It also suggested the setting up of an autonomous corporation to run the four airports with sufficient autonomy on financial matters. These four airports were planned under autonomous body to develop and manage them on commercial basis.

Formation: IAAI was constituted by an Act of Parliament in 1972, for the management of international airports at Bombay, Calcutta, Delhi and Madras which together handles more than 85 per cent of the total traffic. An autonomous statutory authority, the IAAI is concerned with the management, planning and development of the four airports. It will develop professional expertise in planning, design and execution of airport terminals to enable it to provide similar services at other airports in the country.

The development of the four international airports will be closely co-ordinated to meet the growing air traffic.

The IAAI which came into being in February 1972, finalised the programme drawn for the new international air terminal to be built at Palam in consultation with Airport de Paris and the structural genius, Buckminster Fuller.

The new terminal will be built in a modular fashion so that similar self-contained units for passengers and baggage facilities are added as the traffic grows in the coming years.

No effort had been spared to ensure that the three new air terminals had the advantages of the most modern technology and design to keep ahead of the times.

The airports are pivots of economic activity and regional development. There should be a healthy competition between the IAAI and the DGCA to make the airports and air terminals, prestige symbol of the country.

The creation of the IAAI is the first major place of legislation in aviation since 1953 when the domestic airlines were nationalised. The new responsibility vested in the authority would need utmost dedications, imaginative, innovation and proper co-ordination to make them effectively, functional.

Functions: The main function of the Authority is to manage the international airports efficiently. It is the duty of the authority to provide such services and facilities as are necessary or desirable for the efficient operation of air transport services. Air navigation services, however, continue to be provided by the Central Government. Its functions are to:

1. Plan, develop, construct and maintain runways, taxi ways aprons and terminal and ancillary buildings at the airports;
2. Construct residential buildings and create townships for its employees;
3. Establish and maintain hotels, restaurants, and rest-rooms at or near the airports;
4. Establish warehouses at the airports for the storage or processing of goods;
5. Arrange for postal, money exchange, insurance and telephone facilities for the use of passengers and other persons at the airports;
6. Make appropriate arrangements for watch and ward at the airports;
7. Regulate and control the plying of vehicles and the entry of passengers and visitors, in the airports with due regard to the protocol functions of the Government of India;
8. Develop and provide consultancy services in India and abroad in relation to planning and development of airport or any facilities thereto;
9. Establish and manage helipads and airstrips;
10. Provide such transport facilities as are, in the opinion of the Authority, necessary to the passengers travelling by air;
11. Form one or more companies under the Companies Act, 1956, or under any other law relating to companies to further the efficient discharge of the functions imposed on it by the Act;
12. Take all such steps as may be necessary or convenient for or may be incidental to the exercise of any power or the

discharge of any function conferred or imposed on it by the Act.

In the discharge of its function, the Authority is required to have due regard to the development of air transport service and to the efficiency, economy and safety of such service; on the financial side, it is required to function on business principles.

Organisation: It consists of the following members:

1. Whole-time Chairman—appointed by Central Government.
2. D.G.C.A.—ex-officio.
3. Minimum 6 and maximum 13 members appointed by the Central Government.

The Chairman is assisted by a whole-time member and the management of each airport is entrusted to an Airport Director. There are six departmental heads to assist the Chairman and the wholetime member in running the authority, besides Four Airport Directors, each in-charge of one of four international airports.

Programmes of IAAI: Various programmes for improving facilities for airport operations and amenities and services for passengers and public has been planned and taken on hand by the IAAI. These activities are:

1. Acquisition of land;
2. Construction of terminal building;
3. Construction and improvements of pavements for aircraft operations;
4. Improving facilities provided for passengers and public like air-conditioning, restaurants, car parks, surface transport, portage etc.
5. Lighting of runways, taxi-tracks, aprons and provision of other visual aids;
6. Provision of safety services e.g. crash fire tender, rescue vehicles etc.

Facilities Provided by IAAI

1. Snack Bars and Restaurants: A number of other facilities are being provided by IAAI for the convenience of passengers and visitors at India's four international airports. Inside the terminal building at Bombay and Delhi, a number of snack bars, besides restaurant at Delhi, are being run by Chefair. In Madras and Calcutta also these facilities are being provided.

2. *Coach Services and Parking Facilities:* Coach services from airport to city terminal and vice versa have been introduced at Delhi, Calcutta, Madras and Bombay. Car parking facilities are now available at Delhi, Madras and Bombay on payment of a small fee.

3. *Information About Arrival and Departures:* For providing information about departure and arrival of flight, closed circuit TV system has been installed at Delhi airport. Digital clocks, which are electrically operated, have been installed at Bombay airport for giving accurate time. These facilities will also be provided at other airports as well.

The four international airports at Delhi, Bombay, Calcutta, and Madras—the gateways to the country—handle over 85 per cent of country's total air traffic. These airports currently handle more than four-fifth of air traffic in India.

As regards to the exposure of urban population to noise pollution, India is at the cross-road of East and West and most of the flights from these countries arrived or departed at night. The Civil Aviation Department should take up the question of rescheduling the flights of various international airlines so as to relieve the pressure at nights at the Bombay and Delhi airports.

The extension of the international arrival hall had been designed and constructed entirely by its own architects and engineers.

It is now possible to clear nearly 300 passengers in an hour with the opening of the International Arrival hall extension at Palam airport. It had more than doubled its clearing capacity. This has been made possible by increasing the number of customs counters.

Some closed circuit TV sets have been provided for flight announcements in the visitor's gallery. The completion of the extension hall marks the first phase of the project undertaken by IAAI to expand the airport.

A new private lounge has also been opened for passengers not entitled to use the VIP lounge.

Airports are the first point of entry of international passengers coming to India. They have today replaced the seaports on the gateway of this country. According to tourists statistics 85 per cent of all tourists coming to India, disembarked at these air ports. The rest of the tourists 7.1 per cent came by sea and 7.9 per cent by road. Apart from serving as the point of entry for the international tourists, airports are also the focal points of air services for various tourist centres. It is thus essential that we ensure a warm welcome at airports.

An air passenger belongs to an elite class. He is sophisticated and expects facilities commensurate with the expenses he incurs on air travel. As he visits a number of airports, he is in a position to compare facilities available at different airports. He expects comfort in the plane, an efficient and quick services at the airports and good accommodation and surface transport. There is a need for comfortable and convenient passenger handling facilities inside the terminal building and least frontier formalities and quicker clearance.

Airports must be well equipped with facilities to handle passengers. India, because of her geographical situation in the international air route pattern, has an important position on the world aviation map. The International Airports Authority of India is planning to meet the requirements of the growth of passenger traffic and the increase in the number of aircraft through the international airports. The size of the country, the large distance that separates the main centres of its population, and its potential for tourism are some of the factors which underline the need for development of modern, well equipped airports. Over and above to these factors of enormous increases of projected air traffic, coming in of larger and faster aircrafts, and the time required for expanding airport facilities, a comprehensive study of requirements till 1990 has been made by International Airport Authority.

While planning the airports the factors which will help speedier movement of passengers must be kept in view. In the arrival area, customs, immigration and health counters should be increased. The baggage handling areas should be provided with the most modern devices. The terminal facilities in the departure and arrival areas be planned on a large scale to ensure speedy clearance of passengers and their baggage. The successive steps to help passengers to embark on disembark from aircraft and tourists from the airport to the city in the shortest possible time have to be planned. Keeping the passengers in the terminal for lesser time helps in the better use of the available space within the terminal. The parking areas should be spacious and well organised. The group handling equipment required by the aircrafts, better aerobridges and step ladders, fuel tankers, bulk cargo loading vehicles, toilet and fresh water carats, passenger coaches, baggage trains etc. require a greater attention.

Air transport has a key role in furthering and promoting tourism in the subcontinent because it provides the initial point for the foreign tourist who is an acknowledged patron of various kinds of big and small industries on the alien soil. The Air India and Indian Airlines have expanded their passenger capacities and have also equipped themselves with several other ancillary facilities. These air transport authorities must seek co-operation and support from all the departments of the government and private agencies working in the field.

Charter Flights

Charter flights which are very common elsewhere in the world have not found favour with the government till recently for security reasons. But since 1982 there has been some change in the thinking of the government. In fact, an impending tie-up arrangement between Air-India and Travel Corporation of India and one Swiss company had been effected in mid-1982 for running 25 charter flights from Europe to India and back. This is certainly a good beginning and it is hoped that many more such charter flights would be operated in the years to come.

In the operation of charter flights, there are certain unsettled issues like (i) Should charters be allowed to land only on existing gateways to India or should they be allowed to other areas too? (ii) Should the operation be open to all international airlines or to only the A-I?, etc. As far as the first question is concerned, it is good if the charters are allowed to areas other than the gateways also so that the pressure on the gateways to handle additional flights could be eased. But this is opposed on security grounds. Further, tourists also would like to land in the 'metros' first. Regarding the second question, the A-I feels that it should be given the sole right. Perhaps the A-I could be given monopoly rights for charter flights if it could quote competitive prices. Of course this depends on charter demands, size of groups requiring charter flights, size of crafts, etc. But the Billimoria Committee recommended that charter flights be operated by Vayudoot. (From the point of Tourism Industry, it is immaterial who operates the charter flights. What is important is that more tourists should be attracted.) "India can be an all-year beach holiday destination," charter flights could assure us of at least 50 charter tourist arrivals a day, year round, a reasonable estimate when one considers the extent of the beach area available. In terms of foreigners entering the country this would result in a growth rate of only 2.1 per cent, but tourism earnings would rise by 3.9 per cent. Therefore, if the government's targeted tourism growth rate of 18 per cent is projected in terms of charter tourist arrivals it would result in an encouraging 32.57 per cent increase in tourism earnings. Quite obviously charters are the answer to India's drooping tourism."[4]

Road Transport

The development of road travel is bringing about fundamental change in the development of tourism in the growth of resorts, hotel and other services.

Road or motor transport plays an important part in the field of tourism in US and European countries. Unlike the other forms of transport, the cost of a transport kilometre has very little effect on the amount of travel budget. There are two types of vehicles required for tourists:

1. Tourist Coaches
2. Tourist Cars

Tourist coaches or buses are good for group travel ranging from 8 to 30 persons. These large or mini buses are used for sightseeing purposes. Special motor-coaches equipped with large glass panes, trained guides, public address system and other amenities should be constructed for sightseeing in large cities.

Tourist cars are good for those tourists who wish to travel in great comfort and privacy by themselves or with their companions. These cars are required by the foreign tourists who may be doing both business and sightseeing.

With the operation of Asian Highway, the overland movement of visitors from Middle East and South-East Asian countries will be on an increase. New forms of accommodation and travel services are required by the motorists. In America, the transport of lakh of people from railways to roads as the main form of inland transport, has indicated likely developments elsewhere. Motorways, drive-ins with quick means, special cafeteria services, auto courts, and motels are the other forms of travel services which are taking the place of the old railway resorts. In Britain, there is the development of holiday camps and adaptation of motel and the site caravans, are taking over the hotel industry for lucrative middle class family market. With the growing predominance of private car travel, international tourism is becoming more and more influenced by road developments. Motorisation has grown to different degrees according to the geographical and economic conditions of the different countries. Long distance tourism will use the means used by aviation and sea travel and railways (auto train-couchettes). The motor cars will play an important role in the final access to the place of stay. The number of people using their cars to go on holiday will depend largely on the state of infrastructure i.e. the roads and motorways. It all, will increase the importance of the means of accommodation connected with road tourism i.e. motels, camping sites, apartments, villas, tourist bungalows, holiday villages etc.

The first impression formed by a tourist is gained from the airport facilities and the transport uses. In the field of transport, we generally depend upon:

1. *Indigenously Manufactured Cars:* These are in short supply. The waiting period is too long and there is no certainty of delivery.

2. *Imported Luxury Cars:* These cars are released by STC after many preliminaries and to maintain these cars, there is the problem of replacement of parts. Moreover, there are lot of restrictions on the inter-state movement of cars.

3. *Paucity of Coaches:* The number of luxury coaches in the country is very small. Tax licensing systems and collection systems differ from state to state which causes delay.

In the beginning, tourist buses for sightseeing were introduced in important cities in India, but they were not popular with tourists as they do not come to the required standard. It is hoped that ITDC would provide clean, comfortable and efficient road transport to the international visitors. One of the complaint made by the motorists is about the time wasted at state boundaries and checkposts in connection with Octroi etc. According to Estimate Committee, 1956, "The Committee understands that the tourist coaches run from Scandinavian countries to Rome—12 and 13 states—without any check or hindrance, but motor vehicles cannot run free from one state to another, without encountering difficulties at state boundaries."[5]

It is suggested that to save the time and paper work and stoppage of vehicles, the system of some of the Western countries can be adopted in India by introducing All India Road Permit to operators and transport companies and mechanical tax booths should be installed throughout.

As regards the future of road tourism, it is to be mentioned that motor buses and coaches and air coach tourists are likely to become increasingly popular for long journeys and touring. They afford a very convenient form of packaging the whole travel product. Fares in these coaches is cheap than any other form of transport. Although, the average speed is low, these are very comfortable and they exploit the scenic attractions of the countryside more fully and more intimately than is possible by any other means. These coaches have an under floor diesel engine, excellent seating and visibility of passengers. They have perfect ventilation, heating, airconditioning and fitting with bars, toilets, and adjustable seats. Another attractive feature of coach travel is the close relationship between passengers and driver. The drivers are specially trained and make a positive contribution to the enjoyment of the journey.

Our national highways and approach roads must be immediately improved. They should not only be all weather roads, but should have adequate facilities for cars and passengers. Today one can travel in a hired car or coach in the whole of Europe with one permit. There is a need for liberalising the issuance of all India permits for tourist vehicles, without getting involved into what state gets more permits. The import of tourist cars, coaches and air-conditioned equipment should be placed on the same footing as the import of raw materials and machines for other export industries.

With the growing predominance of car travel, international tourism is becoming more and more influenced by road development. New form of accommodation and travel services are required for the tourists. Motorways, holiday camps, caravan sites, drive-ins with quick meals, special cafeteria services, and motels are required for their convenience.

The road tourism have a bright future in India. Tourist coaches, motor coaches, air-coaches tours are likely to become increasingly popular for longer journey and touring.

Road transport is particularly useful for short distances and for carrying light and valuable articles. Motor vehicles are the most popular form of road transport and are used where the roads are in fairly good condition.

Transport units should be opened at various places. It should have its own transport units throughout the country to serve the clients. The lack of quality road transport continues to affect tourism image. Visitors continue to be provided for too often with sub-standard transportation at a substantial fee even where facilities to international standards are available from the ITDC. The hire rates for tourist vehicles particularly imported limousines are not only uneconomic but are unrealistic and one of the most discouraging factors in the expansion of transport capacity of acceptable standard. Unless more inducement and encouragement is provided, the tourist transport capacity will fail to keep pace with the requirement and this essential segment of the infrastructure will continue to be inadequate and deficient in both quality as well as in adequacy.

A scheme to finance tourist transport was introduced in 1970. Under the scheme the financial assistance on easy terms to tourist car operation was provided to the approved car operators. In the year 1971, certain modifications were made in order to make it available to the operators. Loans are given to the operators under this scheme.

Rail Transport

The part of the railways in tourist flows shows considerable difference from country to country. In the past, the railways were the only means of satisfying the needs for tourist travel. They remain an important form of tourist holiday and business transport for long journeys. Today, they play relatively a smaller part in tourist movement due to the difficulty the railways have in competing without adequate modernisation of their out of date equipment. There is a greater competition from the motor car, the aeroplanes and motor coaches. The consequences of these changes from one means of transport to another is a change in the structure of tourist traffic. Efforts have been undertaken by the railways to profit from the technological revolution by modernising their methods and achieving greater efficiency. In the place of those types of travellers who abandoned the railways for other transport, come other travellers with lower purchasing power. The railways remain to these newcomers to tourism, as the ideal form of transport. The price elasticity of demand of tourists confirm this phenomenon. Every increase in prices results in a negative elasticity of demand for the railways and coaches and a positive elasticity for the private motor cars and airways.

Travel by train is a fascinating experience. It offers the tourist an insight into the large country and its people. It passes through buildings, towns, slumbering villages and green vegetation, and takes one back into glorious past.

All tourists who came to India in old days necessarily travelled by rail and accounted for a fair amount of revenue to the railways. We find that railways were very familiar to the tourists in India in the past. The tourist has to use railway facilities wherever he goes to places not linked by air, or whenever he feels a more economical and leisure mode of travel would suit him better. In spite of the various incentives and facilities offered by the railways, it is seen that the railways are not much popular with the tourists. Tourists have to apply 15-30 days in advance for the proposed journey. The visitors coming from affluent countries find the catering services very much unsatisfactory. According to the study Team of NPC in Japan "The quality of meal was excellent and along with meals—sale of liquor was permitted." In USA 'a fullfledged bar service was available in the cocktail lounge which was attached to the dining room."[6]

The Indian Railways have been trying to adopt themselves to the new conditions of modern tourism. The services have undoubtedly been largely improved and adopted to the needs and wishes of the clientele. The different fares introduced have been intended to stimulate the tourists, by many advantageous conditions to make excursions and trips from the place of vacation, with a view to encouraging tourists from overseas to travel by train during their stay in the country. Some seasonal or overall tickets have been introduced both for the individuals and group travel. The railways services are being improved. The fast trains, joining large cities, over medium distances, are appreciated for their speed and comfort. The railways can count on the new categories of people becoming tourists. Special tourist trains of students and pilgrims are an important factor for the railways with their qualities of mass transportation at low costs. The auto-couchette trains would have a large success among tourists who can avoid long drives in reaching to their destinations, but still have their car available. The special tourist railways known as rack railways, funiculars and telepheriques, can open regions and areas to tourism in general and winter tourism in particular. Improvement in the marketing of railways services, further discrimination in fares, the introduction of deluxe first class trains at a first class fare would bring increased revenue and increased traffic for the railways.

The railways led the way in providing the integrated tourist service. They offer catering and hotel accommodation. These were introduced as a by-product to carry passengers in comfort. The tourists should be provided Western style food from restaurant-cars as well as at important railway stations. The catering aspect of the railways in India is oriented to meet the requirements of the domestic passengers, but it should also provide the Western style food for those who are ready to pay for it. There is some improvement in the recently introduced trains in terms of speed, cleanliness, catering and other services. The Indian Railway spans more than 60,170 kms. in routes and connects 7,077 stations, serving the different parts of the vast subcontinents. It is the longest in Asia and the second largest network under the single management in the world.

For long distances, air traffic will grow faster than other modes of travel. But because of economic condition in the country, for a considerable time to come, long distance travel by rail will continue to remain popular unless as a result of some very significant technological developments, the cost of air traffic can be brought down within the reach of the common man.

The introduction of new equipment-electrification and diesel trains have increased the traffic considerably. Improvement in the marketing of railway services, the introduction of deluxe first class trains at a first class fare plus a supplement on routes where no other form of transport can compete, would bring increased revenue and increased traffic for the railways. Railways have a great part to play in stimulating and creating traffic particularly on routes where they can offer the speediest and cheapest form of transport.

The railways led the way in providing integrated tourist services. They offer catering and hotel accommodation, which are introduced as a by-product to enable them to carry passengers in comfort. Railways must regard their catering services as a form of promotion and they would not expect to make a profit nor a loss in running.

Various Steps Taken by Railways to Promote Tourism

The Indian Railways has adopted number of measures in order to promote both foreign and domestic tourism:

1. *"Travel as You Like"*: The 'travel as you like' tickets introduced by the railways offer a special concession to overseas tourists. These tickets are valid for 21 days from the commencement of the first journey. The special feature of the ticket is that the tourist can travel to any place in the country irrespective of the distance by paying in foreign exchange.

2. *Concessional Return Tickets:* Both for foreign and domestic travellers, the Railways issue during the season, concessional return tickets for hill stations, at one and a half single journey fares. Overseas tourists who may stay in India for a short time and who have not drawn up plans for extensive travel can also avail themselves of a 10 per cent concession for travel by air-conditioned class.

3. *Group Tourism:* Tourists coming in higher portion may also avail of the facility of special trains with restaurant cars which run to desired schedules and with the desired class of accommodation. On trains in which air-conditioned class accommodation is not normally provided, a special air-conditioned coach can be arranged for parties of 12 to 14 tourists.

4. *Homes on Wheels : Palace on Wheels:* The Railways provides facility of special tourist cars for organised parties of tourists. There are air-conditioned, first and second class tourist cars with bathrooms, kitchens, sleeping and sitting accommodation. These may be called as 'homes on wheels'. Tourists cars can be kept in occupation by tourists till their itinerary is over. Recently, railways with the co-operation of Rajasthan Tourism Development Corporation has introduced 'Palace on Wheels.'

5. *Preparing of Itineraries:* With a view to encouraging well-planned and organised tourism by individual or parties, the

railways have drawn up itineraries for standard circular tours for which special tickets valid for three months are available at 3/4th the normal fare in all classes, except air-conditioned. Tourists have freedom to frame their own programmes and obtain circular tickets. The middle class traveller can avail air-conditioned two-tier sleeper coaches on the deluxe trains connecting Delhi with Calcutta, Bombay and Madras. The Railways also offers sleeper coach accommodation in second class. In two-tier and three-tier coaches, sleeping accommodation is provided for a small additional charge.

6. *Introduction of Important Trains:* The Railways have introduced number of train services. For journey between Delhi and Calcutta and Delhi and Bombay, the travellers could not do better than glide on the Rajdhani Express which takes fast about 17 hours to cover 1,445 kms. distance ex Delhi to Calcutta and takes just 18 hours to cover the distance, between Delhi and Bombay. These inter-city trains offer air-conditioned comfort in slumberette chair cars or elegantly furnished sleeper cars.

7. *Trains for Tourist Centres:* The famous hill resort of Darjeeling in the North-East is reached by a 2 ft. gauge train between Siliguri and Darjeeling. Another line between Kalka and Simla in the north-west is served by diesel passenger trains and diesel rail cars. The Blue Mountains in the south have also a railway marvel to offer the line between Mettupalayam and Ootaccamund.

On the western side, between Bombay and Poona, a little known station at Neval is connected by train with pleasant Mathern hills.

A visit to Taj Mahal at Agra can be by the elegant Taj Express in the morning and after visiting the Taj and other monuments in the neighbourhood, a visitor can return to Delhi the same evening. Similarly there are other trains as the Deccan Queen between Bombay and Poona, the Flying Ranee between Bombay and Surat, and Black Diamond Express and the Coalfield Express for travel between Calcutta and Dhanbad, the Golconda and Krishna Express between Hyderabad and Vijayawada, the Vridaban Express between Madras and Bangalore and the Vishwanath Express that links Delhi with Varanasi, the cultural capital of India.

8. *Other Facilities:* The railways have arrangements for retiring rooms, air-conditioned suites etc. at important places where for a reasonable charge, sleeping accommodation with toilet facility is

provided. There are railway restaurants and restaurants in important trains which serve Indian and Western style meals. In the absence of restaurant cars in a train, meals can be ordered through the guard of the trains.

Facilities to Travel Agencies: The authorised Travel Agencies are allowed to issue railway tickets to the overseas tourists. Free travel to conductors with parties of tourists is also allowed. Break journey are allowed without the normal limitations on such tickets. Facilities are also given to travel agencies for reservation of accommodation in retiring rooms and conveyance.

Special Trains for Domestic Tourists: The railways cater the needs of domestic tourists by introducing holiday specials during summer, the pilgrims specials, the Kisan specials, students and youth specials and the various 'Bharat Darshan' tours.

Air-conditioned Tourist Cars: The demand for the tourist cars come from some of the following categories of railway users:

(a) Buddhist pilgrims from abroad as well as from different parts of the country for journeys to a number of places of Buddhist interest on the North-Eastern Railways;

(b) VIPs and mountaineering expedition travelling to and from Nepal;

(c) Upper class passengers for journeys to various hill stations;

(d) Upper class business tourists and high officials in private and public sectors.

Indrail Pass

Travel as you like—by any train you like—from North to South and East to West. See the bewildering variety of flora and fauna that India is, see its National Parks and Wild Life sanctuaries; see its colourful people heralding religious festivals and seasons with folk dances and songs, simple yet robust and vigorous; see its ancient monuments and temples; the footprints of history, that links the pre-historic past with its present; see the glory of its snow-capped mountains, its gurgling rivers and relax in the quiet backwaters of Kerala—in fact SEE INDIA—a country that is a continent.

Buy an INDRAIL PASS—valid for 7—15—21—30—60 or 90 days, as desired by tourists—fares payable in US dollars or sterling pounds—travellers' cheques on foreign banks and rupee payments acceptable subject in certain conditions—an all inclusive fare (no extra reservation charges—no meal charges by Rajdhanis—in fact—no extra charges at all). These tickets are available at:

1. Northern Railway Tourist Guide Office, Baroda House, New Delhi;
2. Travel Agencies: New Delhi offices of SITA World Travel (India) P. Ltd., Travel Corporation (India); Mackinnons Travel Service, Cox & Kings, Ambassador Travels.

The Railways help you, your itinerary and guarantee train reservations for making stay in India, a colourful and a memorable event.

The Jha Committee (1963) recommended that:

(a) Bed rolls should be available for tourists at short notice even at smaller station of tourist interest;

(b) The tourists should be able to obtain Western Style food from restaurant cars as well as at important railway stations. The caterings of the Indian Railways is necessarily oriented to meet the requirements of the bulk of the passengers who are Indians. When their catering staff tries to produce a Western style meal, it usually sets out a five-course dinner consisting of Western dishes—but poorly cooked. If the provision of the Western style meals of a good quality is likely to mean more expenses, there should be no objection to supplying them on demand at higher prices which the tourist would be willing to pay;

(c) Since tourists as a rule, use the railways for going to lesser known places of interest, facilities should be made available to them to make return or onward reservations from intermediate stations.

Standard Circular Journey Tickets

To facilitate organised tours by individuals or groups the railways issue standard circular journey tickets at nominal rates for specified periods. These tickets are issued at fares as for two single journeys, the distance of each single journey being taken as half of the total distance for ten different itineraries covering most of the important pilgrim centres and places of historical, cultural or other interests.

Such tickets are available only for a set of itineraries stipulated by the railways. On specific requisition these tickets are issued to the tourists also for itineraries for their own. As on November 1, 1983, there were as many as 10 such standard circular tours provided by the Southern Railway alone. These different circular tours put together connect/cover almost all tourist centres in the railway network of the Indian Railways. Such circular tickets are available with other zonal railways also.

Home-on-Wheels Cars

These are specially designed coach cars which provide, besides sitting and sleeping accommodation, bathings and cooking facilities in the car itself. These 'self-contained' cars thus serve the twin purpose of transportation and accommodation with tremendous amount of flexibility, privacy and economy. There are luxury, I class and II class, cars available on request for sight-seeing, excursion, etc. These cars will be attached to any train of the tourists' choice except the superfast and other prestigious trains.

Advance Reservation

To facilitate foreign tourism, the railways allow reservation 360 days in advance as against the normal 120 days. A special quota of berths up to the last minute is provided for foreign tourists in all the zonal headquarters of the Indian Railways.

The above promotional measures are good as far as they go. But it is essential to see that these measures are implemented well in actual practice. Measures such as these should not give the impression that everything is done for the benefit of tourists. In fact much more could be done with no additional expenditure.

The level of passenger satisfaction depends on the general level of comforts and facilities provided by the railways. It should be said to the credit of the railways that physical comforts in most of the trains have improved. Now trains are becoming faster. Seats and berths are being progressively cushioned. Bathrooms and other facilities have improved, and so on. But what is to be immediately done is to see that the existing facilities are well maintained by the railways and properly used by the public. It is not unusual that fans do not work, lights do not burn, taps are dry, switches are missing, compartments are unswept, bathrooms are dirty, etc. A passenger, particularly a tourist, will be very much handicapped by these shortcomings. All these could be attended to if the railways take a little more care, without much extra financial commitment.

Improved and more coaches with sleeper berths, better seats, clean toilets, more fans and better lights would go a long way in making rail journey more comfortable. Computerisation of reservation is very much needed to reduce the service time at the reservation counter. Besides the entire system of reservation—instant reservation, cancellation and reallotment, etc.,—should be modernised to the benefit of all concerned. A pilot computer system is installed in New Delhi. Other metropolitan cities would also be covered progressively.

On enquiry the tourists have made specific references to certain shortcomings. Most of them were critical of the inordinate delay at the reservation counters, too many forms and procedures for reservation/cancellation, overcrowding, slow speed of some trains, lack of civic sense among the co-passengers, irregularities in reservations including unhelpful attitude of certain personnel both at the counters and in trains, etc. Accidents which occur too often these days indirectly tarnish the image of the railways and would indirectly deter the tourists. Accidents can't be avoided but certainly human failures could be.

Sea Transport

Travel by sea or maritime transport is one of the oldest forms of transport. Its position has changed from the time when it was the sole method of intercontinental transport. The development in the field of air transport and the resulting advantages of speed and fare have halted the growth of the passenger sea traffic. The general development of travel has brought some benefit to the shipping companies. Shipping has for years been a form of international transport. When there was regular reduction in the traffic, the shipping companies invented cruises. Cruise boats give improved profits from better utilization of capacity, especially in the winter off-season. In addition, special prices are being offered to encourage off-season travel on regular services. Long distance liners and car ferries have been introduced. Passenger ships with greater degree of comfort, particularly in the tourist class accommodation, could find an expanding future. Cruising, integration of services with other forms of transport, greater liaison of agents and more promotion etc. would be necessary. Sea transport have a great future if some adjustments are made therein. They are still the major international carriers on long routes. They have upto the present time managed to offer cheaper transport at minimum rates than the airlines.

Cruising may represent some continuing interest in the sea. The Caribbean and the Mediterranean are the two areas where the cruising takes place for sunlust for the industrial population to a significant scale. The tourist sea traffic will have in the future its new orientation of cruise traffic. The growth of the traffic will depend on the qualities of the service and the pricing policy.

The development and growth of tourism depends to a large extent on the adequacy of available transport services. In the international case, the air transport is the most important. There is a need for a close collaboration between the interested parties. The official tourist organisation would take on these tasks. The future will find accommodation and airlines closely correlated and co-ordinated. The tourist traffic coming from the expansion of air travel possibilities cannot grow without an adequate development of accommodation. There is an acute need for closer co-operation between hotels and aviation to remove the intermediaries. Pan American Airways visualised this relationship and the company organised Intercontinental Hotels (PAN AM-Inter-continental) as a wholly owned subsidiary. Similarly Trans World Airlines purchased Hilton International Company (TWA Hilton) which operated more than 40 hotels around the world. Further proof of the desirability of this relationship came in India, when Air India started Hotel Corporation of India (HCI) as its own subsidiary.

It is hoped that some new steps in this direction will take place in future. Considering the economic importance of tourism, additional infrastructure is vitally needed. The infrastructure must be sufficient at the circle and terminal points in the tourist flow. Regional and local infrastructure and the necessary services, better petrol stations, service stations, motels, ferry boats etc. need to be provided. Committees of transport experts, hoteliers, engineers, architects, economists, lawyers should be set up to co-ordinate investment infrastructure. The development of land areas and transport should not prejudice as the development of tourism depends on natural and geographical factors. Regarding the seasonal charatacter of tourism, it is established that the reductions in the transport fares only are not sufficient to change the habits of tourists. If reduction could be had in both transport and accommodation prices, it could be expected that a traffic holiday makers would occur to the tropical countries during the time of the off season in the northern regions. India possesses relatively little of the infrastructure necessary for modern traffic. In order to realise the huge project of Asian Highways, which will join south Asia with the Middle Eastern Europe over a distance of 55,000 kms., a co-ordination committee at governmental level helped by the International Transports and Communication Committee (ITCC) is trying to co-ordinate the numerous and important activities and harmonise, the policies of mobilisation of the necessary financial and technical resources. Considering the role of transport in the development of tourism, there is an urgent dynamic need for a programme for the development of transport in the Asia and Far East. Among other things it requires a closer co-operation between transport and tourist enterprises. The earlier it is done the better results will follow.

Waterways as a mode of transport is not popular in India. For instance, in 1960, 32.8 per cent of the international visitors used waterways to come to India. But this figure is reduced to 6.3 in 1980 and further to 4.6 in 1982. Even this small percentage is largely accounted by tourists from Sri Lanka. In the present state of strained relations between India and Sri Lanka, the percentage is likely to come down.

However, Port Blair and neighbouring islands have potentialities of developing tourism with the help of waterways. Various steps are being taken here by the government to develop this natural facility mainly with an eye on promotion of tourism. The backwaters of Kerala and the Water Transport Corporation of Kerala provide ample opportunities of developing transport and tourism.

The latest thinking in the line of developing ocean transport to India is the use of hydrofoils and hovercrafts. These water crafts reduce the journey time and would avoid inclement weather. Hovercrafts are amphibious air-cushion vehicles while hydrofoils are a cross between a ship and an aircraft which flies just above the water irrespective of the weather and waves. This vehicle could be conveniently used as an alternative to overland transport provided there is the physical facility. In foreign co untries, hovercrafts and hydrofoils are popular, especially in Miar.ui beach resort. "The feasibility of introducing hydrofoils between the oil-rich Gulf countries and India deserves urgent examination. Later they may be introduced between Bombay and Goa and some ports on the Eastern Coast."[7]

It is heartening to note that the Committee set up to study the possibility and feasibility of introducing these modern passenger water transport (PWT) has come out with a green signal, though a detailed investigation would however be needed before adopting the PWT service on a commercial scale. In its report the Committee says that "While PWT may not make a significant impact on north-south traffic, the much shorter water route distances in the case of east-west or cross harbour services tilt the balance decisively in favour of PWT."[8] A cost-benefit study of the PWT vis-a-vis overland transport modes should be done. The hovercrafts are likely to be introduced between Rameswaram and Talaimannar and Madras and Rameswaram in Tamil Nadu for transporting passengers. There are potential routes for hydrofoil service like Puri-Calcutta, Bombay-Verawel and West Coast to Laccadive Islands. Perhaps, tourists tired of overland modes for a change may prefer these PWT which are speedier and are suitable for all weather.

Accommodation Facilities

Accommodation facilities constitute a vital and fundamental part of tourist supply. Among the important inputs which flow into the tourist system is tourist accommodation which caters to international tourists forming a vital component of the tourism superstructure and an important feature of the total tourist image of the country. An adequate supply of accommodation suitably tailored to the requirements of the tourist market is one of the basic conditions of tourism development. The provision of accommodation facilities and their growth should, at the same time, be regarded in a much broader context as they make an important contribution to the economy as a whole, by stimulating economic development, social contacts and commercial activities.

In the promotion of tourism, of all the constituents of the tourist industry, accommodation sector thus constitutes the most important segment. Tourism is, to a great extent, dependent on the type and quantity of accommodation available. Accommodation is a very important part of the tourism infrastructure and the expansion of tourism inevitably brings about the development of accommodation. It is rather the core of the tourist industry. Accommodation is, in other words, the matrix of tourism, and is thus the obvious choice to play a distinctive role in the development of this expanding industry.

The United Nations Conference on International Travel and Tourism held in Rome in 1963 considered, in particular, problems relating to means of accommodation. The conference acknowledged the essential importance of means of accommodation, both traditional (hotels, motels) and supplementary (camps, youth hostels, etc.), as incentives to international tourism. The conference recommended that governments should consider the possibility of including tourism projects, and particularly those relating to accommodation, in the list of projects eligible for loans from their industrial or other corporations, and that, where required, they should establish special financial corporations for tourism. It also recommended that governments should give sympathetic consideration to the possibility of granting special facilities and incentives for accommodation projects.

Many countries have recognised the vital importance of accommodation industry in relation to tourism and their governments have co-ordinated their activities with the industry by providing big incentives and concessions to hoteliers, which have resulted in the building up of a large number of hotels and other type of accommodations. For example, availability of hotel sites on liberal repayment terms, special concessions in the form of long-term loans, liberal import licences and taxation reliefs, contributions to the equity capital, cash grants for construction and renovation of building, and similar other concessions are provided to the industry. Many countries in the world offer most of these incentives.

Accommodation for travellers may be conveniently viewed in two ways. The traveller who left his home required accommodation at his destination and for journeys which cannot be completed in a single day. For this he needed overnight accommodation. Inns were perhaps the first such accommodation units which catered to the needs of travellers in early times. Inn keeping has been a very ancient profession. In ancient times and during the Roman Empire many such inns were established which provided food, drink and also entertainment to weary travellers. However with the decline of the Roman Empire by about 500 A.D., the institution of inn keeping lost its importance and for many years there was not much development. Since people travelled very infrequently and there being not much trading activity, there was not much need felt for inn keeping.

Later, it was the Church which came to the rescue of the travellers. Travel grew again for religious pilgrimage purposes. Travellers in thousands visited religious centres. Many monasteries and cathedrals welcomed the travellers and made their stay a comfortable experience. The accommodation provided was free. By the fifteenth century, inns had developed in several countries of Europe, specially in England and France. During the seventeenth and the eighteenth centuries, the facilities provided in the inns were expanded. Some of the inns had as many as 30 or more rooms. English common law declared the inn to be a public house and imposed social responsibility on the inn-keeper for the well-being of the traveller. Even today a hundred old coaching and posting inns are still operating in England as hotels as part of Trust House Limited. Some of these were built about four hundred years ago.

In the United States of America another type of accommodation unit known as the 'tavern' was opened in the year 1634 by a man called Samuel Coles. Coles had come to the New World in search of a fortune in the year 1630 by a ship. By 1780, taverns were popular meeting places where people used to come for eating, drinking and entertainment. Many important events were associated with taverns. In the year 1783, General George Washington bid farewell to his top ranking officers at the Fraunces Tavern in New York city. The famous Boston Tea Party was planned in a tavern called Green Dragon.

In India the concept of shelter for travellers is not new. In fact it is as old as its recorded history. The historical records are replete with mention/references of *viharas, dharamsalas, sarais, musafirkhanas,* etc. These establishments provided a home to all wayfarers, be they pilgrims, scholars, adventurers or merchants. The shelter under various names have always been a part of India's culture as a valuable institution providing a vital service.

The ancient Buddhist monks were probably the first to institutionalise the concept of a shelter in India. The cave temples scattered all over the south-western region of India have both a Chaitya (sanctuary) for worship and prayer and a Vihara (monastery). These monks, altough living in their quiet retreats, away from towns and villages, were nevertheless mindful of the needs of travellers and pilgrims who found shelter and food at these monasteries. It is interesting to note that these monasteries are located on the ancient trade routes between important deities of the region. It is gathered from some inscriptions that merchants gave liberal donations for the construction and maintenance of these establishments. Mere charity was obviously not the motivation in these displays of generosity. The trader travelled with their merchandise and money on these routes and the Viharas were their 'hotels.'

In the medieval period this ancient institution gradually assumed a more secular character. Although religious centres invariably had 'dharamsalas' and 'musafirkhanas' attached to them the caravan 'sarai' appeared as an exclusive traveller's lodge with a 'Nanbai' or the cook attached with it. Sher Shah Suri, the Great Afghan Emperor and the builder of the Grand Trunk Road, is credited with having built caravan sarais at regular intervals all along this highway creating favourable conditions for commerce and travel. However, he was not alone in this venture. The Mughals built such facilities all over their empire. Later kings, Rajas, Nawabs, rich businessmen and philanthropists built sarais making travel less arduous. At approximately the same point in time, the inn was the Western counterpart of India's sarais. With the expansion of commerce, travelling became profitable and with it emerged the business of providing comfortable shelter and good food to the growing number of travellers. The sarais in India like inns in Europe or the stagecoach stations in the USA of the eighteenth and nineteenth centuries stood all along the well-travelled routes. They provided food and shelter to the travellers and fodder to their horses. The amenities these early hotels offered would seem to us to be primitive but they conformed to the life style of that age.

With the passage of time the age-old institution of the sarai or the inn adapted itself to the ever changing and constantly growing requirements of the market and has evolved into the modern hotel. From the age of the bullock cart and horses through the age of the rail road into the era of the jumbo jet and supersonic aircraft, the hotel industry developed with the simultaneous development of transportation systems. It also reflects the standard of living and the life style of the society in which it operates.

With the growth of travel in the eighteenth century there appeared in London the prototype of the modern hotel with the opening by one David Low in 1774. The next fifty years saw a gradual increase in the recognizable ancestors of the modern hotel in London and in resorts such as Brighton and Buxton and also certain other places. In the United States of America, hotels emerged from taverns by the simple expedient of a change of name. By about 1800, the terms tavern and hotel were used to describe the same thing. By the year 1820, 'hotel' became the accepted term to describe a place where people stayed for the night and took their meals on payment. In the 1820s the first tourist hotel appeared in Switzerland.

The demand for some kind of accommodation away from home is an important function of travel. It is, therefore, not surprising that the main influence on the development of accommodation facilities has been developments in the mode of passenger transport. In the field of mass passenger transport, railways could perhaps be credited with being the pioneers. The evolution of the railway system in the eighteenth century greatly affected the quality and the quantity of accommodation used in conjunction with travel. The growth of the railways also brought to a speedy network of stage coach services. By the mid-nineteenth century the use of the stage coach as a means of travel had almost ceased. The industrialization in its wake brought increased urbanisation. The great number of people who flocked to various urban towns in search of employment and also entertainment needed some kind of accommodation. The need for accommodation enabled promising and enterprising people to build hotels and inns in many such urban towns to cater for an increasingly local market and also to serve the large number of travellers carried by the railways.

Until about the middle of the nineteenth century the bulk of the journeys were undertaken for business and vocational reasons, by road and within the boundaries of he individual countries. The volume of travel was relatively small and was confined to a fraction of the rich segments of he population in any country. Inns and similar establishments along the main highways and in the principal towns grew to become the hallmark of the accommodation for the travellers. The traveller could reasonably expect at most inns a clean and comfortable accommodation when he wished to eat or spend the night. It provided the bulk of accommodation *en route.* This trend continued until the end of the nineteenth century, as most of those who did travel did so by coach.

Emergence of the Hotel

Although the earliest hotels date to the eighteenth century, their growth on any scale occurred only in the following century when the railways created sufficiently large markets to help make large hotels possible. During this period a large number of hotels grew up at important destinations. The hotels were developed along the main railways and highway routes in major towns. Substantial development of the hotels thus awaited the volume and the type of traffic only the railways could bring. With the development of railway systems in many other countries within and outside Europe, the number of hotels also increased. These hotels catered to the increasing volume of traffic.

The 1960s also saw the introduction of Thomas Cook's railway and hotel coupons. Starting in 1868 Cook arranged regular circular tours of Switzerland and Northern Italy from England. By the 1890s, 1,200 hotels throughout the world accepted hotel coupons. Thus we find that railways greatly influenced the development of hotels during the early twentieth century.

The demand for accommodation of tourists was thus met by a variety of facilities ranging from inns, taverns, private houses and hotels. The main changes in the demand for tourist accommodation have come about from changes in tourist transportation and in the popularity of different forms of holidays. After the introduction of the motor car and the aircraft, a large number of hotels sprang up at various tourist areas and destinations. The growth of hotels continued until the 1950s. Hotels as a unit of accommodation dominated the scene all over the world.

Hotels provide accommodation, meals and refreshments for irregular periods of time for those who may reserve their accommodation either in advance or on the premises. In broad terms hotels provide facilities to meet the needs of the modern traveller. The dictionaries define hotel in several ways: 'a place which supplies board and lodging,' 'a place for the entertainent of the travelles,' 'large city house of distinction,' and 'a public building.'

The common law states that a hotel is "A place where all who conduct themselves properly, and who, being able and ready to pay for their entertainment, are received, if there be accommodation for them, and who without any stipulated engagement as to the duration of their stay or as to the rate of compensation, are, while there, supplied at a reasonable cost with their meals, lodging, and such services and attention as are necessarily incident to the use of the house as a temporary home."

A definition of the hotel as a business entity worthy of study was presented by hotel operators during the consideration of the hotel business to authorities of the National Recovery Administration, in Washington in 1933. This definition, as formulated by Stuart McNamara, was:

"Primarily and fundamentally an hotel is an establishment which supplies board and lodging, not engaged in interstate commerce, or in any interstate commerce, competitive with or affecting, interstate commerce (or so related thereto that the regulation of the one involves the control of the other), but is a quasi domestic institution retaining from its ancient origin certain traditional, and acquiring, in its modern development, certain statutory rights and obligations to the public, where all persons, not disqualified by condition or conduct, prepared to pay for their accommodation, are to be received and furnished with a room of place to sleep or occupy if such accommodations are available, and with such services and attention as are incident to their use of the hotel as a home, and/or with food, at stipulated prices, and with or without contract as to duration of visit, and which conducts, within the confines of its physical locations, this business of supplying personal services of individuals for profit. Incidental to such fundamental and principal business, the hotel may furnish quarters and facilities for the assemblage of people for social, business or entertainment purposes, and may engage in renting portions of its premises for shops and business whose contiguity is deemed appropriate to an hotel."

Types of Hotels

Over the years the concept and the format of hotels have changed a great deal. There are various types of hotels catering to the increasing demands of tourists. The size, the facade, architectural features and the facilities and amenities provided differ from one establishment to another. In addition the landscape in a particular destination area also greatly influences the architectural features of a hotel. Following are the main types of hotels.

International Hotels

International hotels are the modern Western style hotels in almost all metropolitan and other large cities as well as principal tourist centres. These hotels are luxury hotels and are classified on the basis of internationally accepted system of classification. The hotels are placed in various star categories. There are five such categories ranging from 5 star to 1 star depending upon the facilities and services provided. These hotels provide in addition to accommodation all the other facilities which make the stay a very comfortable and interesting experience. Various facilities provided include well appointed reception and information counter, banquet halls, conference facilities, etc. There are also a number of shops, travel agency, money changing and safe deposit facilities. Restaurant facilities, bars and banqueting are an integral part of the business of a hotel. The various services provided in these hotels include international and the local cuisine, food and beverage service and speciality restaurant service. These hotels also provide entertainment for the guests in the form of various dance and music programmes, sports and games.

A number of these hotels belong to the luxury category. There are some international chains which own a large number of such luxury hotels. Hotels belonging to international chains are mostly owned by public companies and controlled by a Board of Directors. These hotels have various departments which are managed by persons qualified and experienced in the field of hoteliering. The chief of the hotel designated as General Manager is responsible for the overall management and operation of the hotel through his departmental heads. International hotels are suitable for metropolitan cities and for other large business and commercial towns and principal tourist centres. The potential of these hotels is, therefore, limited to these areas: A number of this type of hotels have conference/convention facilities and are suitable for holding meetings, conventions and conferences.

Resort Hotels: Resort hotels cater to the needs of holiday-maker, the tourist and those who by reasons of health desire a change of atmosphere. Resort hotels are located near the sea, mountain and other areas abounding in natural beauty. Rest, relaxation and entertainment are the key factors around which resorts are built. The primary motive of a person visiting resort hotels is rest and relaxation which he is looking far away from his routine busy work life. The resort hotels in order to provide special services to the visitors are built with a view to give a visitor special welcome and an atmosphere of informality. The type of services and amenities located in resort property include recreation facilities such as swimming pool, golf course, tennis courts, skiing, boating, surf-riding and other various indoor sports. Other important amenities include coffee shops, restaurants, conference rooms, lounge, shopping arcade and entertainment. Emphasis on resort hotels, however, is on recreational facilities. The clientele of resort hotels is mostly persons with considerable income looking for relaxation and recreation. Resort hotels rarely attract commercial patronage.

Resorts can be of various types and can be classified on the basis of climate and also topography. Broadly they fall in the folllowing categories:

(i) Summer resorts,

(ii) Winter resorts,

(iii) Hill resorts,

(iv) All reason resorts, and

(v) Health resorts.

Majority of the resort hotels are seasonal establishments which work to capacity during the high tourist season. Generally the high tourist season is the period when there are holidays at educational institutions. However, in recent years many of the resort hotels with a view to extend the season provide certain special facilities and offer various concessions to the guests. The concessions provided include reduced tariffs, free entertainment, sightseeing, gifts, etc.

Commercial Hotels: The commercial hotels direct their appeal primarily to the individual traveller as compared to international or resort hotel where the focus is on the group travel. Most of the commercial hotels receive the guests who are on business although some have permanent guests. As the hotel caters primarily to people who are visiting a place for commerce or business, these are located in important commercial and industrial centres of large towns and cities. These hotels are generally run by the owners and their success depends on their efficient running and comforts and facilities they provide. In some of the large industrial towns, fully licenced commercial hotels exist compete with restaurants, grill room, functional accommodation and a garage for those travelling by automobile.

Residential Hotels: These hotels can be described as *apartment house* complete with hotel service. These are often referred to as apartment hotels. The tariff of rooms in these hotels is charged on monthly, half yearly or yearly basis and is charged for either furnished or unfurnished accommodation. These hotels which are located mostly in big cities operate exclusively under the European plan where no meals are provided to the guests. These hotels were developed in the United States of America where people discovered that permanent living in hotels offers many advantages. Services and amenities provided in these hotels are comparable to those of an average well regulated home. These are very popular in the United States and western Europe where these are also known popularly as Pension.

Floating Hotels: As the name suggests, these hotels are located on the surface of the water. It may be on sea water, river water or on a lake. All the facilities and services of a hotel are provided in these hotels. These hotels are very popular in many countries. In many countries old luxury ships have been converted into floating hotels and are proving very popular among tourists. The atmosphere they provide is exclusive and exotic. In India, floating hotels in the form of *house boats* are very popular with tourists.

Supplementary Accommodation

Although hotels have been and still are the principal form of accommodation, there has been a growth and development of some other forms of accommodation over the years. It can be of various types and can be classified on the basis of its location, type of construction, type of property, type of management, etc. It is, therefore, difficult to classify. Different terms have been used to indicate similar functions of various accommodation units. It is not possible to give clear cut definition of various types of accommodation. The various accommodation units differ in a number of respects. A study of the different types of accommodation indicates that their diversity is a reflection of the specific nature of each one and their names simply indicate various ways in which one and the same function can be fulfilled or the need can be satisfied.

Hotels although a very important part of the tourism infrastructure are not the only type of accommodation available for the tourists. Tourist accommodation need not be viewed from the point of view of hotel industry alone. In addition to hotels, the demand for tourist accommodation is met by a variety of facilities. There are a series of other installations able to offer to the tourists lodging, food and corresponding services. This is popularly known as supplementary accommodation and is in fact an important segment of tourism.

Supplementary accommodation consists of various types of accommodation other than the conventional hotel type. It may be described as premises which offer accommodation but not the services of a hotel. All the establishments under the heading of supplementary accommodation are designed to offer accommodation in the broad sense of the term, namely, the possibility of stay overnight and meals in return of cash payment per day and on the basis of services provided. In supplementary accommodation the standard of comforts in modest compared to that of an hotel. On the other hand, however, there are certain inherent advantages in this type of accommodation. The biggest advantage is that of price. The supplementary accommodation as compared to the conventional type of accommodation is moderately priced. In addition the atmosphere in the accommodation is informal and there is more freedom with regard to dress, etc. There is also more emphasis on entertainment and sports resulting in increased social contact among the guests.

Supplementary accommodation plays a very important role in the total available tourist accommodation in a country. This type of accommodation can cater to both international as well as domestic tourist traffic. In fact in some countries more tourists utilize this type of accommodation than in hotels. In France and Italy as also in some other countries in Europe and elsewhere there are more campers than there are hotel clients. Following are some of the principal forms of supplementary accommodation:

(i) Motel,

(ii) Youth Hostel,

(iii) Camping Sites,

(iv) Pension,

(v) Bed and Breakfast Establishments, and

(vi) Tourist Holiday Villages.

Motel

The concept of motel and motel-hotel originated in the United States of America. Motel was meant for local motorists and foreign tourists travelling by road. Primarily designed to serve the needs of motorists, motels almost exclusively meet the demand for transit accommodation. They serve the function of a transit hotel except that they are geared to accommodate motor travelling guests for overnight stay.

The important services provided by motels include parking, garage facilities, accommodation, restaurant facilities, public catering and recreational facilities. With a view to provide the above services to the motorists, all the motels are equipped with filling stations, repair services, accessories, garages, parking space, elevator service to the automobile entrance, restaurants, etc. There is also equipment and tools available which the guest can use himself if he wishes to repair his vehicle. The price charged for accommodation and meals/refreshments is much cheaper as compared to that in hotels. Motels are mostly located outside the city limits in the countryside along with the main highway and preferable at an important road junction. Since these establishments cater mainly for persons travelling by road, their development is linked with the development of new motorways along which these are necessarily located. Motels are of different types. Some motels provide just the minimum services while others are well furnished with comfortable accommodation and excellent facilities. The accommodation provided in a motel is of Chalet type which is furnished having a dining hall with fixed menu. Shopping facilities for travelling public are also provided for in a motel.

In many countries, specially the United States of America motel accommodation is ranked with hotel accommodation and subject to general standards applicable to hotel industry. In countries like Norway, France, Ireland, Turkey, etc., specific legislation has been introduced for motels, which includes requirements for the approval of plans, easy access of cars, minimum capacity, provision of restaurant where necessary, minimum standards for facilities and provision of petrol pump or service station where they exist, model classification standards similar to those for hotels. For instance, in France, there are three categories designated by stars, the classification being based on location, sanitary fittings and collective amenities. An increasingly important segment of the accommodation industry, motels are looked upon as distinct asset which has enabled the industry to meet the changes in travel patterns and personal preferences of modern day traveller.

Youth Hostel

In the form of a movement, youth hostels made their first appearance in Germany in about the year 1900. The movement which spread rapidly all over the world was based on the educational principles emphasising the need by youth of large cities to travel on foot throughout the country. In order to provide some sort of accommodation and services the dormitories in the inns were equipped with cots, mattresses, sheets and blankets. Large rooms in inns were used as dining and living areas providing full board at low cost to the guests. There was also provision of additional kitchen where travellers could themselves prepare their own meals. Since the movement was started with a view to encouraging youth to travel in order to learn and know more about the country and also to socialize, it had an educational value. As such, no service was provided in the inn. The persons staying in the inn were themselves required to look after the inn. Subsequently, exclusive youth hostel buildings were constructed to accommodate young travellers.

Youth hostel can be defined as building which offers clean, moderate and inexpensive shelter to young people exploring their own country or other countries and travelling independently or in groups on holiday or for educational purpose. It is a place where young people of different social backgrounds and nationalities meet together and come to know each other. The objective of youth hostel is, therefore, not merely to provide accommodation and board, but also to serve as centres which offer opportunity to young people coming from different parts of the country as also young travellers from abroad to know and understand each other. It is a place of friendship, recreation and out-of-school and college education.

The youth hostels are equipped to accommodate youngmen and women who travel on foot, by bicycle or other means of locomotion and who, at very little cost, are provided with place to sleep, eat or to make their own meal. The services, provided include accommodation, meals and also recreation. The charges for these services are very modest. The hostels are also equipped to enable the users to prepare their own meals if they so desire. The accommodation provided in the hostels is for a limited number of days.

In most of the countries, youth hostels are developed and managed by non-commercial organisations whose main aim is the development of youth tourism. Since Second World War, the number of such hostels has increased greatly. These hostels are now planned to provide comfortable accommodation as also such other services and facilities which are required by youth. Also the number of those using these hostels has grown tremendously. Many hostels receive increasing number of groups and organise stays for winter sports or sailing.

The construction of youth hostels is based on certain norms laid down from time to time all over the world. International requirements for these include provision of separate dormitories for men and women, appropriate and clean toilets, wash rooms for both men and women, a kitchen where hosteliers can prepare their own meals, common rooms, living accommodation for warden and a left luggage room. There is also a provision of a kitchen where warden and staff can prepare meals for supply to hosteliers, separate small room for instructors, a dining room and classroom for school parties and a warden's office. Some youth hostels have playgrounds attached for the use of hosteliers.

Caravan and Camping Sites

Caravan and camping sites constitute a significant accommodation category in many holiday areas. These are very popular in some European countries as also in the United States of America. These are also known as open-air hostels, tourist camps or camping grounds. Camping, originally practiced by hikers on foot is increasingly giving way to car camping. The sites are usually located within the large cities in open spaces. Equipped to receive mobile accommodation in the form of caravans, the camping sites provide facilities for parking, tent pitching, water, electricity, toilet, etc. Though the services provided generally include restaurants, recreational rooms, toilets and at certain places a grocer's shop, the type of services often vary from place to place. Some countries have enacted legislation establishing the minimum facilities that must be provided which include health and sanitation standards and prices to be charged for parking and use of various services and facilities.

Pension

This type of accommodation is very popular in certain European countries. Particularly in Italy, Austria, Germany and Switzerland these establishments are used extensively by the tourists. Pension is also described as private hotel, a guest-house or a boarding house. Catering facilities are optional and are usually restricted to the residents. Many of them stay for a longer and such definite periods as a week or a fortnight. The reservation of accommodation is made in advance. Mostly managed by a family, pension accommodation is much cheaper than hotel accommodation.

Bed and Breakfast Establishments

Also known in some countries as apartment hotels and *hotel garnis,* they represent a growing form of accommodation units catering for holiday as well as business travellers. These establishments provide only accommodation and breakfast and not the principal meals. These are usually located in large towns and cities along commercial and holiday routes and also resort areas and are used by en route travellers. Some of these establishments are very popular with holiday-makers.

Tourist Holiday Villages

Tourist villages were established in some European countries after Second World War. These villages are situated at warm sea sides and in the regions which offer certain facilities for the tourists. In certain countries like Italy and Spain, tourist villages are located in the regions which are economically not developed thereby helping the regions economically. The villages are mostly promoted by important clubs, social organisations and also by tourist organisations.

The village complex is a centre of accommodation providing extensive sports and recreation facilities, riding, swimming, tennis, volleyball, football, sauna, mini-golf, badminton, table tennis and yoga. These provide both board and lodging. The atmosphere in these villages is kept as informal as possible. Telephones, radios, newspapers and TV are banned unless there is an emergency. Wallets and other valuables are locked away at the beginning of one's stay. Instead of money one uses colourful beads which can be worn anywhere as bracelets, necklaces, etc. The staff are chiefly educated young people who live on an equal basis with the holiday makers. The accommodation provided is usually in multiple units and may provide for self-catering. The furnishing provided in the rooms is minimal. The easy mixing of guests is encouraged by the banning of advance booking of tables in the village restaurants so one rarely finds oneself sitting with the same group twice.

The holiday villages are usually based on family units, each providing a convertible living room, bath/shower and sometimes a kitchen. The villages are self-sufficient providing almost all necessities required by the residents. There is also a small shopping complex where one can buy articles of daily need. The services of a doctor are also available in the village. The accommodation is sold for a week or a fortnight at an all inclusive price. In Spain and Italy, these are classified into three categories according to the services and amenities provided.

Club Mediterranee can be considered to be pioneers in the development of concept of 'tourist villages.' The organisation has been consciously built around a philosophy which stresses that people who live and work in cities need holidays in totally different surroundings. The atmosphere of the hundred-odd holiday villages which they operate round the world is kept as informal as possible. When Club Mediterranee started its first "Vacation Village" on the Spanish island of Majorca in 1950, its initial 2,500 vacationers slept in army-surplus tents, helped cook meals, and washed dishes.

Today the atmosphere is vastly different. Its hundred-odd vacation villages in about 25 countries are luxurious, upscale complexes that cater to sun-seeking, high-income couples and singles. Telephones, radios, newspapers and TV are banned unless there is an emergency. Wallets and other valuables are locked away at the beginning of one's stay. Instead of money one uses beads of different colours which can be worn anywhere, as bracelets, necklaces, etc. The club's staff are known as G.O.S. (gentils organisateurs), who are mainly educated young people who live on an equal basis with the holiday makers staying in the village. The staff is trained to act as vacationers' friends and hosts rather than as hotel employees. There are from 90 to 100 GOSs for the average 600-bed village. Accommodation in the basic villages consists of furnished units with all the facilities. The easy mixing of guests is encouraged by the banning of advance booking of tables in camp restaurants so one rarely finds oneself sitting with the same group twice. Each village has a wide range of entertainment and sporting facilities like music, water-skiing, tennis and yoga classes.

The activities in the 'villages' are increasingly being diversified in recent times. There is emphasis on guided tours of countries where resorts are located, along with lectures on local customs, history and language. Business-conference and convention sales also are being stressed. Nearly all the activities and services—plus lodging and virtually unlimited food and wine are covered by a flat fee.

Despite its informal atmosphere and also image, the club now ranks as the 10th largest hotel chain in the world. It has come a long way from 1950 when it started with 2,500 members and a tent village in Majorca.

Classification, Registration and Gradation

Tourist accommodation is one of the important components of the total tourist product. It is thus an individual component. As an individual product it is intangible, often bought in advance of its use. The tourist at the time of making purchase thus cannot inspect or accept or reject. Accommodation as such, raises some issues in its development and in its marketing, both as an individual product and as a part of a package. It creates a need for reliable and accurate information for both the tourists and the travel agents and, therefore, may equire supervision and control. An individual operator needs to bring information about his accommodation to the tourist before he sets off on his journey and also when he reaches his destination. Similarly the tourist on the other hand, needs to know in detail what accommodation is available at what price in particular destination from which he can make a choice about what and where to stay. Schemes of classification, registration and grading of the tourist accommodation are intended to meet these requirements.

The United Nations Conference on International Travel and Tourism held in Rome in the year 1963 also emphasised the need for some sort of regulation of the accommodation with a view to safeguard interests of the users. Considering that special attention should be given to relations between the public authorities and the operators of tourist accommodation facilities, the conference advocated the adoption of a hotel trade charter codifying the regulations applicable to the hotel industry and, in particular, giving official tourist organisations powers enabling them to perform the activities devolving on the state in that field.

The conference observed that many states classify tourist hotels or are considering doing so. Acting upon the recommendations put forward by IUOTO and the International Chamber of Commerce, the conference advocated the standardization of methods of classification and in particular the sub-division of hotels into five categories each identified by a conventional sign (stars) in conformity with sets of standards appropriate to different climatic conditions. The conference also considered the question of classifying supplementary means of accommodation such as tourist bungalows and camps.

Classification

Classification separates accommodation into different classes or categories on the basis of certain criteria, for example, by type of accommodation such as hotels, holiday camps and caravan sites. A scheme of classification seeks to present information about tourist accommodation in a form which will enable the user to find information he requires easily and quickly and to be able to compare it with similar types. Apart from having the information classified by location, a tourist needs to know the availability of accommodation which meets his requirements as to type, price and other criteria.

Registration

The aim of registration, on the other hand, is to provide a complete list of register of tourist accommodation within a particular definition. A registration scheme results in an inventory of accommodation which can be kept up-to-date. In order to be comprehensive, it normally has to have statutory legal authority and is administered by a government authority or a statutory body. Because of the wide range of accommodation used by the tourists, a scheme of registration should normally cover all forms of accommodation used by them.

Gradation

Grading separates accommodation into different categories or grades on the basis of judgements such as standards of amenities and service. A grading scheme provides qualitiative judgements on the amenities and facilities of a particular accommodation unit in a form which enables the user to choose the quality of accommodation he requires. This may refer to the physical facilities, food and other services of the establishment, various amenities provided etc. The establishments are graded individually or collectively by way of giving them numbers, letters or symbols.

The schemes of classification, registration and grading in operation in various countries differs. Some countries incorporate only registration, some others classification and some grading. The standards adopted also differ from country to country.

Volume and Geographical Distribution

According to WTO estimates, based on a survey conducted by the Secretariat in the year 1978-79, the total capacity of hotels and similar establishments, like motels, boarding houses and inns, was 16.3 million bed-places in 1977. The largest accommodation capacity is however available in the continent of Europe, 8.8 million bed-places in the hotel industry proper. This constitutes more than half the total bed-places available all over the world. This is followed by Canada and the United States of America, with 4.6 million bed-places. The share of the developed countries in the total world accommodation capacity is estimated to be approximately 85 per cent.

In several European countries, hotel development is

concentrated in small and medium-sized hotel constructions. In many countries, within the framework of general expansion of the accommodation sector, the increase in hotel accommodation was outstripped by the increase in supplementary means of accommodation, such as camping and caravaning sites, rented rooms, apartments, etc. This type of accommodation has become the main provider of lodging for domestic tourism and has also started to play a very significant role in international tourism. In the Americas the total capacity of hotels and similar establishments increased significantly in several countries of the region.

In East Asia and the Pacific region, several countries are currently enjoying a hotel building boom. In South Asia, the countries of the region are undertaking great efforts to develop accommodation sector. In the Middle East, hotel construction in the region is mainly concentrated on luxury class hotels intended chiefly to cater for business travellers. In view of the high profitability, there are many hotel projects which are under construction. In the African region accommodation facilities are concentrated in the northern part of the continent.

Table 4.3

Distribution of Hotel Bed-places in the World

Region	*Number of countries*	*Available bed places in hotels and similar establishments (in thousands)* 1976	1977	*Percentage change 1976/1977*
Africa	37	239.0	263.0	10.0
Americas	32	5,955.2	6,160.0	3.4
East Asia and Pacific	17	840.6	872.0	3.7
Europe	32	8,632.6	8,791.3	1.8
Middle East	8	113.9	124.4	9.2
South Asia	7	104.1	113.4	8.9
Total	133	15,885.3	16,324.0	2.8

Source: World Travel (W.T.O.)

The contribution to National Income by the hotel and restaurant industry is computed and given in Table 4.4. It could be seen that its contribution to National Income had increased from 0.5 per cent in 1960-61 to 0.8 per cent in 1970-71 and to 1.0 per cent in 1975-

76 which level it maintained in 1979-80 also. The corresponding figures for the tourism industry as a whole work out to 1.0, 1.6 and 2.0 percentages. The trend is encouraging though not the magnitude.

Table 4.4

Contribution to National Income by Hotel and Restaurant Industry and by Tourism Industry (at Current Prices)

Year	*Contribution by hotel and restaurant industry*		*Contribution by[1] tourism industry Percentage to total*
	Rs. in crs	*Percentage to total N.I.*	
1960-61	70	0.5	1.0
1970-71	279	0.8	1.6
1975-76	625	1.0	2.0
1979-80	890	1.0	2.0

1. Computed at twice the contribution of the hotel and restaurant industry.

Source: The Economic Times, March 30, 1983, p. 5.

The contribution of world tourism to World Gross Product (GWP), excluding the Communist countries, was put at 6 per cent for 1979. Indian tourism industry must grow three times the present rate to reach the world level, even assuming that tourism industry in the rest of the world remain static! But unfortunately things are not that encouraging. India has to take very bold and far-reaching policy decisions to catch up with the rest of the world.

Changing Profile of the Accommodation Sector

The accommodation sector has undergone substantial changes in recent years. New developments in tourism and transportation, changes in the organisation of travel and technological innovations are some of the factors which are responsible for these changes. In addition, increasing consumer demand among tourists due in turn to the improvement in living standards and economic conditions has also changed the profile of the accommodation sector. All the above factors seem to have influenced the structure of the hotel industry as a whole. The tendency among middle income groups to take holiday at any time of the year has encouraged accommodation operators to offer novel kinds of arrangements which are now available in addition to traditional hotel accommodation.

New types of accommodation, particularly holiday villages suitable for family type tourists, condominiums and apartment houses, private villas and camping facilities have proved very successful and to a certain degree are replacing traditional hotels and boarding houses. These changes reflect changes in demand with new, often younger groups entering the international travel market and also new approaches to the problem of providing facilities in a very competitive industry with a highly seasonal demand.

The probable future developments in the accommodation sector were the subject of study undertaken in WTO's 1978-79 research programme. Some conclusions which emerge from the study are as follows:

(a) a significant growth in accommodation supply will continue to be contributed by chain operators, including airlines. This expansion will result mainly from the further development of management contracts and franchise agreements;

(b) there will be a continuing move towards the further diversification of accommodation. The development of budget accommodation, covering budget hotels, an also supplementary means of accommodation, is likely to continue as mass tourism stimulates new demands for competitively-priced accommodation;

(c) the standard of accommodation will continue to rise. Demand for recreational and sporting facilities will increase in both business and leisure accommodation;

(d) rising building and operating costs, growing environment and conservation pressures, as well as the need to keep staffing levels at a minimum, will influence design and construction of accommodation units;

(e) advances in technology will both influence the traditional construction methods, for example, more frequent use of prefabricated building techniques, as well as traditional methods of hotel operations.

Notes and References

1. Burkart, A.J., and Medlik, S., *Tourism—Past, Present and Future,* Heinemann, London, 1974, p. 107.
2. *Illustrated Weekly of India,* April 20, 1980, p. 9.
3. Draft IV, *Five Year Plan* (Revised).
4. *The Indian Express,* Sept. 30, 1982.
5. Report of the *Estimate Committee,* 1956, p. 43.
6. Report of NDC-*Hotel and Catering Industry, USA and Japan,* p. 51.
7. *Tourism Recreation Research, India,* Vol. VIII, No. 1, June 1982, p. 9.
8. *The Economic Times,* October 11, 1983, p. 1.

5

Civil Aviation and Tourism

The Organisational Structure

The Constitution of India enshrines a federal and parliamentary democratic Republic for the governance of the country. The Union Government, which is headed by the President of India controls and administers some 97 subjects of the Central List and other 47 subjects enumerated in the Concurrent List of the VII Schedule. During emergencies, which are of three varieties, the Union-State Relationships can be significantly altered and revised in a manner that the Central Government can become paramount and quasi-federal in its day-to-day administrative working within the framework of the Constitution. Civil Aviation as a subject appears in the Union List and is administered by a Cabinet Minister in the Union Ministry at New Delhi.

The transactions of various Union Ministries of the Government of India are executed through the Ministries and Departments, their Attached and Subordinate Offices, Public Undertakings and other establishments under them. The Ministries and Departments are administratively responsible for the execution of national policies within the sphere of their specific responsibilities. They are also responsible for the implementation of thesc policies within the framework of the broad principles embodied in the Constitution or specific Acts passed by the Parliament of India. During last two decades, a number of corporations have been established by the Union Government. These corporations and public undertakings function under the administrative control of the relevant Ministry.

A Secretary to the Government is the administrative head of the Ministry. He is the principal adviser to the Minister on all matters of policy and administration. He is also responsible for the advice given to the Minister. Besides Secretary, there are some Joint Secretaries also. Their number depends upon the volume of work in a Ministry. A Joint Secretary is in-charge of each wing. He is subject to the general control of the Secretary. Some Ministries also have the posts of Additional Secretaries. An Additional Secretary is given charge of an important wing in the Ministry. A Ministry is divided into Divisions, Branches and Sections. A Section Officer takes care of a Section. A branch which consists of two sections is normally under the charge of an Under Secretary. Generally, two branches constitute a Division which is under the charge of a Deputy Secretary.[1]

The Ministry of Civil Aviation and Tourism looks after the development and growth of air routes and aerodromes along with operations of aeronautical communication services for the safe and regular civil air transport in the country. It has its branch offices in State capitals and important cities of India. Administratively the Ministry operates through an International Airports Authority and two Air Corporations which in turn have their attached offices[2] and subordinate offices in the capital and in the field.[3] The functions of the Ministry cover the entire length and breadth of the country covering the network of national air routes. Similarly, the aviation operations on international trade routes also fall within the administrative purview of this Ministry. Air India which is one of the major sources of foreign exchange earning for the country though autonomous is attached to the Ministry of Civil Aviation for purposes of administrative regulation.

The evolution of civil aviation administration in the Central Government dates back to the year 1919. This year it was formally allocated and placed in the Department of Commerce and Industry of the Government of India. An *ad hoc* agency known as Indian Air Board has been rendering advice to the department on all significant matters pertaining to civil aviation. It also provided assistance in regard to technical matters, such as the work of inspection from the Royal Air Force. The year 1921 witnessed the bifurcation of the Department of Commerce and Industry into two full-fledged departments of Commerce and Industries.

Naturally, some of the subjects which were formerly

administered by the combined Department of Commerce and Industry including 'Civil Aviation' were now transferred to the Public Works Department of the Central Government. This arrangement could not last long. After a period of two years in 1923, civil aviation, meteorology and some other allied subjects were added to the list and put under the administrative control of the Department of Industries and Labour. This change was effected on the recommendations of the Inchcape Committee (1922)[4] which favoured the merger of the Public Works Department in the Department of Industries. Up till this time there was not a single officer in the department who was employed exclusively to look after the work of civil aviation. After sometime, however, the need for a special organisation to administer, the subject was felt. This need was further accentuated because of the signing of the International Convention for Navigation by India in 1919.[5]

The growing realisation of the country's role in the field of international civil aviation brought heavier administrative responsibilities on the department. This led to the creation of a full-fledged Civil Aviation Branch in the Department of Industries and Labour in January 1927. The branch was to be looked after by a Director of Civil Aviation who was to be appointed for the discharge of administrative duties in the field. He was also provided with some secretariat staff to assist him. Later on, this Civil Aviation Branch of the department got converted into the Directorate of Civil Aviation and assumed the status of an attached office under the Department of Industries and Labour.[6]

In November 1937 the Department of Industries and Labour again got bifurcated into the Department of Labour and the Department of Communications. This time the subjects 'civil aviation' and 'meteorology' were transferred to the latter i.e. Department of Communications. In 1941 the Department of Communications was further saddled with the additional responsibility of 'railway inspection' which was formerly a function of the Railway Board. A year later the Department of Communications was again separated into two Departments namely the Department of Posts and the Department of War Transport. The Department of Posts and Air was assigned the works relating to Posts and Telegraphs, Civil Aviation, Meteorology and Railway Inspection. In 1946 this Department of Posts and Air was redesignated as the Department of Communications. In August

1947 with the advent of independence the Department of Communications attained the status of a Ministry and was given the name of Ministry of Communications in the Union Cabinet.[7]

The year 1953 represents a major landmark in the history of development of the administration of civil aviation in India when the air transport industry was nationalised by the Government of India.[8] It resulted into the establishment of two Air Corporations, one for the operation of long-distance international air services and the other for domestic air services and for services to neighbouring countries. Both the Corporations were initially placed under the administrative control of the then Ministry of Communications. Four years later in 1957 when the Ministry of Communications got amalgamated in the Ministry of Transport civil aviation administration came under the charge of the new Ministry of Transport and Communications. This Ministry organised itself into two Departments, viz., the Department of Transport and the Department of Communications and Civil Aviation. In September 1963 the Department of Communications was reorganised and subjects like civil aviation, air corporations, railway inspection and meteorology were transferred to the Department of Transport.

Consequently, the Department of Transport was raised to the status of a Ministry and was designated as Ministry of Transport. The year 1964 witnessed yet another major reshuffle when the subjects like civil aviation, meteorology and railway inspection were again pinched out from the Ministry of Transport and placed under the Ministry of Civil Aviation. Two years later the sheer necessity of integrated work pattern forced the two Ministries combine to form the new Ministry of Transport and Aviation in January 1966. This Ministry was organised to have two Departments, namely the Department of Aviation and the Department of Transport, Shipping and Tourism. The subject 'Tourism' came to the Department of Aviation in September 1966. The same year the Department of Aviation was given an extended name of the Department of Aviation and Tourism. By March 1967 the functions and responsibilities of the department became so important that the Union Government decided to elevate the Department of Aviation and Tourism into the Ministry of Tourism and Civil Aviation.[9] The present organisation of this Ministry is outlined in Chart 5.1.

Chart 5.1
Ministry of Tourism and Civil Aviation, Government of India, New Delhi

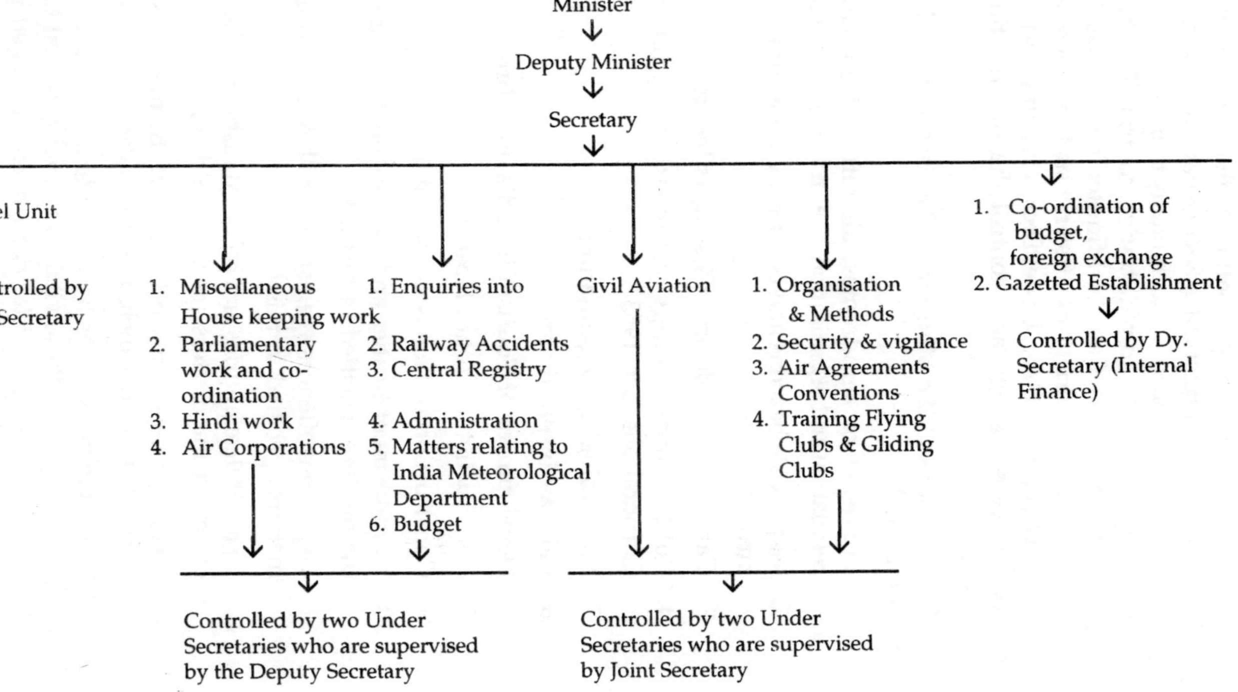

The administrative organisation of the Ministry of Tourism and Civil Aviation consists of a Secretariat, two attached offices and two subordinate offices. Additionally there are five big public undertakings under its administrative control. The Ministry is generally headed by a Cabinet Minister who is assisted by a Deputy Minister. A variety of officers[10] such as Secretary, Joint Secretary, Deputy Secretary, Under Secretary, Junior Analysts and Section Officers manage and control the organisation of the Secretariat.

The functions of the Ministry of Tourism and Civil Aviation are as follows:[11]

1. Provision of aerodromes; aircraft and air navigation; regulation and organisation of air traffic and of aerodromes
2. To provide beacons and other provisions for the safety of aircraft
3. Carriage of goods and passengers by air
4. Public undertakings established under the Air Corporations Act, 1953
5. Meteorological Organisation
6. Railway Inspectorate
7. Development of Tourism in India and abroad
8. Construction of Youth Hostels
9. Construction of Hotels in the public sector
10. To implement treaties and agreements relating to any of the matters specified in this list
11. To prevent offences against laws with respect to any of the matters specified in this list
12. To institute enquiries and collect statistics for the purpose of any of the matters specified in this list
13. To charge fees in respect of any of the matters specified in this list but not including fees taken in any court.

All these functions cover a very wide area of activity. The Ministry has to perform these vital and developmental functions in collaboration with other sister departments engaged in allied activities in other ministries. To handle policy matters pertaining to these well defined responsibilities of the Ministry, the Ministry has to operate through attached offices called as the Department of Tourism and Directorate General of Civil Aviation.

Department of Tourism, New Delhi

(An Attached Office)

The Ministry of Tourism and Civil Aviation has the Department of Tourism as one of its attached offices. It performs both the promotional and organisational functions. Its major functions relate to the creation of the infrastructure for tourism in its multiple aspects. It is charged with the responsibility of tourist publicity both in India and abroad. The Department works in close co-operation with the India Tourism Development Corporation which is one of the public sector undertakings under the care of the Ministry. The Director-General of Tourism who is the head of the Department enjoys the ex-officio status of Joint Secretary to the Government of India.[12] The department is organised into six sections. These sections are:[13] *(i)* Travel Trade and Promotion, *(ii)* Planning, *(iii)* Hotels, *(iv)* Publicity, *(v)* Research and Statistics, and *(vi)* Administration. Each of these sections looks after the specific functions assigned to the care of the department. As the department is responsible for the overall development and promotion of Tourism as Industry in the country its activities range from field publicity to market research on tourist traffic every year. Being an attached office it concerns with the staff functions some of which are:[14]

"1. Development of tourist infrastructure;
2. Publicity at home and abroad with a view to promoting tourism;
3. Compilation, collation and dissemination of tourist information in India and abroad; attending to enquiries from tourists, tour operators and the travel industry such as airlines, steamship companies and hotels, and assisting them;
4. Co-operation with international travel and tourism organisations at Government and non-Government levels;
5. Facilitation work such as simplification of frontier formalities, either directly or in co-operation with the Union Ministries and the State Governments;

6. Regulation of activities of various segments of the travel trade, such as hotels, travel agents, shikar out-fitters, guides, tourist car operators and shopkeepers;
7. Compilation of statistics and market research on tourist traffic to India."

The Department of Tourism has to remain in active contact with the activities of other international tourist organisations all over the world because the decisions, recommendations and activities of these agencies bring their inevitable impact on the tourist markets of the country. The Department is a member of the following international organisations:[15]

1. The International Union of Official Travel Organisation, Geneva
2. The South Asia Travel Commission, Kabul
3. The Pacific Area Travel Association, San Francisco
4. The American Society of Travel Agents, New York
5. The Universal Federation of Travel Agents Association, Hong Kong

The overseas tourist offices provide a direct link between the Department and the travelling public abroad. Some of the functions of these tourist offices include handling of enquiries, dissemination of accurate information, advertising, publicity, public relations with the Press and the travel trade. Additionally they also supply information to the Department about latest trends in tourism in various areas of their functioning. There are fifteen such overseas offices located in principal towns of several countries of the world. The Table 5.1 explains their coverage.

Then there are dozens of tourist offices located inside the country. They furnish information to tourists regarding tourist attractions and various facilities available to the national and foreign tourists. These offices also help the Department in exercising some degree of control over various segments of the travel trade. They further ensure that the services for tourists are maintained efficiently and are available at reasonable cost. Four such regional offices are located at major ports of entry, namely, Bombay, Calcutta, Madras and New Delhi. A large number of these field offices have been set up at other major centres of tourist interest.[16]

Table 5.1

Overseas Tourist Office	*The area covered*
1. New York 2. San Francisco 3. Chicago Sub-office	U.S.A. including Hawaii, Guatemala, Bermuda and Caribbean Islands
4. Mexico	All countries in Latin America
5. Toronto	Canada
6. London	United Kingdom and Eire
7. Geneva 8. Paris 9. Frankfurt 10. Brussels 11. Stockholm 12. Milan	Continental Europe
13. Sydney	Australia, New Zealand and Fiji Islands
14. Tokyo	Japan, the Philippines, Hong Kong
15. Singapore	Singapore, Kuala Lumpur and Thailand

Directorate General of Civil Aviation, New Delhi

(An Attached Office)

This attached office of the Ministry of Tourism and Aviation was born in the year 1927. Headed by a Director-General of Civil Aviation the Directorate is responsible for various kinds of regulatory functions in the area of civil aviation. Its major function is to provide for the required infrastructure conducive for the growth of civil air transport operations in India. The following are the main activities of the Directorate:[17]

"1. The construction maintenance and management of terminal buildings, runways, aprons, etc. of civil aerodromes;

2. the provision of navigational aids and communication facilities to civil air transport;

3. the enforcement of Air Transport Regulations, including safety requirements, such as the certification of the airworthiness of aircraft, licensing of pilots, navigators, and other aircrew, and regulation of air traffic; and

4. enquiries into air accidents and incidents affecting the safety of aircraft."

For purpose of its administrative working the Directorate General of Civil Aviation is organised in 10 regular Directorates. The principal among them are Air Routes and Aerodromes, Communications, Aeronautical Inspection and Training and Licensing. The Chart 5.2 indicates the organisation of the Directorates in the Directorate General. The Director General of Civil Aviation (D.G.C.A.) is assisted by two Deputy Directors General. Both of them have Directors under them who look after the work in the technical branches of their respective Directorates. The Director General is the administrative head who is responsible to the Minister of Tourism and Civil Aviation, Government of India. He is administratively responsible for the control and regulation of all operations pertaining to civil aviation in the country. He advises the Ministry on major policy matters in the area of aviation. Aviation being a specialised activity the D.G.C.A. retains a very substantial control over critical areas of policy making and policy implementation. The Directorate for Air Routes and Aerodromes looks after the construction and equipment of aerodromes, their planning, administration and regulation of air traffic operations. It also serves as a liaison with Air H.Q. India, on air route operations and development. The other Directorate for Aeronautical Communications is responsible for planning, organisation, equipment, administration and operation of the aeronautical communication service for safe and regular operation of air transport. It provides the much needed liaison with Air H.Q. on radio organisation for Joint Air Force and Civil Aviation purposes.[18]

The Directorate of Aeronautical Inspection has the responsibility to ensure the airworthiness of the aircraft. This entails the supervision of materials from their origin to their incorporation in the aircraft and the day-to-day maintenance of the aircraft. It also supervises the licensing and working of the personnel and allied organisations engaged in the work. The Training and Licensing Directorate has especially been created to train Indians in different technical branches of civil aviation. The Civil Aviation Centre of Allahabad imparts specialised training in various technical branches of aviation. In 1946 a Communication School was also started at Saharanpur which was later on transferred to Allahabad in December 1950. This school trains Radio Operators and Radio Technicians for the Ministry. To train Pilots and Air Traffic Control

Chart 5.2
The Directorate General of Civil Aviation

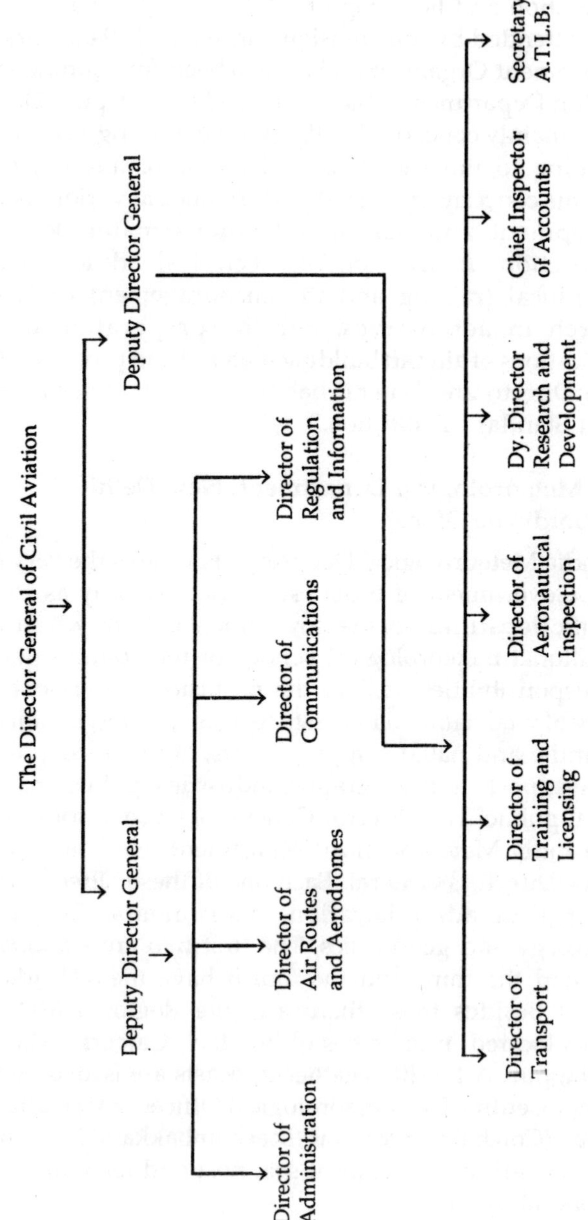

Officers the Directorate has been running one Flying Training School and other Aerodrome School at Allahabad since 1948. The examination and licensing of pilots and other aircrew personnel is also attended by this division. Since April 1946, a Research and Development Organisation has also been functioning in the Civil Aviation Department which is headed by a Deputy Director. This wing is mainly concerned with research into engineering problems pertaining to modifications and repair of aircraft, operational problems concerning aircraft performance at various aerodromes, development and use of indigenous materials for aircraft construction. It also tenders technical advice in advanced aeronautical training and the encouragement of fundamental research in aeronautics. For the preparation of standard specifications of aircraft building material and processes this section of the Directorate General has been closely associated with the Indian Standard Institution.[19]

India Meteorological Department, New Delhi

(A Subordinate Office)

The India Meteorological Department is one of the very old offices of the Government of India established as early as 1857.[20] It is a scientific department of the Government of India which constitutes the national meteorological service of the country. Its functions and responsibilities include the provision of services to a wide variety of vital national interests such as civil and military aviation, mercantile and naval shipping, ports, agriculture, public works, railways, posts and telegraphs, industries, public health and the general public. The Director General of Observatories is the head of the India Meteorological Department. He is assisted by four Deputy Directors General. Each one of these Directors General is in-charge of administration, instruments, forecasting and climatology and geophysics. The first two are stationed at New Delhi and the third and the fourth have their Headquarters at Poona.[21] Besides these there are five Regional Meteorological Centres located in the cities of Bombay, Calcutta, Madras, Delhi and Nagpur. All India weather forecasts are issued by the Poona Weather Centre. The Meteorological Offices of Calcutta (Alipore), Bombay (Colaba) and Madras (Meenambakkam) issue time signals for the benefit of the ships at sea, post and telegraph offices and the general public.[22]

The India Meteorological Department organises and maintains the basic network of meteorological observatories. These observatories prepare weather reports, compile meteorological statistics and supply climatological data. In addition to this, these observatories furnish weather forecasts, information regarding earthquakes, geomagnetic storms and solar flares. The study of the environmental sciences of meteorology, seismology, terrestrial magnetism, atmospheric electricity, ionosphere as well as astronomy and astrophysics is also a part of the functions performed by this Department.[23]

The meteorological organisation renders valuable service to civil aviation. For the provision of weather service to national and international aviation the organisation consists of six Main Meteorological Offices, twelve Dependent Meteorological Offices, fourteen Supplementary Meteorological Offices and forty-four Current Weather Observatories. There are four Meteorological Watch Offices which serve the four Flight Information Regions of Bombay, Calcutta, Madras and Delhi. These offices are attached to the Main Meteorological Offices at the international airports at the four places.[24]

Commission of Railway Safety, Lucknow
(A Subordinate Office)

The origin of the Railway Inspectorate can be traced back to the year 1908 when it was a part of the Railway Board. In May 1941, this Inspectorate was transferred to the Department of Communications[25] and today forms a subordinate office of the Ministry of Tourism and Civil Aviation. This transfer was made effective on the recommendations of the Pacific Locomotive Committee of 1938. The Committee had suggested that the railway inspection work should be undertaken by a Department other than the one responsible for the running of the railways. Later on the Railway Inspectorate was renamed as Commission of Railway Safety.[26] The main function of the Inspectorate is to enquire into railway accidents.

The head of this organisation is called Commissioner of Railway Safety. He is the Principal Technical Adviser to the Government on the matters with which the Commission is concerned. He directs the technical activities of the Commission and issues instructions for the guidance of Additional Commissioners in respect of holding statutory inquiries into serious accidents. His functions include the inspection of new railway lines prior to their being opened to passenger traffic. He carries out periodic inspections of railway lines. He makes recommendations regarding the introduction of new types of locomotives and rolling stock. Additionally he also co-cordinates the work of Additional Commissioners in their dealings with the Railway Administration. The Commission consists of five Circles of Inspection.[27]

India Tourism Development Corporation, New Delhi

This organisation was incorporated on 31st March 1965 by an amalgamation of three separate undertakings, namely the India Tourism Transport Undertaking Limited, the Hotel Corporation of India Limited, and the India Tourism Corporation Limited. Popularly known as I.T.D.C. it has been functioning since October 1, 1966. The Ashoka Hotels Limited,[28] and the Janpath Hotels Limited[29] have also been amalgamated with the I.T.D.C. since March 1970.[30] The activities of the Corporation include the construction of Hotels, management of Tourist Bungalows, restaurants on behalf of the Department of Tourism and providing shopping, transport and entertainment facilities to the tourists. The production of tourist publicity material for the Department of Tourism and operation of duty free shops at International Air and Sea Ports are also some of the main functions of the I.T.D.C.

The Ministry of Tourism and Civil Aviation broadly supervises and co-ordinates the working of the Corporations which are autonomous in their functioning. On 1st February 1972 yet another statutory Corporation namely the International Airports Authority of India has been constituted by an Act of the Indian Parliament for development, control and management of the four international airports of Bombay, Delhi, Calcutta and Madras. The Authority and the two Air Corporations, working in collaboration under the auspices of the Ministry, run and manage the airways of the country.

Administrative System

Tourism in India has been a very popular activity since ancient time. Scholars, historians, settlers and seekers of knowledge have visited India from times immemorial. The growth of religious movements has been conducive to the development of Domestic

Tourism. The Shankaracharya laid the foundation of domestic tourism by establishing four maths at the four corners of the country. People in India have been travelling for pilgrimage or to attend religious or cultural fairs. The Pandas at the various religious centres, and the local 'Dharamshalas' and 'Sarais' have been the foreunners of modern travel agents and the hoteliers. Before independence domestic tourism has remained mostly confined to the summer exodus from the plains to the hills. Some scholars and colleges might have taken their students on holiday trips but the concept of 'Bharat Darshan' is of very recent origin. International tourism to India during British days was essentially confined to visitors from the United Kingdom and few from European countries.[31]

The air transport has facilitated the entry of more foreigners to India. Several ancillary industries like Tourist Guides, Taxi Services, Hoteling etc. thrive on the tourist budgets. The data about the foreign tourists handled by Aviation Administration of India indicate that not only their number has increased but also even the average expenditure of the tourist has almost doubled from 1964 to 1969. Consequently, this has added to the foreign exchange earnings in two ways: firstly, by bringing more foreign tourists to India and secondly, by making them spend more on items and services allied to tourism. Although there is marked increase in the number, per capita expenditure and the total foreign exchange earnings year by year but a detailed examination of the figures indicates that per capita expenditure of the tourists inside the country has made a bigger contribution to country's foreign exchange earnings. Here again the civil aviation administration has done its job in creating ancillary industries and making the tourist spend which he would have otherwise not cared.

The five year period under review registers a four time increase in the net foreign exchange earnings from air travellers to India. This is quite an advance over the past but the number of foreign tourists who arrive in India by air has not increased in the same proportion. Actually, the average tourist visiting India has started spending almost the double. This proves that air transport or civil aviation administration is contributing to national income in a sizable number. The transport capacity of the airlines during the period under review has also expanded and obviously they are carrying double the passenger load. This increase in sheer numbers of tourist inflow is immensely helpful in providing other sorts of big and small jobs to various kinds of employment sectors, local, regional and national, in one way or the other.

Tourists are generally attracted by measures such as provision of adequate and cheap accommodation, availability of cheaper travel facilities, effective advertisement, well connected transport services from airports and railway stations to tourist centres, building up of a new image abroad and above all making the tourists feel at home in the country of their travel. An example, how tourists can be attracted to the centres through a planned strategy based on market research and psychological studies is provided by Khajuraho, a place of historical and cultural attraction in India. The network of well developed air services to Khajuraho have attracted more than a lakh of foreign tourists to this spot every year. In terms of annual turnover Khajuraho crossed Rs. 60 lakhs in the year 1972. This tourist centre has generated a lot of employment potential and income by providing new job opportunities to guides, clay modellers, photographers, hotelkeepers, shopkeepers and a host of other varieties of artisans.[32]

The demand for tourist services are sustained by cheaper and comfortable accommodations without much procedural wrangles. The development of tourist restaurants, lodgings and big hotels equipped with modern amenities need to be clustered around tourist centres, airports and nearby places. This requires a policy and a well-planned administrative effort to execute that policy. The Ministry of Tourism and Civil Aviation was constituted for the first time in India under a Cabinet Minister in 1967. It set for itself some result-oriented objectives that mark the beginning of a period of interrupted growth in the field. The Department of Tourism was assigned specific functions and was made "responsible for the development and financing of a tourist infrastructure, the regulation of existing facilities, conducting of studies, compiling tourist statistics and maintaining liaison with international travel and tourist organisations."[33]

In 1966 came another landmark when the India Tourism Development Corporation (ITDC) was set up to consolidate the work done earlier by three separate Government undertakings:

1. the Hotel Corporation of India,
2. the India Tourism Transport Corporation, and

3. the India Tourism Corporation.

In the year 1970, the Ashoka Hotels Ltd. and the Janpath Hotels Ltd. were amalgamated with India Tourism Development Corporation and handed over to its care. Some of the functions assigned to the India Tourism Development Corporation include "provision of comfortable tourist accommodation, better tourist transport facilities, special services such as duty free shops and entertainment, and other publicity services for tourism promotion." In October 1971 an advisory body on tourism in India called as the Tourist Development Council was constituted and strengthened by inclusion of members of State tourism authorities, as well as that of the travel trade and other related groups. Later, the National Tourism Board was established in May 1972 to advise the Ministry on proposals for the Fifth Five Year Plan period. The Board comprises representatives of the Government, the travel trade and allied fields.[34]

The India Tourism Development Corporation is an autonomous public sector undertaking and is primarily engaged in developing an infrastructure of the tourist industry in India. It is a national organisation providing a wide range of tourist services throughout the length and breadth of the country. The India Tourism Development Corporation emphasises upon those services which are essential for the promotion of tourism. Some of these services are:[35]

(a) Comfortable accommodation for tourists;

(b) Better cars and buses for sight-seeing;

(c) Special services such as duty free shops and entertainment; and

(d) Publicity that sells India's tourist attractions abroad and also makes Indians aware of what their country offers them for a holiday.

The India Tourism Development Corporation started from an initial capacity of 129 rooms or 196 beds at the end of March 1969 which expanded into 1676 rooms or 2432 beds in four years time. Similarly 3 transport units of 43 cars and 11 coaches have expanded into regular transport units at 14 centres with 120 cars and 30 coaches.[36] The Duty Free Shops of the India Tourism Development Corporation at four International Airports of Delhi, Calcutta, Madras and Bombay offer the tourists a wide range of products at bargain prices. These shops also provide a show window for the handicrafts and handlooms manufactured in India. These duty free shops earned as much as Rs. 85,000 in foreign exchange during one sample year of 1967-68.. The sale proceeds from these shops in 1971-72 ran into Rs. 3.35 million, which represented a forty times increase in four years time. The total earnings of the Corporation were nearly Rs. 65 million in the year 1971-72. This represented a 16 per cent increase over the incomes of the previous year. These financial successes apart the growth of India Tourism Devclopment Corporation can be measured from the fact that starting "from a small number of activities limited to few tourist spots, it has extended its range of services to the whole of India right from Gulmarg to Kovalam."[37]

The Growth of Infrastructure

By nature the tourist industry has to be structured upon several vital segments which need to be related and co-ordinated with each other. If India wants to increase the number of foreign tourists she needs airports big enough to handle mass arrivals expeditiously and improved internal transport system by road, rail, air and water. A whole range of tourist accommodation from five star luxury hotels to modestly priced but incontrovertibly serviced Travellers' Lodges is a prerequisite. Ancillary tourist services such as duty free shops and entertainment need to be deverloped. A powerful and persuasive communications media should net the "visitors whether they come to India to seek sun and sand or wildlife or spiritual solace or they just belong to the increasing host of students, businessmen and convention travellers."[38]

India's hotel needs far outstrip accommodation availability. Efforts are to be made to improve several categories of hotel accommodations to meet the needs of various classes of travellers, domestic as well as foreign. The creation of additional hotel facilities are to be prompted in the public as well as private sectors. The Union Ministry of Tourism has approved 95 new hotel projects out of which 39 were approved in 1972 and have been in various stages of progress. After completion, these hotel projects will add another 9,073 rooms to the existing capacity. Naturally, the India Tourism Development Corporation emerges as "the largest hotel chain of the country."[39]

A tourist expects a warm welcome with a clean and comfortable place to stay, good food and pleasant surroundings. For this the India Tourism Development Corporation has started managing hotels, lodges, restaurants and motels. In New Delhi alone there are five India Tourism Development Corporation hotels providing an accommodation of 1,250 rooms of 1,700 bed capacity. The Ashoka started its operations in October 1956. It has 5 restaurants, 486 centrally air conditioned rooms, India's largest Convention Hall, a swimming pool and one of the finest shopping arcade of any hotel in the world. The Akbar was opened early in 1972 and has 163 centrally air conditioned guest rooms and suits, conference and banquet facilities, a swimming pool, two restaurants and a bar. Its strikingly contemporary decor fashioned entirely from Indian materials has earned international acclaim. The Janpath, Ranjit and Lodhi hotels cater to travellers 'on a budget' of tourist variety.[40]

The Hotel Ashoka at Bangalore is another fine hotel built by the India Tourism Development Corporation, in May 1971. It is also the first-five-star hotel in south India. It has 91 centrally air conditioned rooms containing 182 beds, four restaurants, a conference hall, swimming pool, shopping arcade, tennis courts and a golf course next door. At the lake city of Udaipur, the Laxmi Vilas Hotel has been expanded to provide more rooms and conference facilities. A hundred room transit hotel at Calcutta's international airport has recently been built by the India Tourism Development Corporation. Kovalam Grove, on Kerala's beach, the first of its kind in India has been added to this hotel chain. It provides a beach resort of international standard with a distinctively Indian taste. Other plans include "a luxurious new 100 room Kovalam Palace Hotel, having facilities for water sports, Kathakali performances, Yoga instruction and Ayurvedic health remedies, including traditional oil massages."[41]

India offers tourist attractions very much off the beaten track. The India Tourism Development Corporation has plans to offer foreign tourists clean, comfortable accommodation and wholesome food even in remote places. Presently, it runs 19 Travellers Lodges and Hotels all over the country. At Mahabalipuram twenty beach cottages have been constructed. The motel at Khajuraho has been provided with 40 more rooms. The Jammu Hotel has been commissioned recently. Work has also started on a fifty room motel-cum-tourist reception centre at Varanasi, India's religious seat of learning.[42]

The Department of Tourism has classified the various hotels in India on 'star' basis. This star ranking system is based on an evaluation of hotel facilities. To enforce its ranking procedure, the Department of Tourism has a system of inspection and recognition of hotel facilities. These recognised hotels are listed and communicated to the travel trade. The number of star ranking of hotels in India is given in Table 5.2.

Table 5.2
Star Ranking of Hotels

Ranking	*No. of Hotels*
5-Star and 5-Star Deluxe	9
4-Star	12
3-Star	45
2-Star	52
1-Star	28
Unclassified	32
Total	178

Source: Annual Report of the Department of Tourism, Government of India, New Delhi.

It is generally complained that hotel accommodation for tourists, who visit India, is unsatisfactory. Cities like Bangkok, or Geneva alone have more tourist beds than that obtained in the whole of India and too when the tourist influx continues to mount every year in the country. In the year 1970, India had 178 hotels, with less than 10,000 rooms, which catered to the needs of 2,80,821 tourists who came from foreign lands.[43]

To accelerate hotel development programme the Ministry of Tourism and Civil Aviation, Government of India, has started a special loan scheme known as the Hotel Development Loan Scheme since 1968. The scheme provides financial assistance to the private sector for the development of hotel industry in the country. Loans totalling Rs. 12.34 crores have been approved for 31 hotel projects. These hotels are to provide 2,776 room accommodation to the foreign tourists in the year 1975.[44] The year-wise break-up of the number of projects and rooms is indicated in Table 5.3.

Entertainment facilities constitute an essential ingredient in the tourism product. The development of entertainment forms which can combine evening's enjoyment with a glimpse of the country's artistic traditions and cultural heritage are the prerequisites of tourism promotion. The most notable of these are the Sound and Light shows (Son et Lumiere). The popular Son et Lumiere spectacle at Red Fort in Delhi evokes the history of this magnificent monument through a play of lights and synchronised system of sound. The spectacle has drawn some 1,30,000 people every year. At the Sabarmati Ashram of Mahatma Gandhi in Ahmedabad, a new Sound and Light show presents the life and times of the Father of the Nation and provides a colourful glimpse of freedom struggle of the country. At the Shalimar Gardens in Kashmir another Son et Lumiere depicting the spectacle of Mughal glory has started. The India Tourism Development Corporation offers the foreign visitors the best performances of Indian dance, music, theatre, painting and crafts right in the Banquet Halls of its hotels.

Table 5.3
Hotel Development Loan Scheme

Year	*No. of Projects*	*Room Accommodation*
1969-70	1	115
1970-71	2	118
1971-72	2	198
1972-73	6	553
1973-74	10	830
1974-75	10	962
Total	31	2,776

Source: Reports of the Department of Tourism, Government of India, New Dellhi, 1969-1974.

Similarly the unmatched wildlife resources of India offer a major source of interest to international tourists. The development of wildlife sanctuaries needs special attention to draw tourists who do not have the like of which in the countries back home. The Department of Tourism has initiated background studies related to various aspects of nature-oriented tourism and on the proper protection and management of the wildlife resources of the country. The Department has provided assistance in the development of selected national parks and sanctuaries, meeting the construction cost of rest houses, their furnishings, kitchen equipment and other accessories. The Department of Tourism has set up rest houses for foreign tourists at Bandipur, Bharatpur, Corbett Park, Dandelli, Gir, Jaldapara and Kaziranga sanctuaries. The ecological problems are endangering wildlife all over the world. The Indian tiger also faces the threat of extinction. A 4-crore rupee Tiger Project is an international effort to save this magnificent beast, in which the Government of India and the World Wildlife Fund are collaborating. A special "Project Wildlife Tourism" which is included in the Fifth Five Year Plan covers nine tiger sanctuaries and several other areas which are inhabited by similar species facing trouble.[45]

In their efforts to conserve the tigers some 26 European children have recently made an air journey to India in 1975. They raised funds at their own to see tigers in the wild. Air India provided these children with passage between Amsterdam and New Delhi. These children belonged to countries like Austria, Belgium, Finland, Great Britain, the Netherlands, Norway, Sweden and Switzerland. The Indian children, who also raised funds for themselves, joined their European counterparts for a tour of Corbett National Park in Uttar Pradesh and Ranthambhor in Rajasthan. These two sanctuaries constitute the chain of nine such major reserves which have been established by the Government of India under the Tiger Project, 1975.[46] Two Safari parks have also been set up at Hyderabad and Borivili (Bombay). They represent the first venture of their kind in India. These safari parks are quite popular in East Africa. They permit tourists to view wildlife in its natural settings.[47]

A Flying Start to Tourism

The civil aviation administaration in India forms the hard core of infrastructure of tourism in the country. The two Air Corporations serve as functional wings of the Ministry of Tourism and Civil Aviation. The services of Air India and its promotional activities in foreign countries act as incentive for tourist traffic to India. In 1971-72, it contributed revenue in foreign exchange to the tune of Rs. 7.41 crores. The foreign exchange earnings of the Indian Airlines Corporation have been exclusively from these foreign tourists. During the year 1971-72, it totalled at Rs. 9 crores with an enhanced income of Rs. 12 crores in 1973-74.[48]

The Department of Tourism has to work with other Ministries

and authorities to ease travel and customs regulations for the tourists. For instance, visitors no longer require a visa for a stay of less than 21 days and customs procedures have been simplified. Training facilities are extended to customs staff and facilitation arrangements for the foreign tourists have recently been improved at the four international airports of the country.[49]

The world statistics about private organisations indicate that there are over 1,00,000 organisations which hold their annual national conventions in various parts of the world. Together they are reported to have over 100 million members, making a world conference potential of over $20,000 million each year. In an effort to procure some of this lucrative business to India, the Department of Tourism, Government of India, has set up a special cell which has been planning to project Delhi and Bombay as suitable venues for international conventions and conferences. The Ashoka Hotel and the Vigyan Bhawan offer convention facilities of international standard in the metropolis of India. Conference services are being built into hotel development schemes all over the country, including Bombay.[50]

It is said and perhaps rightly that tourism is a person-to-person business. It is a service industry dependent on public participation. To make tourism a success, government efforts alone are not enough. Public understanding and co-operation of all right from the customs officer to the taxi driver or from the hotel attendant to the shopkeeper and the man-in-the-street are absolutely essential. Press campaigns in leading newspapers and magazines are helpful in creating awareness of the tourism industry and motivating public participation. Advertising campaigns on behalf of the Department of Tourism advocate welcoming the tourist by slogans such as "Welcome a visitor, send back a friend." It further explains the economic necessity of doing so, as well as the need for preserving wildlife and historical monuments as a part of our national wealth.

It should be a matter of serious concern to the Government of India that some 400,000 tourists fly over India every year without having a stopover in the country. This number represents an untapped reserve, which if attracted to India, can earn foreign exchange and net revenue in millions of rupees. Naturally, the tourism development should immediately be concentrated on attracting these numbers.[51] It should be anticipated imaginatively that the tourists of tomorrow are going to need and want things different. They cannot fly half way across the world for facilities which they can find on their door-steps. India needs to develop a basic tourist development philosophy. She must certainly provide the basic amenities and comforts which tourists have come to expect, but she must not surrender a very real and a very significant national identity, which is apparent to anyone with perception and which Indians have held on to cover centuries despite immeasurable obstacles.[52] The international tourist market is extremely competitive and there is a constant need to keep alive an awareness of India as an exciting destination to motivate traffic. Moreover, this has to be done on a planned basis utilising a wide range of media available for image building.

Kashmir has been a star attraction of tourists visiting orient from all parts of the world. Traditionally known as the Switzerland of the East, this heavenly land has done relatively very little to attract the foreign and even domestic tourists to its scenic valley and salubrious climate. The politics of the region has positively retarded its face-lifting for tourism purposes and the potential available has not been exploited to the optimum. It is estimated that about two lakh tourists visit Kashmir annually, besides about four lakh pilgrims who visit the shrine of Vaishno Devi, near Jammu.

The state plan for tourism hardly makes any mention of augmenting the accommodation during the period though the total Plan outlay was fixed at Rs. 6 crores against Rs. 4 crores in the Fourth Plan. Most of the allocation was utilised for developing tourist centres like Gulmarg, Pahalgam, Kokernag. The Plan provides for only Rs. 50 lakhs for building additional accommodation. This apparently is not enough, because the tourist traffic is likely to be doubled by the end of the Plan period. This made it imperative that accommodation for tourists was substantially increased if not doubled in case the target was to be achieved. It was estimated that in Kashmir, about 5,000 beds were available for tourists, most of which were at Sonamarg, Yusmarg, etc., where the occupancy was limited. This also included the accommodation in house-boats. As such, it was surprising that the state was able to cater to nearly two lakh tourists in a limited season which started in May and ends in October. The number of tourists coming to Kashmir in July and August was extremely small and these two months were known as lean months. The attempts at attracting tourists to Kashmir in winter months were still at the experimental stage and the number of tourists who come to Gulmarg in winter months were in hundreds only. As such, the state had to adopt entirely a new strategy to achieve the target.

Yet another point which has been overlooked by the planners is the need for adequate buses. It is very difficult to get buses for travelling between Jammu and Srinagar or for sight-seeing in Kashmir. In case realistic allocations are to be made for catering to five lakh tourists in terms of additional accommodation and transport, the meagre allocation of Rs. 6 crores is not adequate. As such, the survey to be conducted by experts in tourism should be used for creating more beds that the state requires. The survey should also suggest what type of accommodation is required and how it can be done within the limited means available. For instance, there is no reason why the occupancy rate of house-boats, which is around 30 per cent, should not be increased. A major drawback in this respect is lack of hygienic standards in house-boats, absence of arrangements for disposal of sewage and lack of proper supervision which leads to unfair practices by house-boat owners. Similarly it is no secret that tourism in Kashmir, over the years, has become more oriented for catering to the needs of the affluent. Middle-class tourists are being squeezed out. A middle-class tourist contributes much more to the state exchequer than a rich one who stays in a five-star hotel. It is obvious that despite our efforts for attracting affluent tourists, the mainstay of the tourist industry are middle-class tourists. Yet another factor which makes it necessary for the state to change its approach is that the state lacks resources for building accommodation for the affluent on a large scale. It is necessary to spread the gains of tourism to a wider section.

Efforts were made to introduce direct charter Air India flights between Kuwait and Srinagar from summer 1976. The Government of India had also opened a tourist office in Kuwait. The airports of Srinagar and Jammu were expanded to take heavier planes. The publicity media geared up to project Kashmir in foreign countries. The Tourism Development Corporation prepared a film to project Islam in Indian cutlure. This film, on the one hand, helped us in projecting the country's image abroad especially in Arab countries and on the other, it helped in attracting more tourists from these areas.

The India Tourism Development Corporation has made efforts to raise the quality of publicity material about India to international standards of excellence. Reputed designers, writers, film-makers and other specialists have been enlisted for the task. As many as Rs. 75 lakhs were spent on the production of high quality publicity material and 6 million pieces of tourist literature were produced for distribution in India and abroad in one year i.e. 1972-73. The range of materials now includes brochures, posters, films, photographic presentations and other sales aids. Simultaneously, tourist products are also being developed by the ITDC for market sale in the country. These include picture postcards, maps and guide books in international formats.[53]

A new scheme of close collaboration with Air India in matters of tourism was introduced in Europe in 1968 to intensify promotional efforts by the Department of Tourism overseas. This was called 'Operation Europe.' Under the scheme, a chain of new tourist offices were added at Geneva, Stockholm, Brussels, Milan and Vienna to the existing offices at Frankfurt and Paris. The Operation Scheme was later extended to the United Kingdom and to the United States of America. A number of new Tourist Promotion offices have been located at Washington, Boston, Dallas, Detroit, Miami and Seattle under the scheme called Operation USA. Operaions Europe and USA have proved quite successful and revenue yielding. The Department now proposes to extend the scheme to East Asia and Australia also. Presently, the Department of Tourism has offices in Tokyo, Singapore and Sydney. Additional offices in this region need to be opened to encourage tourism promotion. Another office at Beirut can prove very useful to cover the travel market of West Asia from where more tourists can come in near future.

The planned efforts made in the field of tourism development have started bearing their fruits. Some 4,00,000 tourists came to India during the year 1973. This number represents an increase of 16.6 per cent over the 1972 arrival figure which was 3,42,950 only. Despite the disturbing situation in Bangladesh in 1971-72, the overall percentage increase in the number of arrivals of foreign tourists was as high as 13.9 per cent. Based on these trends, the Department of Tourism had set a target of 1 million tourists by the end of the decade i.e. 1980. The figures point out that the international tourists spent a total sum of 21.7 billion US dollars in the year 1972 only. India's share of this turnover was approximately 0.01 per cent. It is true that tourist earnings of India have maintained a steady improvement, yet there seems to be a vast market waiting which needs to be tapped with ingenuity and imagination.

Next to oil, tourism stands as the largest industry of the world.[54] It involves a massive movement of millions and millions of people from one end of the globe to another. The civil aviation system plays the most significant role in making this movement possible, profitable and prompt. The post-war years have witnessed a phenomenal growth of international tourists and tourism everywhere include India.[55] The liberalisation of foreign exchange rules and other travel restrictions which characterised the pre-war years have contributed their bit in encouraging larger number of people to travel. International tourism in the early nineteen sixties was mainly limited to Europe or its neighbouring countries. The newly independent countries of the former colonial world have recently started attracting tourists and taking increasing benefit from its growth. From 1950 to 1970 international visitor arrivals, including vacationers,[56] excursionists,[57] businessmen and others, in all countries grew from 25 million to 168 million. This covers to an average yearly growth rate of 10 per cent. The international tourism receipts during this period have also risen from $ 2.1 billion to $ 17.4 billion which marks a rise of 11 per cent per year.[58] In some of the developing countries this growth rate has been even higher because some of these distant destinations have become increasingly and easily accessible in shorter span of time with the expansion of civil air administration inside and outside the country. Table 5.4 illustrates a comparative data on international tourism in some of the major countries of the developing and developed world:

Taking the year 1970 as the base year for the above data it appears that India is not doing badly in international tourist market. The comparisons of Indian situation with European and South American countries will not be fair for the simple reason that tourists generally come from developed countries and because of their ethnic and cultural orientations they generally prefer to visit the countries of the European continent. It is the reason why that Spain tops the list of the countries by attracting as many as 2,41,05,000 tourists in one year i.e. 1970. Canada, America and

France come close to the approximate second. India's performance in attracting 2,81,000 tourists in one particular year compares well with countries like Pakistan, Indonesia and Philippines.

Table 5.4
Tourist Arrivals

Developing World	*No. of Tourists*	*Developed World*	*No. of Tourists*
1. Ethiopia	53,000	Austria	88,67,000
2. Kenya	3,44,000	Belgium	68,89,000
3. Tanzania	63,000	Canada	1,39,98,000
4. Philippines	1,44,000	Denmark	1,11,12,000
5. Thailand	6,29,000	France	1,37,00,000
6. Indonesia	1,29,000	West Germany	77,15,000
7. Turkey	4,84,000	Hungary	63,20,000
8. India	2,81,000	Italy	1,27,19,000
9. Iran	2,99,000	Spain	2,41,05,000
10. Nepal	46,000	Switzerland	68,40,900
11. Pakistan	1,22,000	United Kingdom	67,51,000
12. Jamaica	3,09,000	USA	1,31,67,000
13. Argentina	6,95,000	Japan	7,71,000

Source: Computed from Tourism Sector Working Paper, World Bank, Washington, June 1972 and Report of the Department of Tourism, Government of India, New Delhi, 1971.

It almost equals with Iran which attracts more tourists but earns less foreign exchange in gross foreign tourism receipts. The actual 1970 figures for India and Iran for this period is 51 and 42 million US dollars respectively. The undivided Pakistan of pre-1970 period (which included the present Bangladesh) could attract even less than half of the quota of tourists, who visited India. Its gross foreign tourism receipts were less than one-fifth of the Indian receipts in that particular year. Countries like Hong Kong, Thailand and Greece have their special and unique travel attracting reasons and must not be compared with India. Yet the Indian tourist industry has registered a record rise and an appreciable progress in the post-war years especially since the year 1947.

It is estimated that in 1972 about 200 million people crossed the international borders and spent money equivalent to 21.7 billion US dollars. Obviously, this makes tourism a major source of revenue and employment in the countries around the world. The International Union of Official Travel Organisation (IUOTO) has projected that by the year 1980 some 280 million tourists will be on the move. It will result into a consequent massive increase in tourist spendings in which all countries, big or small, can hope for the due share of their receipts. For example, the British Bahamas, with a population of 1,85,000 have entertained as many as 14,63,591 visitors in the year 1971. In Tunisia, tourism generates the largest source of foreign exchange earnings, exceeding revenues from oil and phosphates which constitute the leading export commodities from that country. In case of India, it is the tenth largest earner of foreign exchange to national economy.

The number of tourist arrivals in a country do not determine the foreign tourism receipts of the country. The average daily expenditure of a foreign tourist in a particular country depends upon a number of several factors that make him spend his country's money and thereby contribute to the foreign exchange receipts of the country of his travel. The numbers of tourists and the quantum of tourism income do not indicate direct relationship. For instance, the tourist arrivals in countries like Ethiopia and Tanzania are 53,000 and 63,000 in a year respectively but the gross foreign exchange receipts for the period vary from 6 million to 14 million US dollars for both these countries. This is mostly because when a foreign tourist in Ethiopia on an average spends US $ 28 per person per day, it works out to US $ 24.8 for each tourist visiting Tanzania. Table 5.5 about the gross receipts and average daily foreign tourist expenditure in some of the countries of the world explain the fact that the countries which earn more from tourism do not necessarily attract a larger number of tourists through their aviation administration.

The table reveals that the position of India in tourism market compares well with her neighbours like Pakistan and Nepal. It is very happily placed as compared to the countries of the African world. But the countries of Europe and Latin America are certainly earning much more from tourist industry than what India has been able to eke out. As compared to Pakistan, India has earned five times but a country like Nepal which earns only 2 million US dollars as compared to 51 million US dollars of India make her foreign visitors spend $ 13 per person per day which is only $ 8 in case of India. The average daily foreign tourist expenditure in India is perhaps the lowest in the world.

Table 5.5
Foreign Exchange Earnings and Average Daily Tourist in Some of the Countries of the World

Countries	*Gross foreign tourism receipts (dollars in million)*	*Average daily foreign tourist expenditure (dollars in million)*
1. Ethiopia	6	28.0
2. Tanzania	14	24.8
3. China, Republic of	89	38.8
4. Hong Kong	293	83.2
5. Philippines	32	30.5
6. Thailand	104	30.0
7. Indonesia	16	25.0
8. Greece	194	13.0
9. Israel	104	28.7
10. Spain	1,681	15.7
11. Turkey	51	13.7
12. Yugoslavia	275	12.2
13. India	51	8.0
14. Iran	42	20.1
15. Nepal	2	13.0
16. Pakistan	10	9.3
17. Bahamas	221	45.5
18. Argentina	77	16.2
19. Jamaica	95	40.0
20. Mexico	575	21.0

Source: Computed from Tourism Sector Working Paper, World Bank, Washington, June 1972.

Tourism everywhere and especially in developing countries is a growing industry. It has been estimated that by the year 1980 almost 250 million tourists will be in transit all over the world each year. This increase is certainly dependent on the innovations and attitudes of the seventies. The Boeing 747 which is called a veritable palace in the skies and the increasing accent on leisure amongst the people of the developing countries has started contributing to this increase in the numbers. But what is significant is the rate of growth of international tourist receipts in developing countries whose economies are gaining faster than the total world growth of tourism as an industry. This further indicates that the potential for the growth of tourist industry in developing countries is far higher than that obtained in other parts of the world. The situation can be taken advantage of by India.

The phenomenon of rapid growth does not occur by itself but has to be made to happen through rigorous planning. "Spain is the classic example of the benefits of a self-induced tourist boom. It has been brought about by a well planned development of tourist resorts and holiday spots, which has led to the building up of one of the world's most up-to-date hotel systems, with over 4,65,000 hotels beds, located in strategic tourist attraction spots."[59]

Singapore is another country where the Singapore Tourist Promotion Board has steadily increased hotel accommodation, developed a complete resort complex and have improved many other tourist conveniences. Today, with an area less than half of India's capital city i.e. Delhi, Singapore receives 5,00,000 tourists every year. A large number of these international tourists are delegates to international conferences and conventions who are attracted to Singapore's first-class hotels and efficient tele-communications network. The careful planning by the Tourism Promotion Board has made tourism one of the most significant industries in the Singapore economy. "In fact, the earnings from tourist services have gone upto 5 per cent of the gross domestic product of the country, which was only 1.5 per cent a decade ago."[60]

India has been somewhat slow in causing the growth of its tourist arrivals and receipts. A comparative study of the tourist figures with that of India's neighbours in the developing world makes this evident, as is illustrated in Table 5.6.

Table 5.6
Increase in Tourist Arrivals and Receipts of India and Her Neighbours

Countries	*Arrivals percentage increase*	*Receipts percentage increase*
India	20.0	19.9
Ceylon	22.3	39.6
Nepal	35.3	N.A.
Indonesia	31.5	21.2
Singapore	32.4	N.A.

Source: Report of the India Tourism Development Corporation, New Delhi, 1971.

Tourist traffic in India has been showing an encouraging trend ever since the 1950s when the foreign visitors numbered around one lakh. This was the first time when some serious efforts were made to make India known to people abroad. Soon after, however, it was realised that apart from catering to the requirements of the overeas tourists, steps had also to be taken to promote domestic tourism. The two go together in respect of infrastructural facilities. The Second Five Year Plan, therefore, accepted tourism as a national development endeavour. This led to the setting up of the India Tourism Development Corporation in 1966. Table 5.7 provides facts about India's place in world tourism.

The figures below (Table 5.7) vividly bring out the fact that though the tourist arrivals index in India has shown a phenomenal increase of about 47½ times as compared to the base year 1951, the country's share in terms of world arrivals presents a very low score of less than even 33 per cent.

Table 5.7

Tourist Traffic in India 1951-1980

Year	*Arrivals in India (Number)*	*Index*	*Arrivals in World ('000)*	*Arrivals in India as % to World Arrivals*
1951	16829	100	13185	0.13
1955	33269	198	24010	0.14
1960	123095	731	71139	0.17
1965	147900	879	115000	0.13
1970	280821	1669	169000	0.17
1975	465275	2765	221749	0.21
1980	800150	4755	298153	0.27
1981-82	853148		302.80	
1982-83	916350		320.30	
1983-84	1001173		338.80	
1984-85	1091510		358.30	
1985-86	1185690		375.80	
1986-87	1284270		400.30	
1987-88	1387250		422.80	
1988-89	1494630		446.30	
1989-90	1606410		470.80	
1990-91	1722590		496.30	
1991-92	1843170		523.60	
1992-93	1962526		541.30	
1993-94	2125875		569.80	
1994-95	2398750		587.40	
1995-96	2587921		802.50	

Source: Department of Tourism, Ministry of Tourism and Civil Aviation, Government of India, New Delhi, *The Business India*.

The compound growth rate of tourist arrivals in India between 1951 and 1981 was 14 per cent as against the world average of 8.2 per cent, and India's share of world tourism traffic went up five-fold, but it is still a meagre 0.29 per cent. In absolute terms, India's foreign tourism went up from a 4.32 lakhs in 1961 to 1.28 milllion in 1981, inclusive of all tourists in the South Asia Region. In 1989-90 total number of tourist arrival in India was 16,06,410 which increased to 25,87,921 in 1992-96.

India's performance in attracting tourists as compared to her neighbours like Nepal, Ceylon and Singapore is understandably poor. A foreign tourist who comes all the way to India naturally and logically plans to visit some of these small neighbouring countries of the Orient. These small countries do not spend enough money on tourist publicity also, yet the tourist infllow to India always and quite naturally has a spill-over to Ceylon, Nepal and Indonesia. But what is significant from the point of tourist industry in India is that there are thousands and thousands of tourists, who visit Ceylon, Nepal and Singapore and quite meticulously avoid India from their itinerary. Such tourists are to the extent that when Singapore and Nepal can effect 32.4 and 35.3 per cent of increase in their tourist arrivals, India has failed to push this number beyond 20.0 per cent. The aviation administration in India cannot be held directly responsible for this tourist behaviour but it should certainly investigate the causes and not permit the loss of revenue to its tourist industry by default.

From 1.40 lakh tourists who arrived in India by way of air, sea and land in 1961, the number of tourist arrivals in India rose to 2.8 lakhs, excluding nationals of Pakistan, during the year 1970. The largest number of tourists in India came from the United States, France, Germany and the United Kingdom constituting about 63 per cent of the total in 1971. The tourists from the eastern and far eastern countries were mostly from Ceylon, Malaya, Japan and Australia, constituting about 27 per cent of the total arrivals in the year 1971. The measure of tourist demand has been worked out by means of average stay of foreign travellers in India in terms of days. This average stay span has declined from 25.1 days in the year 1965 to 22.7 in the year 1970. This again brings to light that "exchange earnings of India can be stepped up either by making foreign travellers spend more days in India or by attracting an increasing number of tourists to India's scenic places through a vigorous image projection campaign abroad.[61]

The Role of Airlines in Promoting Tourism

The aviation administration plays a very major role in the promotion of tourism and tourist industries because the majority of the tourists everywhere travel by air on the international as well as domestic sector. In order to attract a constant flow of tourists to this country, the Air India has introduced special discount fares. The new youth fares also help to release the untapped potential that exists in this sector. Studies in the field demonstrate that youth travel is increasing quite rapidly in the world and the largest number of tourist groups are from among the people who fall in the age group from 20 to 29 years. To cater to the needs of this group the Air India has introduced special group fare schemes. These devices have enabled the Air Corporations to increase their net revenues and also to help in the promotion of tourism and tourist trades in all parts of the country. All these efforts netted some 67,000 more tourists to India during the year 1973 than the figure of the preceding year.

A new development is that tourist arrivals from Australia and West Asian countries are recording a sharp and unprecedented increase. The 1973 tourist arrivals to India viz., 4,09,895 included nationals of Pakistan and Bangladesh. This figure records an overall increase of 19.5 per cent over the tourist arrival figure of 1972. Thus the target of welcoming four lakh tourists by the year 1973 has been exceeded by about 10,000 despite the fact that there has been a serious dislocation in the aviation administration due to a lock-out during the later part of November and throughout December of the year 1973.[62]

The inflow of additional tourists from Western Europe and South Asia has been especially notable during the year 1973. Similarly the number of tourist arrivals from Western European countries including United Kingdom has also recorded a marked increase of 33.7 per cent during the year. The tourists from South Asian countries have also registered an increase of 20.9 per cent as compared to the actual figures of 1972. The most encouraging feature of the tourist inflow has been a 33.5 and 27.1 per cent additional arrivals from Australia and West Asia respectively. Certainly the affluent countries, comprising North America and Europe together with other countries, including Japan, Australia and New Zealand accounted for the major portion (i.e. 70.8 per cent) of the tourists inflow to India in the year 1973. Most of these visitors to India came by air, the actual break-up of figures being

3,48,000 i.e. 84.9 per cent by air, 29,512 i.e. 7.2 per cent by sea and 32,377 i.e. 7.9 per cent by road.[63]

In the sample year 1973, 1,36,740 tourists disembarked at Delhi's Palam airport which retained its leading position as the point of disembarkation for tourists coming to India. Bombay followed quite close where 1,30,389 tourists landed in 1973. Madras and Calcutta accounted for 35,760 and 29,711 tourists respectively. These figures indicate that the number of tourists arriving through overland routes has also gone up from 9,768 in 1972 to 32,377 in 1973.[64]

Thus tourism is a growing industry of promise and potential. It vitally concerns and effects the planned economic development going on in a developing country like India. The aviation administration has a key role in furthering and promoting tourism in the sub-continent because it provides the initial starting point for the foreign tourist who is an acknowledged patron of various kinds of big and small industries on the alien soil. Because of its rich flora and fauna and an image which ancient culture of the country has bequeathed as a legacy, the tourist industry in India is favourably poised for an increasing tourist traffic and potential tourism market. The Indian Airlines and Air India have expanded their passenger capacities and have also equipped themselves with several other ancillary facilities and tour plans which can be called conducive for tourist attraction and tourism development in a country like India. Tourism in case of India is capable to sustain several small industries and employment giving agencies in all sorts of big and small towns of a country like India. But tourism itself as an industry cannot survive, and, still less thrive without a support structure, which civil aviation administration alone can provide. The performance of air aviation in India during the last few decades has been seriously handicapped by the absence of infrastructure so very essential to attract tourists from far flung corners of the globe. The aviation administration has to realise this fact that while transporting foreign passengers they are not only carrying passengers, but are taking people on board who are more than passengers. In this venture, the aviation administrators have a legitimate right to seek co-operation and support from other departments of governments and private agencies working in the field. But then, relatively speaking, it is the aviation administration of India which meets the foreign tourist at its source point and that

Table 5.8
Average Length of Stay of Foreign Tourists in India

(In days)

Tourists from	*1976*	*1978*	*1980*	*1981*	*1982*	*1984*
North America	28.4	25.7	26.6	27.4	28.4	30.3
Central and South America	15.1	17.6	19.2	18.5	21.6	21.4
Western Europe	25.3	23.7	25.2	25.0	26.8	27.5
Eastern Europe	19.7	16.9	18.8	18.7	21.9	26.2
Africa	35.9	32.9	33.6	32.9	36.3	31.9
West Asia	28.9	27.5	22.7	22.2	22.4	29.9
South Asia	31.8	24.4	22.1	21.2	24.6	27.6
South-East Asia	45.1	41.7	38.7	34.1	35.5	34.1
East Asia	12.0	13.2	12.3	14.4	19.4	20.6
Australasia	22.5	22.4	25.8	26.0	28.1	25.7
Stateless	54.5	55.6	69.4	67.7	46.9	50.9
Grand average	27.2	25.2	25.4	25.0	26.7	28.4

Source: Government of India Tourist Statistics.

Table 5.9
Vital Facts About Indian Tourism: Arrivals, Growth and Receipts

Year	*Tourist arrivals (Numbers)*	*Percentage of growth, over previous year*	*Tourists Arrivals in World ('000s)*	*Arrivals in India as % to World Arrivals*	*Gross Receipts from Tourism (In crores)*	*Percentage of growth over previous year*
1	2	3	4	5	6	7
1976	5,33,951	14.7	2,35,276	.23	225.0	—
1977	6,40,422	19.9	2,49,628	.26	283.0	25.8
1978	7,47,995	16.8	2,64,855	.28	330.0	16.6
1979	7,64,781	2.2	2,81,011	.27	384.0	16.3
1980	8,00,150	4.6	2,98,153	.27	482.0*	25.5
1981	8,53,148**	6.6	3,15,295[E]	.27		
1982	8,50,178**	0.8	3,32,438[E]	.25		
1983	10,91,510		338.80		1,030.6	
1984	11,85,690		358.30	377,834	1,075.3	
1985	12,84,270		375.80			
1986	13,87,250		400.30	425,336		

(*Contd.*)

1	2	3	4	5	6	7
1987	14,94,630		422.80	—		
1988	16,06,410		446.30	4,78,809		
1989	17,22,590		470.80	—		
1990	18,43,170		496.60	539,005		

Source: Department of Tourism, Ministry of Tourism and Civil Aviation, Government of India, New Delhi.

* The figure of Rs.482 crores has been complied by the Department of Tourism. This, however, doesn't include earnings from Pakistan and Bangladesh also money spent by Indians domiciled abroad but still holding Indian Passport, and Foreign airlines crews.

** Figures excludes nationals of Bangladesh and Pakistan, including these, the total were 1,279,210 for 1981 and 12,88,162 for 1982.

E Estimated.

too in his own land. Several administrative agencies in this field can undertake co-ordination work and come to assistance and support of aviation administration. The growing figures of tourist traffic and foreign exchange earnings of India explain the development of aviation and tourism in the country. But the evolution of the two needs to be linked up in an organic whole and a policy conducive to national interest has to be evolved and launched for the implementation of integrated plans of tourist development and aviation growth in India.

Charter Policy

For a long time in India, we did not commit charter in principle, but had to deal with so many restrictions that it practically became a non-starter. Now, for the first time, the charter policy was announced in 1984-85 and we are thankful to Air India, the Ministry of Civil Aviation, the DGCA, though we had to do some very hard work. We remember those days—Dr. Bhatt and many of us, as well as, of course, Air Marshal Raje—had to do a lot of solid work to make the charter policy a success.

Basically, what are the conditions for successful charter operations? Normal scheduled airlines today are not possible as far as India is concerned. It is impossible to get additional aircraft.. So India has visions of having a quantum jump in tourist arrival by a sort of additionality: charters are a must. Now, the conditions for a successful charter operation is to have a market from where a large number of people come to a specific destination—let us say from the United Kingdom to Spain, United Kingdom to Italy, United Kingdom to Greece or Canada to the Bahamas, the market place from where large number of people go to a specified destination. One difficulty about India is that we do not really have a single tourism market.

India is also a very vast country with tremendous attractions. Similarly, our tourism market is also pretty divesified. We do not really have a single country which dominates the Indian tourism scene as, for example, Japan dominates the tourism in Hong Kong and Taiwan and the Mauritians dominate the tourism scheme of Singapore. We do not have that sort of market, but then there are countries from where a large number of people come. What do we give them? It was thought that a beach holiday could be an excellent opportunity, and we remember Dr. Sidhu was there when we identified five or six beaches in India which could provide a beach holiday.

Now, what is the market? It is mainly North Europe. The United States is far away. A charter basically has to be point to point, and from United States to India, it is a very long distance by charter. Again, when people come to India, they would like to see other places also. People do not mind going to the Maldives or Sri Lanka or Seychelles and going back after 15 days of not doing anything except lazing in the sun, lazing on the beach. But if you bring them to India, they will say how can you come to India and go back without seeing the Taj Mahal, etc.

So, basically, we decided to identify a beach holiday as a sort of product to be offered to Europeans, the market being North Europe, particularly in the winter months, from October till April when it is very cold in Europe, you hardly see the sun, sometimes for months at a stretch. The cold and growing affluence are factors influencing people who are anxious to get away for seven days or ten days to all that sun, to the sea and sand and come back. Initially, in the fifties they were going to Southern France, the Riviera, Spain, Italy and Greece. After sometime they became bored and then they started going to Morocco, Tunisia, Israel and so on, then that also became boring. They wanted to go farther than Mauritius and the Seychelles. Sri Lanka is the Mecca for such tours now since Sri Lanka, on the advice of the Indian consultant, we are told, successfully advertised the beaches of Sri Lanka, Sri Lanka being the land under the sun with coconut-tree filled beaches. And that became a very great success. People would come and spend 15 days, 20 days, one month. Last year, when we were in Mauritius and Seychelles, we saw that many Europeans were regularly maintaining their permanent bases to come to the place of their choice for a short holiday and then go back and these are the conditions where the charter really originated, which means that if you have got surplus airlines, you make that available, and since the market is assured it is possible to give it at a cheaper rate. This, therefore, made it possible for a larger number of people who cannot ordinarily afford or wish to travel by anything but the ordinary commercial scheduled airlines. Then, there are specific dates of departure. They can come back again carrying the return load. It has been estimated by economists that on an average, if you have got 12 flights then it reaches possibly the breaking point, because after the return of the first flight the second flight maybe after a week or after a fortnight to bring some people back again and carry back the first load. Similarly, the last flight of the charter has to come back empty and so making allowance for all that, we believe that after 12 such flights it starts generating resources.

So that is the market. Why can't India provide this? We identified Goa, Madras and Mahabalipuram beaches, Trivandrum and one or two other beaches also, and subsequently maybe the Andamans for charter destination. Goa became the most successful story. We still remember a casual conversation after the announcement of this charter policy. At that time nothing much was happening since there was a communication gap. We were attending the Board of Directors meeting at San Francisco. Well, Daubenfield knows that story well. Temerman from Lufthansa was also on board. He was sitting there and we casually asked about the charter. "Why don't you come to charter," we said. "Will we be permitted to come to charter?", he asked. "What are the rules?" So we told him about the principle. And, by the time we came back within a week, we remember, Daubenfield was telephoning us to say that they had decided to apply for a charter to Goa. That was a single crucial decision. Condor, which is a Lufthansa subsidy, started operating. It was a great success. Lots of problems, however, had to be sorted out. We remember our journey to Goa because things were not prepared well—neither customs, immigration or the Goan administration. We do not know whether Dr. Sidhu remembers the day we paid a day's visit to Goa bringing everybody together. All the problems were sorted out which indicates that where we have the political will, even in our system which is notorious for lethargy, delay and inter-departmental feeling, things can be sorted out. We sent some officials in Goa to the Maldives to find out how they were handling charter and eventually customs, police, health, navy and, of course, the DGCA, and then the Goa charter started.

Now, there are objections from Indian Airlines on several counts. They say their traffic will be affected. To that our answer is that their traffic will not be affected. In fact, it will be an addition of traffic. They will get more business.

Incidentally, the developments which have taken place since then around Goa, certainly are up to our expectations. Whenever people come they spend time in Goa. Then, perhaps in Kathmandu. In between they want to go elsewhere since after some time they get bored. And they want to see something of India. So around Goa, all sorts of new packages have been introduced. Some people go by domestic airlines to Bombay and then to Delhi and on to Agra. Again, they come back to Bombay and go to Goa, spend another week and go back. Some people are spending one week in Goa and one week in Kathmandu. Then they take the Indian Airlines flight to Varanasi, Khajuraho, Agra, Delhi and again they go back. Some tourists from Germany going from Goa to the South—Bangalore to Hyderabad—visit to off-beat places. We saw a large number of tourists from Germany, basically charter tourists, who as we say, not only want to have a beach holiday but who also want to see something of India's ancient past, ancient land, ancient history, ancient culture, ancient civilization and architecture and then go back with vivid memories.

Interesting packages are coming up. We found one enterprising travel agent in Goa. Take them on the steam engine. Take them to the Marmagaon railway station and make them travel on the steam locomotive or the normal train going through the sleeping but very interesting picturesque Goa countryside—three or four stations, they simple enjoy and go back. Today, Vayudoot flights have started connecting Goa with Bangalore, Hyderabad, Pune and so on. In a way, this is where the charter has created new opportunities in civil aviation.

There are routes, new packages, new hotels, new opportunities for travel agents and that is indeed an indication of the shape of things to come in the future. We have now permitted Bangalore for charter, but there a certain infrastructure is necessary. We sent charters to Orissa. Unfortunately, they still felt that the airport should be made suitable for wide-bodied jets. There was an idea of first bringing people to Calcutta and then to take them to Bhubaneswar. But again the charter operators say that will inflate the cost of operation because the people in this income bracket cannot afford the normal scheduled airline. So point-to-point fare, whatever is the discounted fare that is given on the basis of 100 per cent occupancy and assured date and certain date of journey will be taken away if we have to introduce another concept of hopping flights or planes. We are happy that Civil Aviation Ministry is now taking steps to expand the capacity of Bhubaneswar.

Kovalam can be a good destination. But again, you have to build the hotel capacity because there is only one good hotel there and that is not really suitable for it and cannot take a large number of tourists.

Similarly, we notice that this year, a number of one time-charters have come about, a much larger number than before, Dr. Bhatt will bear me out, quite a number of charters. These are one-time charters coming to Delhi, visiting Jaipur and other places and then taking off to some other destination. They are essentially like separate cruises round the world. But of these point-to-point regular charter operations, Goa is the success story. The problem is the rising demand and falling supply. Today it is very difficult to get additional hotel accommodation in Goa. If we had our way, this year, we could have two more charters because Condors want the charter only for Goa. The Swedes wanted to bring a charter to Goa. Hotel capacity is limited and we must remember that Goa is also very popular domestic destination. Hotel capacity cannot be made available for only foreign tourists, since we cannot ignore our domestic travellers. The hoteliers have said that last year there was some trouble in Goa and two or three charters were cancelled. They worry that if charters will not come their capacity will suffer.

So, basically, we have to maintain a delicate balance between domestic tour operators and the foreign charter tour operators and that is what we propose to do. We do not want to really accelerate the process of charter, but it is bound to grow. We shall go on slowly expanding the charter capacity so that it is absorbed in the generally civil aviation-cum-tourism scenario in certain time frame without causing undue severe strain on the system which might be counter-productive sometime.

Well, ladies and gentlemen, that is all. We thought we should share our thoughts with you at this stage. Well, when the history of tourism and civil aviation is written, the introduction of charter operations is going to be one of the major highlights: this is an example of how, when the will is strong, there is a common objective and people are willing to subordinate their narrow departmental views to an overall consideration. Even in our system of delays, various government departments can come together and produce satisfactory results and certainly can for the future growth of tourism charter, play a much bigger role.

The Relationship of Civil Aviation with Economic Development

The rapid growth rate that civil aviation has achieved in India was fair indication that it was playing an important role in the country's economic development. The proportionate contribution of civil aviation to the overall transportation system was increasing, though in absolute numbers it appears small. The growth rates of different modes in transporting passengers within India in the period 1970-71 to 1984-85 are shown in Table 5.10. This was a period with capacity constraints in all modes. The comparatively high growth rates in domestic air transport have been forecast to continue till 2000-01 in the recent report of the Planning Group on Civil Aviation.

Table 5.10

Comparative Passenger Traffic Growth in India

(Million Passener Kilometres)

Mode	*1970-71*	*1974-75*	*1984-85*	*Annual Growth Rates*	
				84-85/ 70-71	*84-85/ 74-75*
Rail	118000	126000	227000	4.8	6.0
Road	169000	219000	658000	10.2	11.6
Air	1545	2232	6454	11.0	11.2

Source : NTPC Report (1980); Working Group on Road Transport (1984); Corporate Plan of Railways (1986).

The expenditures and proposed outlay from the public sector expenditure towards civil aviation since the Fourth Plan period, is summarised in Table 5.11.

Table 5.11

Plan Expenditures and Proposed Outlay for Civil Aviation

Plan	*Period*	*Expenditure (Rs. in crores)*	*Expenditure as % of total Transport Expenditure*
Fourth	1969-74	177	7.0
Fifth	1974-79	294	5.2
Sixth	1980-85	931	6.6
Seventh	1985-90	758 (Outlay)	3.3

Source: Plan Documents.

As may be seen, the outlay for the Seventh Plan period has dropped to 3.3 per cent of the transport sector, resulting in a planned outlay of Rs. 758 crores. This is accompanied by a greater emphasis on the civil aviation sector to find internal resources for funding its developments. It has also been suggested that while improving utilization of its assets, the growth rate of civil aviation be kept in check.

The key factors in the future scenario thus becomes:

(a) an expected high annual growth rate within the country, and a slower growth rate (6 to 6.9 per cent per year) for international travel, with growing emphasis on regional travel;

(b) an expectation that civil aviation ought to become a self-financing sector of transportation.

Based on these factors, the planning for civil aviation ought to tackle the task with three major goals. These can be considered to be:

(a) Plan such that new investments are distributed amongst different organizations based on the relative costs and benefits of the types of services.

(b) Make more efficient use of existing aircraft, manpower, airports and infrastructure etc. so as to minimize costs of the sector as a whole, while meeting air transportation needs.

(c) Making the most efficient use of funds available for investment by effective project/equipment selection, acquisition and execution/introduction.

It is by and large accepted that even after doing this for a period of time, the need for assistance from the public exchequer will continue to some extent. Whatever assistance is to be got can, in all probability be gained if the civil aviation industry as a whole can work together to project the contribution that it makes to the economic development of the country. At present there is an appreciation that aviation does contribute a share to development, but it is an appreciation that is not adequately supported by reasoned analysis.

The lack of a supporting economic data base leaves many decision-makers and the public with the feeling that since market forces do not play a free role in this sector the real economic costs of air transport are hidden and the resultant beneficiaries are only the small, select band of travellers by air. In this presentation, therefore, certain areas, where the relationship between civil aviation and the economy are most noticeable, are identified and the types of planning studies required indicated which would contribute to removing the feeling that "airtravel only benefits the haves."

Possibly the greatest benefit that aviation renders to the economy is the greater speed with which it transports passengers and goods as compared to other modes of transportation. The savings in "time of travel" are significant. Whereas it is possible to roughly measure the savings in time, studies to quantify the economic benefits that it results in have not been done. Table 5.12

Table 5.12

Comparison of Travel Distances and Time by Air and Rail

	City-Pair	*Distance (km)*		*Time (Hours)*			
		Air	*Rail*	*Air Journey*	*Air (1) trip*	*Rail Journey*	*Rail (2) Trip*
(a)	Delhi-Bombay	1193	1384	1.75	4.75	17.25	18.75
(b)	Delhi-Calcutta	1358	1445	2.00	5.00	17.75	19.25
(c)	Bombay-Calcutta	1685	1968	2.35	5.35	32.35	33.85
(d)	Bombay-Madras	1072	1279	1.75	4.75	26.75	28.25
(e)	Bombay-Bangalore	870	1120	1.50	4.50	24.00	25.50
(f)	Bombay-Lucknow	1548	1419	3.00	6.00	27.85	29.35
(g)	Bombay-Goa	432	669	1.00	4.00	23.50	25.00
(h)	Bombay-Bhavnagar	312	761	0.75	3.75	17.00	18.50
(i)	Calcutta-Guwahati	504	991	1.00	4.00	22.50	24.00
(j)	Delhi-Jaipur	245	312	0.50	3.50	5.25	6.75[3]

Notes :
1. Air trip time include 3 hrs for travel to and from airports and waiting, in addition to flight (journey) time.
2. Rail trip time includes 1½ hrs for travel to and from stations, in addition to journey time by fastest direct train or best approximate of connecting trains.
3. Time taken by bus to Jaipur plus one hour of addition in-city travel time is about 6.5 hours.

indicates some of the routes and the savings in time which result from air travel compared to rail, the alternate long distance mode of transport.

Air travel provides comparatively greater benefits over long-distance or terrain limitations, rather than over the short-distances e.g. Jaipur-Delhi. The savings in time are even greater when comparisons are made with sea travel, e.g. Calcutta to the Andaman Islands. In some cases even the distance of travel falls significantly e.g., Calcutta-Guwahati or Bombay-Bhavnagar.

The beneficiaries of the savings in time come from all occupations. The surveys of passenger profile done by Indian Airlines during March—June 1986 provide comparative figures regarding occupations, nationality, reason of travel etc. Some of their findings are summarised in Table 5.13.

Table 5.13

Survey of IA Passengers, Resident Indian Only, during March/June, 1986

(All figures in percentage)

1.	Occupation		
	(a)	Government/PSU employees	22.8
	(b)	Private Sector employees	20.5
	(c)	Businessmen	22.8
	(d)	Housewives	7.47
	(e)	Others, incl, self-employed professionals, MPs' etc.	17.5
2.	Purpose of Travel		
	(a)	Work/Business	70.6
	(b)	Vacation	13.8
	(c)	Personal reasons	15.6

Note: The Survey found that Resident Indians constituted 85.6 per cent of the passengers, while NRI and foreigners accounted for 14.4 per cent of total passengers.

It is thus obvious that business and work travel forms a very high percentage of the total. These findings may not be applicable on a route-wise basis as on certain routes and in certain seasons the proportion of vacationers is higher than those indicated. The same surveys also showed that proportion of passengers travelling on vacation and for personal reasons is about 10 per cent higher on the shorter sectors than on the longer sectors. On the longer routes business travellers account for about 73.4 per cent of the total resident Indian travellers. Continuing with a prior reasoning from this point it is realised that a substantial number of "business hours" are saved due to air travel that would otherwise be lost while making rail, road or sea trips. But even though to the businessman "time is money," the civil aviation industry is still to assess the "value of time" to its largest group amongst its clientele, and thus estimate the economic benefits that it provides. In this connection, more information is required regarding the "reasons of travel" on all our carriers, around the year. If collected on a regular co-ordinated basis the information could also be used for other planning studies, e.g. route/capacity allocation, regional development, infrastructure have wide implications e.g. better on route ATC, reduced distance of travel etc. to reduce journey time or faster processing at airports to reduce the ground time portion of the total trip time etc.

It is often suggested that tourism could be the main reason for encouraging investment in the aviation sector. This view requires examination to identify where the civil aviation sector needs strengthening and where other infrastructure improvements e.g. hotel rooms, road transport, etc. should get greater priority. The IA surveys indicate that domestic tourism cannot be the *raison d'etre* at present for supporting air transportation. The estimates of the domestic leisure travel market are too diverse at this time to permit fair idea of the optimum segments that could be induced to travel by air. One would hypothesize that amongst these travelling on vacation by air there could be significant proportion on LTC. This needs to be verified.

For international travellers, the picture is significantly different. Table 5.14 indicates the numbers of foreign arrivals by air, as compared to other modes.

The fact that air is the preferred mode of international travel emphasises the case for high economic returns due to improved aviation infrastructure, aircraft and services required for international travellers. (But even as we say this, we emphasise that this alone does not take the place of a project-wise economic analysis required prior to any investment). Here also there is a need to categorise the total numbers by reasons of travel i.e., business, leisure etc. as well as other attributes. At present for international arrival categories are treated as a homogenous group. Without such categorisation, further planning of leisure tourism packages, their pricing policy and infrastructural development requirements, and assessment of economic benefits remain unsubstantiated.

Table 5.14

Tourist Arrival in India by Mode of Transport

(Figures in lakhs)

Year	*Air*	*Sea*	*Land*	*Total (100)*
1981	7.67 (89.9)	0.48 (5.6)	0.38 (4.5)	8.53
1982	7.81 (90.8)	0.39 (4.6)	0.40 (4.6)	8.60
1983	8.09 (91.5)	0.32 (3.6)	0.44 (4.9)	8.85
1984	7.64 (89.7)	0.52 (5.4)	0.39 (4.5)	8.35
1985	8.05 (96.2)	0.02 (0.2)	0.30 (3.6)	8.37

Note: Figures in parentheses ( ) indicate per cent to row total.

In the light of a renewed spurt in foreign arrivals we would only highlight the need for such studies, which are without doubt being dealt with by the expert group at present studying tourism. After a period of slow growth, about 6 per cent a year for the last 10 years, 1986 saw over a million arrivals, i.e. just over 20 per cent rise in one year. If policies of liberalized charters, bilateral agreements etc. for encouraging visitors to India are to be introduced they must surely, quickly and substantially be supplemented by infrastructure developments which get us the greatest economic benefits.

Amongst these developments, obviously air travel within India will play a major role. But the extent to which scheduled air services as well as air taxi operations can profitably contribute has to be realistically assessed by full scale technical, economic and managerial studies.

Air transportation plays a major role in the transportation of high value cargo. International air cargo is a small percentage of the total tonnage of cargo trade export and import of India. It accounts for less than one half of one per cent of the total tonnage, but its economic significance can be appreciated by the value of the cargo handled. Table 5.15 presents figures for 1981 to 1985.

The figures for export cargo are already quite notable. Informal observations and discussions indicate that the share of import cargo is also expected to rise. Recent years, however, have seen a slowing down of cargo clearance at airports. The reasons are many and varied, e.g. inadequate capacity on aircraft, cooling-off periods required for security, slow pick-up of cargo imported by government agencies and P.S.U.'s are some of the major factors. Therefore, there is no doubt that investments in facilities, equipment and managerial practices, e.g. consolidated outbound cargo rates or import cargo review committee, to speed up the flow of cargo in both directions would have high economic returns.

Table 5.15

Air-borne International Trade of India vis-a-vis Total International Trade Carried by all Modes

(Value in Rs. crores)

Year	*Export*		*Import*		*Total*	
	All modes	*Air*	*All modes*	*Air*	*All modes*	*Air*
1981-82	7805.9	1622.0 (20.8)	13607.6	1108.2 (8.1)	21413.5	2730.2 (12.7)
1982-83	8903.4	1845.7 (21.0)	14306.7	1924.9 (13.5)	23110.1	3770.6 (16.3)
1983-84	9872.1	2502.5 (25.3)	15763.0	2306.8 (14.6)	25635.1	4809.3 (18.8)
1984-85	11297.4	2661.2 (23.5)	17173.3	2112.2 (12.3)	28470.4	4773.4 (16.8)
1985-86	10420.4	3383.8 (29.6)	18371.3	2381.9 (13.0)	28791.7	5465.7 (19.0)

Notes:
1. Air-borne figures are provisional.
2. Total trade figures w.e.f. 1983-84 are provisional.
3. Figures in parentheses ( ) are percentage to the total carried by all modes.

Source: Ministry of Commerce.

Within India, the transport of high value freight by Indian Airlines has grown from 48,354 thousand kg in 1980-81 to 88,603 thousand kg in 1984-85, an average rate of growth of 16.3 per cent per year. Understandably, this rate is expected to slow down with the introduction of the cooling-off period for security reasons. Shippers will now turn to surface modes of transport and thus be able to utilize the time required for cooling-off to actually move their goods. To encourage higher rates of growth that now aircraft would generate through additional cargo, capacity investment in handling facilities and faster security checking of cargo by electro-mechanical means is likely to have economic returns.

The airlines, airport authorities, government departments etc. provide direct employment to the economy. At present about 54,000 people benefit from such employment. In addition, the foreign carriers also provide direct employment.

In addition to the direct employment, there are a whole range of support services who owe their jobs to civil aviation. This goes beyond the travel and cargo agents, the taxi and bus drivers etc. There is, for examples, the growth of new industrial products and activities that civil aviation invites. The manufacture of aircraft tyres, of fixed and mobile ground support equipment, of the spin-off benefits to computer, communication and navaids technology used in aircraft and infrastructure are all new industrial opportunities. The supply of services e.g. by caterers to Indian and foreign carriers, or car rentals to passengers, are a direct effect of aviation. These benefits are distributed throughout the country through various aircraft maintenance units, training units and numerous other services that form the network of the aviation industry in India.

There has been no detailed study that the author is aware of done since the early 1970s, when the Indian Institute of Management examined data of 1968. It is time that such a study is undertaken to examine the ratios of direct and secondary employment due to civil aviation and its impact on the economy.

Another way in which air transportation serves a national purpose is in the psychological support given to steps of national integration and by opening up areas which are relatively inaccessible due to terrain. Regular air services to and from the Andaman Islands could be held up as an example of such a consideration. Knowing that daily air services would be available to Calcutta and Madras (now these are available every alternate day) and connections abroad, could allay the hesitation that public servants and business houses may have in working in the islands. Air services could thus act as catalysts for the development of the islands. Similar reasoning could also be applied to developing currently backward or inaccessible areas. This is a role that Indian Airlines has played for many years and which Vayudoot has taken on recently. While this aspect has often been touched upon by many, we are unaware of planning studies, either by regional planning bodies or the aviation industry which have assessed its impact on industrialisation regionally.

This role has implicit in it the acceptance that airlines and airports are not to be seen only as economically self-sufficient, commercial bodies in themselves, but can in turn be planned as important infrastructure in regional development. There are numerous difficulties in the way in which the economic costs and benefits of air transportation to a region or a nation can be quantified, but such efforts ought to be made.

An important factor in the economic role of civil aviation is its relationship with the net foreign exchange balance. Since heavy expenditure is made on acquisition of aircraft and support equipment, as well as fuel, there ought to be concerted steps on keeping them well under control and if possible, aiming for a net foreign exchange gain. The Planning Group on Civil Aviation last year examined a consultants report on this subject. The consultant came to the conclusion that the civil aviation sector would suffer a net deficit in foreign exchange, at escalated expenditure but constant yield, to the order of loss of over $ 23.5 billion, whereas IAAI would gain a net $ 1 billion. The consultant recommended numerous steps to control costs on one hand and advised increased fares and yields on the other to reduce the net outflow of foreign exchange.

The Planning Group came to the view that if the yield rates increased at about 7 per cent per annum, which is close to historical for Air India, its deficits could be substantially reduced or even wiped out. In the case of Indian Airlines the annual increase in fares would have to be very substantial. Though the Planning Group did not indicate any rates, the consultants sensitivity analysis showed that the rate of increase would have to be about 17 per cent annually.

The main point for consideration to offset such assessments of net outflow are the actions that the industry must plan to increase indigenisations of maintenance and reduce the imported content of material. This applies not only to aircraft but also to support equipment, communication and navaids, airport equipment etc. Increased foreign arrivals would increase the foreign exchange component of the revenues of all the airlines, and better performance of 5th freedom rights would especially help Air India. This broad issue in itself identifies the critical need for an economic analysis of tourism and its multiplier effect on the economy as well as the financial standing of the carrier.

There is no doubt at this stage that civil aviation in India is intimately involved with the economic development of our country and that it affects plans of regional and urban development. What is missing is an attempt to quantify and relate the two through a co-ordinated, strategic planning process. This last section discusses factors and steps that could be useful in implementing such a process.

A strategic plan rarely, if ever, grows out of a flash of intuition or a stroke of luck. It requires a joint exercise in formulation of objectives based on a study of existing and possible markets. It is supported by systematic information gathering and forecasting to identify opportunities, strengths and existing and likely problem areas. The strategies thus developed require to be implemented with operational and fiscal discipline with a strong bias towards grasping new opportunities built up on a base of research and development.

A number of possible studies have been identified in earlier sections of this paper, but unless they are fitted into a larger framework they will remain ad hoc in nature. To build up such a framework we must determine and evaluate industry performance and the impact on it by differences in performance of each constituent company and organization. A critical aspect of such evaluation is an industry-wide cost analysis per unit (passengers, cargo and aircraft) handled by the system. The differences in costs and benefits that exist for different markets, regional and geographic locations and on various routes will have to be prepared. The differences in strategy, if any, amongst organizations to serve particular user groups should be determined and then differences resolved. This includes financing and administrative strategies and support requirements. Compare the criteria used by different organizations to choose (qualitative and quantitative) strategies to meet stated targets or goals.

The industry must deduce in its studies the economic advantages it provides to a region based on its own distinctive competence as compared to other modes. An extreme example of a set of penetrating questions to ask would be, "what will be the impact on the region if the industry was to totally withdraw its services from it? What will be the effect on the industry? Could the region get adequate services from other modes? How could the region got alternate services, at what cost, for what benefits? Could the aviation industry utilize the resources thus freed to more economic advantage elsewhere?" A prime example could result in a study of trade-offs between short-haul air-services and improved surface transport provisions to tourist centres served from a major metropolis e.g. to Agra and Jaipur.

For the industry to plan future strategy it has to identify major opportunities and hurdles, forecast changes in customer preferences and then strengthen its areas of weaknesses to meet them. It is only when objectives are jointly formulated with regional planners, and stated, that the individual constituents of the aviation sector can develop its desired performance specifications and develop plans of equipment acquisition, allocation of routes and services and above all, the allocation of resources to maximize its own and national economic objectives.

Notes and References

1. *Organisation of Government of India*, The Indian Institute of Public Administration, New Delhi, Second Revised Edition, 1971, p. 45.
2. The Attached Offices are responsible for providing necessary executive direction required in the implementation of the policies laid down by the Ministry to which they are attached.
3. A Subordinate Office, more or less, operates as a field establishment. It is responsible for the detailed execution of the decision of the Government.
4. See Maheshwari, S.R., *The Evolution of Indian Administration*, Laxmi Narain Agarwal, Agra, 1970, p. 96.
5. It was the first systematic attempt to bring air transport under some kind of international regulation prior to the Second World War. The Convention was signed at Paris on October 13, 1919, by 38 nations including India. The Paris Convention established the International Commission for Air Navigation (ICAN). It guided and assisted the growth of international civil aviation during the two decades which followed. It recognised the priniciple of sovereignty of each contracting country over the air space above its territory and territorial waters as well as the right of each nation to impose its jurisdiction over the air above its territory and territorial waters. Necessary

regulations were also drawn up for the definition and determination of such matters as the nationality of aircraft, standard of air worthiness, certificate of competency for aircrew, aircraft documents and procedure for aircraft operation. Dhekney, M.R., *op. cit.*, p. 222.

6. The Organisation of the Government of India, *op cit*, pp. 248-49.
7. *Ibid.*, p. 249.
8. *The Air Corporations Act*, 1953, Government of India, New Delhi, Act No. 27 of 1953.
9. The Organisation of the Government of India, *op cit*, p. 249.
10. *Ibid.*, p. 250.
11. *Ibid.*, pp. 249-50.
12. *Annual Report, 1971-72*, Ministry of Tourism and Civil Aviation, Goverment of India, New Delhi, p. 1.
13. *Annual Report, 1968-69*, Ministry of Tourism and Civil Aviation, Government of India, New Delhi, p. 56.
14. *Ibid.*, p. 56.
15. *Ibid., 1971-72*, pp. 23-25.
16. *Ibid., 1969-70*, pp. 2-3.
17. *Ibid., 1971-72*, pp. 2-3.
18. Dhekney, M.R., *op cit*, p. 216.
19. *Ibid.*, p. 217.
20. The Organisation of the Government of India, *op cit*, p. 253.
21. *Annual Report, 1971-72*, Ministry of Tourism and Civil Aviation, *op cit*, p. 84.
22. *Ibid., 1967-68*, p. 16.
23. *Ibid., 1970-71*, pp. 78-79.
24. *Ibid., 1969-70*, p. 71.
25. The Organisation of the Government of India, *op cit*, p. 254.
26. *Annual Report 1971-72*, Ministry of Tourism and Civil Aviation, *op cit*, p. 108.
27. *Ibid.*, p. 107.
28. The Ashoka Hotels Limited, New Delhi started functioning from October 1956. In the first instance, it was placed under the administrative control of the Ministry of Works, Housing and Supply. It was, however, transferred to the Ministry of Tourism and Civil Aviation in July 1968. *The Organisation of the Government of India, op cit.*

29. The Janpath Hotels Limited was constituted in September 1964 to take over the management of Hotel Janpath, New Delhi. This Hotel was constructed by the Government of India.
30. *Annual Report, 1971-72,* Ministry of Tourism and Civil Aviation, *op cit,* p. 26.
31. Sharma, Inder, "A View from the Top," Indian Hotelier & Caterer, *Official Journal of the Federation of Hotel & Restaurant Association of India,* New Delhi, Vol. XVI, No. 9, September 1972, p. 121.
32. Tourism: A Long Way to Go, Department of Tourism, Government of India, New Delhi, Indian Hotelier and Caterer, *op cit,* p. 132.
33. Tourism: A Progress Report, 1973, Ministry of Tourism and Civil Aviation, Government of India, New Delhi, p. 3.
34. *Ibid.,* p. 3.
35. A Profile of Progress, 1947-1972, India Tourism Development Corporation, New Delhi, p. 1.
36. In addition, the ITDC has a fleet of tourist cars, limousines, coaches and mini-buses, many of them are air-conditioned. Besides car and coach hire facilities at Delhi, there are transport units at Agra, Aurangabad, Bangalore, Bodhgaya, Bombay, Hassan, Hyderabad, Jaipur, Khajuraho, Madras, Patna and Srinagar. Sight-seeing tours are conducted daily by ITDC units at Delhi, Hyderabad, Jaipur, Madras, Patna and Udaipur.
37. *Ibid.,* p. 3.
38. Sundra, M.S., "Tourism: Old Problems and New Hopes," *Indian Review of Public and Co-operative Economy,* New Delhi, Vol. I, No. 1, March-April 1972, p. 23.
39. Tourism: A Progress Report, 1973, *op cit,* p. 4.
40. *Ibid.,* p. 5.
41. *Ibid.,* p. 5.
42. *Ibid.,* p. 5.
43. Why Tourism? Indian Tourism Development Corporation, New Delhi, p. 7.
44. Tourism: A Progress Report, 1973, *op cit,* p. 6.
45. Tourism: A Progress Report, 1973, *op cit,* p. 12.
46. *The Hindustan Times,* New Delhi, January 6, 1975, p. 3.
47. Tourism: A Progress Report, 1973, *op cit,* p. 12.
48. *Ibid.,* p. 14.
49. *Ibid.,* p. 14.

50. *Ibid.*, p. 14.
51. Why Tourism? *op cit*, p. 19.
52. Roy, S.K., "Tourism Planning, National and International Scene," *Commercial Review*, Indian Airlines, New Delhi, Review No. 18, May 1971, pp. 14-15.
53. Tourism: A Progress Report, *op cit*, p. 16.
54. Mahishi, Sarojini, "Building an Image Abroad," *The Times of India*, New Delhi, March 27, 1973.
55. An international tourist, as defined by the International Union of Official Travel Organisation, is a person who visits a country other than that of permanent residence for at least 24 hours, whatever his motive for travel may be.
56. A vacationer, whether international or domestic, is defined by major European tourist services as staying away from home for at least four nights on any one trip and may in some instances include tourists travelling for a combination of business and pleasure.
57. An excursionist is a person who stays in any one destination for less than 24 hours.
58. Tourism Sector Working Paper, prepared by World Bank, Washington, June 1972, p. 3.
59. Why Tourism? *op cit*, p. 4.
60. *Ibid.*, p. 5.
61. Tourism: A Long Way To Go, *op cit*, p. 132.
62. *The Hindustan Times*, New Delhi, June 10, 1974.
63. Report of the Departmenrt of Tourism, Government of India, New Delhi, 1974.
64. *Ibid.*

6

Air Transport and Tourism

In inter-continental or long-distance travel, air transport has been responsible for the "explosion" in world tourism and, in certain areas where the terrain and other conditions prevent normal development of other forms of transport, air travel is the only means of tourism. Historically, it is established that improvements in travel facilities (especially reduced travel time and increased comfort) have encouraged and influenced travel movement and created an upsurge in the volume of traffic. In a period of under eighty years from the first flight of 1903, we have reached the figure of over 850 million passengers travelling by air. It is forecast that by the years 2000, there would be about 2000 million people travelling by air each year. It is expected that, out of these passengers nearly 60 per cent would be tourists and "mixed" business and pleasure passengers.

Air transport is essentially international, large and above all a dynamic and developing industry. Its extensive network spans all continents, serves nearly all countries and scheduled services are now operated by nearly 400 airlines domestically and internationally. Air transport has become the largest single item in international trade (barring oil) and its importance to tourism cannot be over-emphasised. Only air transport has brought tourism on a large industrial scale to many tourist centres, not least to developing countries, thereby contributing in an unprecedented way to their social and economic amelioration. Jets, in particular, have revolutionised travel and Jumbos have dramatically accelerated the revolutionary change. By their achievements in speed, safety, comfort and economy, they have attracted great numbers of travellers. In providing large capacities, there has been an emergence of bulk pleasure and business travel. Air travel also became accessible to families with more moderate means.

Jets, in addition, accelerated travel-related industries and offered untold opportunities for business and international trade New services helped to broaden travel and far-flung new places became closer and easily approachable. Mass travel had arrived and the age of air travel was brought to its own by jets. Tourist traffic grew fast and in mass, especially in Europe, USA and inter-continentally in the fifties. It spread to Asia in the sixties and is adding new dimensions to tourism in other areas of the world. In Africa, it is expected that "the decisive instrument in the development of African tourism cannot but be the aircraft. It is upto the aircraft to carry this mass of inter-continental traffic. But there are other reasons for promoting air transport, particularly the difficulties of surface transport on the African continent. This explains its equally vital role in domestic transport".

The considerable increase in international tourism worldwide is mainly due to air transport, which has facilitated long distance travel, particularly for passengers with higher incomes from the developed countries. It may be recalled that only 16 countries provide over 82 per cent of total international tourist traffic spread over various areas, though domestic air traffic is of greater volume and consequence, as it counts over four times the international tourist traffic. This perspective gives an indication of the magnitude of air transport operations. The UN Conference on International Travel and Tourism held in 1963 at Rome recognised the paramount importance of public and private transport as an element in the growth of tourism; noted that air and sea transport companies had lowered fares; considered the further lowering of international fares for all modes of transport, where economic circumstances so permit, to be essential for the continued development of tourism.

Despite the already revolutionary increase in air traffic and air tourism over the years, it must be recognised that various constraints have exercised a limiting influence on the growth of air transport and tourism. Since these constraints are of continuing importance a brief discussion would be appropriate. These include problems relating to:

(*a*) Facilitation through frontiers;

(*b*) Airport terminal and ground clearance systems;

(*c*) Ground transport between airport and city;

(*d*) Accommodation for tourists;

(*e*) Air fares and costs; and

(*f*) Charters and inclusive tours.

(a) Facilitation Through Frontiers: With the continuing growth of air traffic and the need for speedier handling of air passengers on the ground, it is imperative to eliminate red-tape and streamline clearance procedures. The legitimate inspection requirements of government control agencies have to be reconciled with the objectives of facilitation. Formalities at international airports, either before departure or on arrival, should neither be time-consuming nor frustrating to air travellers.

(b) Airport Terminal and Ground Clearance Systems: The problem of coping with the great expansion in the volume of passengers might be considered in the light of the following:

(i) Design and size of the air terminal complex: The design, the layout and size of air terminals, apart from the operational and navigational aspects, depend mainly on the growth of traffic and volume forecasts for the future, the type of aircraft used and anticipated, the frequency and density of operations, transit, terminating and embarking loads, peaks and valleys in traffic movements, land available for the complex, climatic conditions, availability of utility and other essential services, distance from city centres, etc. Two important aspects of terminal planning have received considerable attention from airlines, airport authorities and governments and these relate to *(a)* forecasting traffic growth and *(b)* assessing the capacity of air terminals. Also, in regard to requirements of high density aircraft, parking arrangements, loading bridge positions, space needs for gate lounges, holding areas and baggage handling facilities standards have been established and the earlier difficulties have been overcome. Efficient systems have been formulated which could be incorporated in the master plan for air terminal development. The objective is to create a concept for the designing of facilities of immediate interest with a built-in potential for future expansion. The problems of getting large numbers of passengers on and off high capacity aircraft

parked in distance, in an orderly and speedy manner, involves the use of loading bridges or mobile lounges or moving caravans which have to be considered in the planning of the tarmac area and the designing of the flow channels of the terminal building. Handling of large quantities of baggage (cargo and mail), along with other activities such as refuelling and cabin servicing, etc. necessitate a large number of other vehicles on and around the tarmac area, which factor also calls for attention when planning a terminal complex. Proper layout of the interior of the building is an important matter in order to speed up the flow of traffic to maintain physical control of movement and to simplify and expedite its clearance. In addition, adequate facilities must be made available for visitors and members of the public to the air terminals. Similarly, space for government control authorities, airlines, concessionaires as well as other users has to be provided and included in the terminal. Large lounges, restaurants, bars, cable and post offices, banks and also facilities like telephones, toilets, adequate car parks and loading bays for coaches are additional and important requirements of a terminal complex.

However, the considerable increase in air traffic has a tendency to outpace the growth of space in airport terminals and it has been noticed in many countries that, by the time a new terminal complex is completed, it is already too small despite better and improved forecasting methods. A simple design that enables passengers to move forward in one direction through government controls without having to back-track, turn into narrow passages or get involved in cross traffic and which avoids bottlenecks and offers adequate number of channels to process passengers, is the best. Airport terminal designing is a special subject which involves high professional aptitude and experience. A layout and design which makes passenger clearance difficult and vulnerable to delay is not appreciated by tourists and there is a tendency to avoid such places.

(ii) Regarding the provision of facilities for embarking and disembarking passengers, the layout of the building contributes much to smooth and speedier flow of passengers. The more satisfactory the design and layout, the faster will handling and clearance of passengers be; and the shorter the time the passenger will be in the terminal, there would be less congestion and consequently less need for extra space. Basically, necessary facilities,

services and equipment must be provided to enable disembarkation from or embarkation to aircraft to be carried out with the least possible delay and difficulty. Mobile loading fingers from the aircraft doors to the terminal gates are now a regular feature of most airports. Yet mobile caravans or coaches are also in use to eliminate walking of large numbers of passengers in the tarmac area and thus guiding and expediting this traffic into the terminal.

(iii) The separation of arrival and departure functions is not only a control requirement, but is essential for moving and filtering traffic through the various formalities with despatch. Although transfer and transit facilities for passengers are necessary and closely connected with arrival, these should be located suitably so as not to create difficulties and confusion for departure. For embarking passengers, pressure on space in the terminal building can be reduced and movement expedited by providing check-in and other formalities in downtime centres, curb-side or parking lot check-in for baggage, allowing passengers to proceed directly to gate positions rather than congregate in the central area. However, for official control checks, adequate numbers and size of channels is necessary to process passengers and their baggage without their having to form long and waiting lines. Walking distances need to be kept to the minimum and the comfort and convenience of passengers generally kept in mind. Special facilities for group clearance of tourists are much appreciated by them and they feel welcome to the place. Expeditious handling of baggage from the aircraft to the tarmac and to the clearance area calls for availability of suitable ground equipment, conveyor belts and other distribution systems. This is an area of likely delay and whatever can be done to speed up the process to put passengers in touch with their baggage for clearance is appreciated by them and by tourists especially.

With regard to actual clearance, it is hoped that health, immigration and customs formalities will be systematically simplified and reduced to the barest minimum for international travellers, thus minimizing the stay of the passengers in the terminal building and maximizing its use for other passengers. The procedures for spot checks or selective sampling and the introduction of three channel systems for customs clearance at many airports may result in still speedier clearance of air passengers. Tourism anxiously awaits greater progress in this direction so that tourists together with their luggage could proceed directly to ground transportation without any delay and frustration.

(c) Ground Transport Between Airport and City: Transportation of large numbers of passengers from the airport to the city is a matter which requires special attention and with increasing number of air travellers, the problem calls for a planned approach between the airlines and the airport authorities in conjunction with the local or national authorities responsible for surface transportation. This transportation not only involves adequate provision of taxi-cabs and coaches or other transport, but development of approach roads and highway systems to prevent clogging of traffic to and from airports. Solutions also lie in rail links, monorails, undergrounds and helicopter services and each case might involve special consideration and planning to meet its requirements. Inadequate transport facilities and delay in movement from airport to town is stultifying and disconcerting to a tourist who sometimes feels vexed that he has spent more time on ground than in the air. Generally ground delays tend to cancel out the benefits of speedy air travel.

Allied to the problem of surface transport at airports is also the matter of providing enough parking facilities for cars and coaches at airports. The demand for adequate facilities keeps on increasing with the growth of air traffic. Special bays for bulk-loading of tourist groups and their baggage is a step in the right direction. However, where parking areas are located away from terminals, shuttle services may have to be provided to facilitate movement and avoidance of long walking distances. Airports that are unable to provide fast, frequent and satisfactory surface transport are not generally liked by tour operators and tourists.

(d) Accommodation for Tourists: It has been stated at the beginning of this section that accommodation is an important column on which the edifice of tourism is built. While concerted efforts are being made by the airlines and other transport industries and national tourism organisations to promote increased tourism and economic, social, demographic factors are favourable to future continued growth, the provision of the required lodging facilities of different kinds and classes is fundamental to tourist arrivals and their patronage. Tours are not encouraged to cities or areas where accommodation is not available and substantial tourist revenue could be lost. It is, therefore, a prerequisite to successful tourism

that lodging facilities (including hotels, motels, holiday cottages, holiday villages, youth hostels and centres, etc.) are available to accommodate the visitors and it is incumbent upon all sections of the tourism industry, especially the hospitality industry and the governments, to ensure that shortages and deficiencies are overcome and that appropriate measures are taken to meet the increasing demand for satisfactory lodgings and services.

(e) Air Fares and Costs: Air transport has had an exceptionally rapid growth rate and has reached high proportions over the last thirty years, particularly due to the jets. The rate of growth in passenger traffic of 1980 over 1979 has been 2.3 per cent and it is hoped that this rate would improve in the next few years. The rate at which air transport develops depends on the influence of many different factors. These influences may be categorised as *internal* i.e., industry and allied factors and *external* i.e., outside industry forces. The *industry* factors include the choice and use of equipments (type of aircraft, frequency, convenience of schedules, passenger comfort, route patterns, traffic densities, primary markets served, etc.). The quality of services, marketing and allied matters or services relate to adequacy of terminal facilities, ground transport, lodging arrangements for travellers, etc. which play a highly significant part in the growth of air traffic. In addition may be considered the activities of airline associations like IATA which contribute to the growth of airline operations in many ways. However, it is the level and structure of air fares that is the determining factor of the growth of air travel. As regards the already achieved growth of air travel, referred to earlier, it must be noted that *(i)* the rates of increase are not the same every year and *(ii)* that growth rates are not the same for different routes, sectors and areas of the air transport industry. Growth rates are not the same because conditions and the factors exercising influence vary.

As regards the *external* forces, these include general economic conditions, demographic and political forces, technological developments, fuel and other costs, economic position of countries using air transport, governmental regulations, route allocations, traffic rights, etc., all outside the control of the air transport industry. Both the internal and external forces are inter-related and influence one another in different ways and have significant impact on the operation and development of air transport. However, both the industry and its users are interested in the ever-expanding role of air travel. It is said that the public want safer, *cheaper,* more reliable, faster, point-to-point transportation and the airline's objective is to give the traveller what he wants and, in addition, to operate at a profit with a potential for future growth as a public service.

Airlines differ in their operating conditions like type of ownership and equipment, economic environment of each country, financial and foreign exchange constraints and traffic rights problems and all these differences affect cost levels which have to be borne in mind when negotiating or considering fares. This is where the IATA unanimity principle for establishing international fares comes. It is well-known and, statistics support the earlier stated view, that the fares charged by the airlines, in general, have a marked effect on the growth of traffic, though the degree to which different markets respond to fare reductions is by no means uniform. Since 1951, the airlines have been able to reduce fares and offer a variety of cheap fares, despite their increasing cost of operations and the higher consumer price index. If, on the other hand, the relationship between the GNP of a national and the increased individual income of an air traveller were to be examined in the light of reduced fares, the advantages of reductions offered by the airlines would become highly manifest. The airlines, despite increasing operational costs, have been able through the years to bring down the price of their services by improved technology and management.

Markets served by air transport vary in size and potential and possess different elasticities of demand in the light of differing demographic features, changes in income levels, expansion of disposable incomes, leisure and increased desire to travel and tour. When demand is inelastic, fare reductions may not stimulate demand sufficiently to produce enough additional revenue to meet the loss in terms of fare reduction. Two considerations are of essence when examining fare reductions: *firstly,* reductions that are designed to improve profitability by bringing in more net revenue after allowing for any extra costs incurred to carry the extra traffic and, *secondly,* reductions that come from passing on to the passenger the benefits of improved efficiency and profitability. These considerations, individually or with their inter-play, determine fare changes, also bearing in mind that large increases in traffic are not always dependent on fare reductions.

Again, the different segments, e.g. government, international and private business-travel, may not be accelerated by reduced fare levels. On the other hand, it is argued that in the sphere of personal travel, massive growth of air travel must be sought and expected and that the elasticity of demand is such as to make the level of fares critical. While a considerable number of special fares, inclusive, excursion group, family and other promotional fares, have already been introduced by the airlines to induce increased travel; they also keep the fare structure under constant review for still other formulations to tap new sources of travel in general and to attract tourists in particular, without having to dilute their revenue from existing traffic.

The tourists, the tour operators and tourism officials and allied industry representatives, who are also interested in the future growth of tourist travel, from time to time stress the need for the airlines to consider additional steps to offer cheaper and more attractive fares, particularly on long hauls and where other means of transport are neither competitive nor satisfactory. The airlines have in the past responded with a variety of reduced fares and charter flights at much lower cost, with the result that tourist movements have been accelerated and a large number of tourists have been able to visit destinations which used to be beyond their financial means. In this context, what is important to remember, assert the scheduled airlines, is that with the unrelenting increases in cost of operations, including fuel, spares, labour, aircraft equipment, competition and other uncontrollable costs, the airline business has been reduced to marginal profitability and the industry has also suffered severe losses in the recent past. They are strongly of the view that, in the light of the difficult economic and financial position, the chances of substantial fare reductions could be unrealistic and unfair and fraught with danger to their financial stability which in turn could damage the established air transportation system. But the clamour for further reduced fares continues.

(f) Charters and Inclusive Tours: The major part of international air passenger traffic, as is well-known, is carried on scheduled services i.e., services provided by flights scheduled and performed according to a published timetable and open to the public at

normal first class, economy, excursion or other established fares. A significant share of the air traffic is, however, carried in other ways i.e., in aircraft of scheduled airlines under charter arrangements, in which case either a scheduled flight might be chartered to a party or spare aircraft capacity may be made available for the charter. In addition, non-scheduled operators or air charter companies or supplementals perform the carriage on their aircraft.

The advantage of charter flights is that the cost of the charter could be much below the published fares on scheduled services for groups and as such is most attractive to tourists, but these charters, apart from own use are for the most part available only to "affinity" groups i.e., to members of a club, firm or other organisations whose common interest in being members is essentially not travel. The fare for the air transport component of an inclusive tour is not offered to the individual members of the public but to tour operators who combine it with the cost of other components and offer the complete package for sale to the public. In the case of inclusive tours, traffic carried on non-scheduled services, where the aircraft may be chartered or is owned by a tour operator, the conditions of service are determined by the governments of the countries of origin and destination of the flight and vary accordingly.

While the "affinity" restriction on charters and group inclusive tours are enforced by scheduled airlines, the charter companies are all for waiving these. The scheduled operators in general do not favour non-affinity charters or inclusive tour groups, as they apprehend substantial diversion of normal scheduled traffic to non-affinity cheap charters. On the other hand, the charter companies urge that they should not be prevented from carrying such traffic and deny the opportunity to public to take advantage of possible cheaper transportation. The pressure from the public for cheaper air transportation through non-affinity charters and inclusive tours has increased and supplemental carriers were authorised in Europe and USA to operate cheap non-scheduled flights for tourists by concerned governments. Scheduled air transportation services operate between and through countries under bilateral agreements entered into by them and are regulated under agreed conditions including type of equipment, capacity, frequency, route patterns, fares and rates, conditions of service, traffic rights and generally are based on reciprocity, equality and mutuality of interest.

As referred to earlier, the civil aviation authorities of different states exercise control on scheduled and non-scheduled domestic and international operations. In regard to domestic operations, they have full and complete jurisdiction. In 1976, the US Civil Aeronautics Board (CAB) recommended deregulation of domestic air operations and to do away with rules in force for nearly 40 years. It authorised specially reduced fares, liberalised charter rules and made licensing procedures easy for new carriers and routes. In 1978, the US Congress approved legislation, including the abolition of the CAB, on the assumption that government regulations precluded efficiency and added costs in airline operations.

The first impact of de-regulation from 1978-1980 helped in offering cheaper flights and it was estimated that nearly 80 per cent of US passengers travelled on discounted fares. But the industry went into difficulties soon due to inflation, high fuel costs, steep interest rates, deep fare cutting and unrealistic route expansion. Many experts believe that de-regulation has created more problems than it has solved, while others support the free market concept as the best suited for the present and future airline operations. Whether the airlines would be able to surmount their difficulties through de-regulation is to be seen. Meanwhile some of them have paid the penalty for extraordinary fare reductions and route expansions by severe losses.

Charters, on the other hand, operate under individual or general permits and have no assured legal status or freedom to operate to other countries. There is no worldwide and agreed policy in international civil aviation regarding charters, as a result of which the growth of international passenger charter services is not planned, co-ordinated and extensive. Charter operations have an important supportive role to play and can, under appropriate conditions, provide the stimulus by cheaper air prices for massive tourist growth in the future. International tourism hopes that this role of charter companies would be strengthened and enhanced by national and international action and co-operation. Governments interested in tourism are urged not to limit, control or discriminate against international charter services and let them operate under "freedom of the skies" in response to market demand. However, it is agreed and considered vital that the charter air transportation could not be allowed to impair in any way the maintenance of the level of essential scheduled air services debilitating the public air transportation system. As regards costs, it is important that full economic costs of performing the services should be established and adopted by charter companies as well so that the development of a sound charter services system could be encouraged and be in a position to promote tourism.

International tourism is a significant industry, with a great potential in the future, particularly in developing countries. As such, policies which encourage and promote all aspects of tourism infrastructure, including scheduled and non-scheduled air transport and other complementary factors for the realisation of the potential offered by international tourism, should be adopted by each country. It has been stressed from time to time that charter operations with their lower air costs are specially relevant and advantageous when a country is situated far away from the main sources of tourist traffic. As distance increases, the cost of an air ticket inevitably mounts and accounts for a growing share of total travel expenditure. To counteract the competitive disadvantage thus induced by distance, the best method may be to encourage charter operations. In this regard, the Caribbean countries have often been criticised for their "open-skies" policies which certainly helped in pushing up the statistics for arrivals without yielding corresponding economic benefits.

However, that economic benefits may be reduced or enhanced depends also upon the nationality of the charter services. The decision of the authorities in a South Asian country has recently been criticised where group traffic constituted two-thirds of the total number of tourists, more than half of whom travelled by foreign operated charters. A recent WTO study showed that nearly 60 per cent of the retail price paid by the tourist for an inclusive tour by charter was retained in the originating country. Not surprisingly, such a policy has been opposed by national carriers, especially when charter movements take place in peak tourist seasons. Such traffic has also a tendency to utilise scarce peak hotel accommodation and other transportation services at group and reduced rates offered to charter passengers. Such charter passengers would be most welcome if large-scale accommodation and other facilities built or under development remain underutilised. So, developing countries have carefully to evaluate the various aspects of charter traffic policies and arrive at a considered decision after examining the cost-benefit equation of these policies. The policy-makers must scrupulously reconcile and balance the relative importance, functions and needs of scheduled and non-scheduled air transportation so as to strengthen both the benefit of tourism in general and the individual traveller in particular. The raison d'etre must be to ensure the maximum of economic and social benefits for each country, both short- and long-term.

Tourism and transport have both grown into vast and complicated industries by the dynamic influence they have exercised on each other. Worldwide tourism has excellent growth prospects and the air transportation industry, more than any other form of transport, will expectedly carry still larger numbers of tourists all over the world in the future. It is hoped that advances in aviation technology and management will make possible greater efficiency, more comfort and lower air fares to the benefit of future tourism. The First World Congress on Air Transportation and Tourism held at Madrid in 1972 made certain recommendations on tourism and the air transport systems of the future, taking into account the expectation that future generations of air transport vehicles would primarily serve international tourism by air and that the comfort and convenience of the air traveller must remain the primary consideration of aircraft manufacturers. These recommendations are:

1. that future generation of air transport vehicles take into account the special needs of bulk markets as well as traditional scheduled markets;
2. that regulatory authorities remove unnecessary restrictions on bulk transportation which impede and discourage the development of more economic air transport vehicles;
3. that future aircraft types be developed not in isolation, but as components of an intricate tourism system, particularly in developing countries;
4. that future air transport systems recognise the essential individuality of the air traveller and pay more attention to his needs as a human being;
5. that there should be closer consultation in the future, between aircraft manufacturers, on the one hand, and tourism authorities, the travel trade and the consumers, on the other;

6. that aircraft manufacturers and airlines pay more heed to the disruptive effect on tourism of the erratic cycle of airliner procurement;
7. that more encouragement be given to action aimed at reducing the extreme seasonal variations which are typical of air travel, particularly in the bulk market; and
8. that more attention generally be given to the improvement of passenger handling and processing at airports (including official formalities) and in particular, to the special needs of the elderly, infirm and inexperienced, for help and information.

These recommendations spell the wishes of the consumers i.e., the air travellers, a majority of whom are tourists and those interested or involved in air tourism of the future. Recommendation number (4) above refers to the individuality of the air traveller and his needs as a human being. As a corollary, a "Bill of Rights for Air Passengers" was formulated for adoption, which may appropriately be reproduced below:

(i) Freedom to travel without arbitrary and discriminatory barriers.

(ii) Continuation of high standards of air safety by all carriers which carry passengers.

(iii) Availability for all people of charter and other low cost air services which will attract a mass consumer demand and ensure economic operation of airlines, whether scheduled or charter.

(iv) Equal treatment in landing and uplift facilities, regardless of the type of air transport.

(v) Truth in advertising by airlines and travel companies and the full utilisation of the mass media about every type of air travel.

(vi) Proper medical facilities in international airports throughout the world.

(vii) Proper information services at airports by national and regional tourist offices.

(viii) Representation of consumer interests in all national aviation and tourism organisations in inter-

governmental bodies such as ICAO and WTO, and such industry groups as IATA and IACA.

While the consumer interests have been well defined in the above "bill" the reconciliation of these interests with those of the air transportation services and other parties, should lead to desirable lower cost holiday travel and other facilities and thereby give a greater boost to the air tourism of future. It is hoped that future developments in air transportation take the direction most conducive to the continued expansion of tourism worldwide.

7

Road Transport and Tourism

Tourism, both domestic and international, has rapidly won considerable recognition as an activity generating a number of social and economic benefits like promotion of national integration and international understanding, creation of employment opportunities, removal of regional imbalances, opening-up of new growth centres in the interior of the country, augmentation of foreign exchange earnings, thus redressing the balance of payment situation, etc.[1] It is significant that many of these beneficial aspects of domestic and international tourism have special relevance to the socio-economic scene in India. Tourism also tends to give support to local handicrafts and cultural activities, both in urban and rural areas. Expenditure by tourists has a multiplier effect and also generates considerable tax revenue for government, both in the Central and State sectors.

It is also relevant that the various multifaceted socio-economic benefits of tourism are achieved with a relatively low level of investment. Tourism also generates a variety of unskilled employment opportunities by providing restaurants, hostels, motels, travel agents, tour operators and professional tourist guides generates high cash flow in relation to the investment promotes national consciousness in developing natural resources and focuses attention to the country's cultural heritage.[2] So it is quite clear that many of these beneficial aspects of domestic and international tourism have special relevance to the socio-economic scene in India.

Though the development of tourism depends largely on the facility of transport communication, residential fooding, guide as a whole, but all of them transport especially road transport is of paramount importance. An attempt is made in this chapter to examine the growth and trend of tourism in Bihar. Further, it would evaluate the role of road transport in the development of tourism particularly in Bihar. Attempt will also be made to give some suggestions particularly in the context of road transport to develop tourism in Bihar.

A Historical Perspective

Tourism, a trade phenomenon of the past, is now turned into a trade by itself. Until Second World War, 'the tourists' visiting places and related tourist activities were treated quite casually. After Second World War, a mass movement of people from their home town to other places for pleasure, has turned the casual tourist business into a world tourism trade.

However, the modern tourism has its ancestry, back in the Old Testament. By and large, the nomad of the past would have had pleasure by seeing different natural and scenic areas while he was moving in search of food and shelter. But, his prime motive would obviously have been to find food and shelter, no pleasure. Once man had settled and the ancient civilizations took place, then the motivations for travel had been changed to trade and commerce. Later on, the religious and educational motivations were also added to travel industry. The religious missionaries travelled wide and returned home with fascinating images of places and people they visited. Their experience in a way whetted the general appetite for travel.

During the same period, the great kingdoms grew adding political and military motivations to travel. In medieval period, the motivations for travel were a combination of religion, war and pleasure. The renaissance period was known for the adventurous travels, mainly for trade and colonialism. It is only the Industrial Revolution that laid the foundations of modern tourism. The population of developed countries had leisure and disposable income to regard a holiday as an essential feature of their life. By 1970, tourism had become no longer the preserve of the wealthy and the leisured people, but rather a mass market. Furthermore, the development of science and technology has shrunk the world to a few hours of travel.

World Tourism Boom

In view of the large volume of tourists flow and their expenditure, the importance of tourism is gradually being recognized by most countries in the world. Tourism is expected to become one of the largest industries in the world at the end of the present century. In 1950, international tourist arrivals were 25.3 million with a total of 2.1 billion United States dollars receipts, which increased to 290 million tourists with international tourists receipts of 106.0 billion United States dollars in 1981. It is estimated that international tourist arrivals may increase to the tune of 1048 million with an estimated international tourists receipts of 1136.0 billion US dollars by 2000 A.D.[3]

As the economic gap between the rich and poor countries are widening, the developing countries have realized the importance of foreign exchange earned by the tourism industry. Therefore, tourism is especially important for the developing countries like India.

Tourism Development in India

India's tourism potentials are immense and of a large variety ranging from world's renowned historical monuments to wildlife sanctuaries of exquisite flora and fauna. Besides, there are cool hill stations, stretches of sunny beaches and varied cultural heritages form unique tourism resources of India.

When looked upon the resources, India's share in world tourism market is very meagre. Although it has increased from 0.06 per cent in 1950 to 0.29 per cent during 1981, it is not up to the mark if compared with smaller countries like Ireland and Greece earning 136 and 80 million dollars every year, whereas, India earns only 54 million dollars. However, the absolute number of foreign tourists have increased from 15,000 during 1950 to 8,53,000 in 1981. But mere increase in the number of tourists flow would not enhance the earnings, as it is evident from the fact that India earns much less than smaller countries. Potentially, yet another 4,00,000 tourists fly over India every year without stopping. With appropriate plans these potentials could be tapped to contribute to Indian economy.

As a matter of fact, it is only the growth of international tourism has been taken into consideration but the domestic counterpart has not yet included in the statistical reports. By and large, domestic tourism is now gathering importance in Indian tourism. Although India shows a continuous growth of tourism industry, very little planning effort has been put in. This may be one of the reasons why India's share in the world tourism market is less. Therefore, the tourism growth cannot occur by itself to give maximum benefit, but it has to be planned. A systematic approach with defined policies to all touristic regions of the country is what exactly India needs.

International tourism in India has grown substantially during the last 15-20 years. The number of foreign tourists arrivals increased from about 17,000 in 1951 to 7,65,000 in 1979 to 12,88,162 in 1982 and 13,04,976 in 1983.[4] The average stay per tourist has also registered an increase over the years. The rate of growth of tourists arrivals in 1979 and 1980 had no doubt been below expectations. The reasons for this are connected, to some extent, with global, factors like the oil crisis and recessionay trends, but, to a great extent tourist arrivals have also been affected adversely by the inadequacy of infrastructure like hotel accommodation, internal transport, particularly air services and comfortable surface transportation, airport facilities, etc. Despite the global factors mentioned above, international tourist traffic has increased at a high rate in many of the developing countries. It is expected that international tourism in the world will develop at much higher rates, keeping in view the growing place it is occupying in the life style of the people in many countries. The share of India in international tourism continues to be very low. It should be possible for India to get a much higher share keeping in view the inherent attractiveness of the country from the tourist point of view. Efforts are required to be made to develop adequate infrastructure facilities to cater to substantially higher levels of tourist traffic.

During the Sixth Plan, the main objectives of the investments in the Tourism Sector was to optimise the use of existing capacity and to increase substantially tourist accommodation in the public and private sectors. It would be ensured that development of tourism does not adversely affect the environmental surroundings or the local culture and ethos of the tourist areas and locations. While taking up schemes for development of tourism, a selective approach was followed with a view to maximizing the return on investments. In the development of tourism, the selected travel-circuit approach was followed the matching facilities was also provided accordingly. Close co-ordination in regard to provision of facilities in the Central, State and Private Sectors in the same areas and locations would be maintained to obtain the optimum results from the available resources. This approach was intended to bring about flexibility in offering a mixed tourism package, help to regionalise tourist traffic and promote repeat visits to increase the overall volume of the traffic.[5]

The broad divisions of responsibility between Central and State Governments will continued to be on the basis that, by and large, the scheme intended primarily for international tourism continues to be in the Central Sector and those meant mainly for the promotion of domestic tourism, in the State Sector. However, India Tourism Development Corporation provides technical assistance to State Governments for promotion of tourism.

An outlay of Rs. 187.46 crores was provided in plan 1980-85 which included a sum of Rs. 115.46 crore under the State Sector and a sum of Rs. 72 crores under the programme of the Central Sector a sum of Rs. 30 crores was provided for Department of Tourism and Rs. 42 crores for the programmes of India Tourism Development Corporation (ITDC). In the Programme of Department of Tourism, the emphasis was on the development of selected beach and mountain resorts, wildlife and cultural tourism training facilities and overseas promotion. In order to encourage private sector to build hotels, it was proposed to continue interest differential subsidy to financial institutions through Industrial Finance Corporation of India. In the programme of ITDC with the completion of existing and proposed schemes, the total availability of tourist accommodation with the ITDC was expected to increase from 2,644 rooms at present to roughly 5,000 rooms by 1984-85.[6]

A number of infrastructural facilities not directly covered by the investments in the tourism sector are extremely important for tourism development, for example, increase in capacity at international and domestic airports to prevent congestion and long queues at peak hours and increase in the passenger carrying capacity of Indian Airlines to enable confirmed booking for internal travel. Investments in this regard are being included in the respective sectors.

India's potential for tourism is as vast as it is varied. While the infrastructure at home is being strengthened, promotional activities are undertaken abroad to attract more tourists. With a view to diversifying tourist attraction, the Department of Tourism has taken up the developing of beach and mountain resorts. A sum of Rs. 30 crores was provided for developing tourism in the Sixth Plan as against the original outlay of Rs. 44 crores and revised outlay of Rs. 23.62 crores in the Fifth Plan. Over the years, the department has been following a two-pronged strategy by strengthening the infrastructure at home and improving the tourist image abroad. To this, a third dimension has been added in domestic tourism development by giving equal weightage to domestic tourism along with international tourism in the Central Sector. This is a new orientation that has been given to tourism since 1977.[7]

Thus, emphasis in the Sixth Plan continued to be on building up tourist infrastructural development of selected areas as mountain and beach resorts and promotion of domestic tourism. The Department of Tourism of the Union Ministry of Tourism and Civil Aviation has both promotional and organisational functions and works in close co-operation with the Indian Tourism Development Corporation. Several States and Union Territories have also set-up tourism departments and offices.

The Department of Tourism has a chain of regional offices at home and abroad. Regional offices are functioning in Bombay and Delhi with sub-offices at Calcutta, Madras, Agra, Aurangabad, Cochin, Jaipur, Khajuraho and Varanasi. These offices work in close collaboration with State Governments, travel agents, hoteliers and carriers abroad. India has tourist offices in New York, Los Angeles, Chicago, Toronto, London, Geneva, Paris, Perth, Frankfurt, Brussels, Stockholm, Milan, Vienna, Kuwait, Bangkok, Tokyo, Paris, Singapore and Sydney. In addition, tourist promotion offices are based at Dallas, Miami, San Franscisco, Washington, Osaka, Melbourne and Tehran. The various tourist offices abroad are functioning under a scheme of close collaboration between the Department of Tourism and Air India for promotion of tourist traffic from the respective regions.

To meet the requirements of these offices, Department of Tourism produces tourist publicity literature in English, German, Spanish, French, Italian, Persian, Arabic, Japanese and Thai languages. In order to boost up domestic tourism literature in

Hindi is also produced. On an average, 60 lakh copies of tourist offices maintain film and photo libraries on subjects of tourist interest.

The department has constructed forest lodges in the bird sanctuary at Bharatpur, and the wildlife sanctuaries at Kaziranga, Sasangir and Jaldapara. The Indian Tourism Department Corporation is managing the forest lodges at Bharatpur, Kaziranga and Sasangir and the one at Jaldapara is being run by the Tourism Development Corporation, West Bengal.[8]

In addition to the construction of forest lodges, the department has also provided facilities for viewing wildlife, such as 4 boats at Bharatpur bird sanctuary, 4 elephants at Kaziranga, 5 elephants at Kanha, and 25 mini-buses have been distributed among 18 wildlife sanctuaries in the country.

At present, there are 119 approved tourist car operators spread over 26 tourist centres. Apart from this, there are 147 officially registered travel agencies in the country and an increasing number of trained and approved tourist guides.

To promote traffic, regulations, relating to police registration, currency exchange control, customs, prohibition and visas have been liberalized. The validity of landing permits has been increased from 28 to 30 days. Tourist from many countries can now come to India without a visa.

Concessional tickets for domestic tourists are issued by the railways for round trip journeys and circular tours. Special concessions are given to students. Indrail pass facilities are available for foreign tourists and Indian residents abroad against payment in US dollar and other convertible currencies. The scheme "Discover India" for travel on IA domestic services in round circle trips with unlimited stop over *en route* is available to all persons permanently residing outside India including Indians. Foreign residents in India are also eligible if they pay in US dollars or similar convertible currency.

Corporation, set up in 1966, is the only multi-unit undertaking for the development of tourism in the country. It looks after the construction and management of hotels, motels and travellers' lodges, provision of transport facilities for tourists, production of tourist publicity and promotional materials, provision of entertainment and management of duty free shops at international airports.

The Corporation has under its management 21 hotels—seven in Delhi, and one each at Aurangabad, Bangalore, Calcutta, Hassan (Karnataka), Kovalam, Jammu, Khajuraho, Mahabalipuram, Mysore, Udaipur, Varanasi, Patna, Bhubaneshwar and Madurai. It also arranges sound and light shows at Red Fort and near at Trimurti Bhawan, Delhi; Sabarmati Ashram, Ahmedabad and Shalimar Gardens, Srinagar. In addition, it runs 13 travellers lodges, 3 forest lodges, 15 restaurants, 16 transport units and 5 duty free shops at airports.[9]

The ITDC also arranges cultural shows for the tourists.

Two hotel projects in Iraq (Masul and Dokan) were to be built by the ITDC as consultants. A joint venture with Lotus Hotel Limited in Limassol Cyprus in ITDC's third overseas hotel project which would also cover management.[10]

New approach to the planning of tourist infrastructural facilities has been given by introducing the concept of travel circuits whereby facility would be developed at tourist centres falling along identified travel circuits.

With a view to attracting more tourists, publicity is undertaken in major tourist generating market of the world through 25 tourist offices located in North America, Europe, Australia, West Asia and East Asia.

The Indian Institute of Tourism and Travel Management was set up in January 1983 with its registered office in New Delhi. The Travel Industry and Management Institute are represented on the governing body. The Institute organised seminars, workshops on hotel management, restaurant management, tourism planning and on functioning areas such as finance, marketing, etc.[11]

In order to consider and recommend measures necessary for the promotion of tourist traffic to India from other countries and from one part of the country to the other. Tourism Advisory Board has been constituted. The Board reviews the tourist trends and suggests appropriate measures.[12]

Trend of Tourism in Bihar

Bihar offers to the tourists a variegated diverse package of glimpses of ancient Indian civilization, culture and scenic beauty. The ruins of the ancient sites of Rajgir, Vaishali, Patliputra as well as international universities of Nalanda and Vikramshila are places of attraction of tourists from different parts of the world. The fascinating forest of Chotanagpur interspersed with attractive water- falls and hillocks have made south Bihar a veritable paradise for tourists. The temples of Gaya, Bodh Gaya, Deoghar, Pawapuri and Parasnath, besides the Sikh Gurduwara at Patna Saheb attract millions of pilgrims every year. Bihar has limitless potentialities of tourist development and with determined efforts and investment Bihar can be transformed into Tourists Paradise and a wonder-land of inland and international tourism.

In the first two plans there was no scheme to promote tourism in the state. Since the time of the Buddha Centenary Celebrations in 1957, Tourist Centres were opened at Bodh Gaya, Gaya, Nalanda, Patna, Rajgir and Ranchi. A separate Directorate of Tourism was also created in 1960-61.[13]

Third Five Year Plan

In the Third Plan, a sum of Rs. 10 lakhs was provided for various tourist schemes. The actual expenditure was about Rs. 6 lakhs. The shortfall in expenditure was due to the paucity of resources in 1962-63 and subsequent years. During this period, however, tourist offices were set up at Dhanbad, Hazaribagh, Jamshedpur, Netarhat, Sasaram and Vaishali. Construction of a Tourist shala at Rajgir and a Rest House at Netarhat was also taken up.[14]

Fourth Five Year Plan

In the Fourth Plan, a sum of Rs. 50 lakhs was proposed for the various tourist schemes. Of this outlay, Rs. 3 lakhs was already provided in 1966-67. The amount needed in 1967-68 was Rs. 15 lakhs and in 1968-71 Rs. 32 lakhs. The schemes include beautification of places of tourist interests, construction of rest houses, cottages and cafeteria, establishment of tourist centres, provision of road and water transport facilities, tourist publicity and strengthening of administrative set up.

Fifth Five Year Plan

An outlay of Rs. 74.52 lakhs had been earmarked for the Fifth

Plan. But, owing to financial stringency, a sum of Rs. 39.63 lakhs only could be made available during 1974-78, out of which Rs. 38.75 lakhs were spent.[15] During this plan period four mini-buses, one car, two motor-launches were added to the fleet of tourist transport service; twelve tourist information centres were established, and a sum of Rs. 16.37 lakhs was spent on construction of tourist centres-*cum*-cafeteria at three places.

Sixth Five Year Plan

In the Sixth Plan (1978-83), emphasis was laid on the development of infrastructure, suited to the needs of the various types of tourists. Improvement of facilities for pilgrim-traffic was also given due consideration. Development of such places of attraction was accorded priority which was likely to stimulate employment for the local people.

During 1979-80, construction and widening of approach road leading to various temples in Rajgir and Bodh Gaya were taken up sanitation and provision of drinking water supply to the pilgrims were improved.[16]

The following programmes were taken up to foster the development of tourism in Bihar during Sixth Five Year Plan 1978-83.

Beautification of Tourist Places

Beautification of tourist places is an important aspect of attracting tourists. It was, therefore, proposed to beautify some selected places of tourists attraction, as for instance Kakolat fall in Nalanda district, hot spring at Bhimbandh in Monghyr district, hot spring at Suryakund in Hazaribagh district and Topchanchi lake in Dhanbad district etc. A sum of Rs. 50.00 lakhs was proposed for this purpose in Sixth Plan (1978-83).

Construction and Establishment of Tourist Cottages, Rest Houses etc.: Accommodation is a major requirement of tourists. Without the provision of accommodation, tourists cannot be expected at any tourist centre, however, important it may be. On the other hand, if suitable accommodation is available tourist may prefer to enjoy a change even at a less attractive place. Hence, construction and establishment of tourist cottages, rest houses, etc., deserve attention in development programmes. Stress was, therefore, laid on construction of house, lomist, cottage,rest houses, etc., with an outlay of Rs. 100.00 lakhs.

Renovation and Expansion of Tourist Bungalows, Rest Houses and Youth Hostels: Youth hostel had been constructed as far back as 1957. Some of them are now in a dilapidated condition. It is, therefore, proposed to renovate and, where necessary, expand them and the sum earmarked for the purpose was Rs. 50 lakhs.

Expansion of Transport Facilities

Tourism and transport go together, and, therefore, the importance of adequate and convenient transport facilities for the desired promotion of tourist traffic cannot be over-emphasised. As such, the transport facility will have to be improved and expanded for the development of tourism in the state. Hence, it was proposed to establish transport units at important places with luxury cars and coaches, where necessary. This programme accounted for an outlay of Rs. 50.00 lakhs in Sixth Plan 1978-83.[17]

Intensification of Tourist Publicity: Publicity is essential for development of tourism; it is vital for attracting tourists. The world at large has to be informed about the places of tourists interests, located in Bihar and facilities available to the tourists. It was, therefore, proposed to intensify the tourist publicity programme at a total outlay of Rs. 15.00 lakhs during 1978-83.[18]

Establishment of Tourist Information Centres-cum-Cafeteria: Dissemination of latest and up-to-date information to tourists is a must for an efficient tourist organization. Information is required before the commencement of journey as well as after reaching one's destination. After reaching one's destination, the tourist, also requires some light refreshment. But, in Bihar we lack such information centres where light refreshment is also available. Therefore, construction of tourist information centres-*cum*-cafeteria at important places was proposed. A sum of Rs. 75.00 lakhs was proposed for this for 1978-83.

Strengthening of the Organisational Set-up : The Directorate of Tourism needs to be strengthened to be able to shoulder the load of the proposed development programmes. Besides, Five regional offices, one each at the divisional headquarters of Bhagalpur, Darbhanga, Saharsa, Muzaffarpur and Hazaribagh need to be established. Establishment of offices at district headquarters at the rate of one each per district is also being thought of. For proper manning of the information centres, tourist bungalows, rest houses, youth hostels, etc., trained personnel are required. It was, therefore, proposed to set-up a training institute. A sum of Rs. 60.00 lakhs was the proposed outlay on all these.

In this manner, a sum of Rs. 400.00 lakhs was proposed during Sixth Five Year Plan, 1978-83 to be utilized, as detailed in Table 7.1.[19]

Table 7.1

(Rs. in lakhs)

Sl. No.	*Items*	*Outlay*
1.	Beautification of tourist places	50.00
2.	Construction and establishment of cottages, rest houses etc.	100.00
3.	Renovation and expansion of tourist bungalows, rest houses and youth hostels	50.00
4.	Expansion of transport facilities	50.00
5.	Intensification of tourist publicity	15.00
6.	Establishment of tourist information centres-*cum*-cafeteria	75.00
7.	Strengthening of the organizational set-up	60.00
	Total	400.00

The overall strategy in the sub-plan also would be to lay emphasis on the development of infrastructure suited to the needs of the various types of tourists.

Beautification of the places of tourists attraction like Netarhat, Ghatshila, Hundru falls, Ranchi lake, etc. would be undertaken. At Ghatshila and Ranchi "Nandan Kanans" one at each place would be established. Tourist cottages would be constructed at Basukinath, Netarhat, Hundru Fall and Rajrappa. A regional tourist office-*cum*-rest house would be suitably strengthened to undertake the regional work load. A regional office in the North Chotanagpur division would be set up.

Out of a total outlay of Rs. 400.00 lakhs for the State Plan, a sum of Rs. 77.00 lakhs was proposed to be earmarked for the sub-plan which would be spent, as detailed in Table 7.2.[20]

Table 7.2

(Rs. in lakhs)

Sl. No.	*Items*	*Outlay*
1.	Beautification of tourist places	5.00
2.	Construction and establishment of tourist cottages, rest houses etc.	20.00
3.	Renovation and expansion of tourist bungalows, rest houses and youth hostels	20.00
4.	Expansion of transport facilities	20.00
5.	Intensification of tourist publicity	2.00
6.	Establishment of tourist information centres-*cum*-cafeteria	5.00
7.	Strengthening of the organizational set up	5.00
	Total	77.00

Sixth Five Year Plan (1980-85)

The outlay approved for the 1978-83 Plan was Rs. 90.00 lakhs, out of which a sum of Rs. 16.75 lakhs was utilized in 1978-79 and Rs. 15.00 lakhs in 1979-80. The approved outlay for 1980-81 was Rs. 18.00 lakhs.[21]

During 1978-79, first floor of tourist complex at Netarhat was completed and furnished. Tourist bungalows at Bodh-Gaya, Rajgir and Vaishali were furnished. Besides, Schemes for provision of other facilities at different places of tourist items were taken. The construction of Paryatan Bhawan at Patna and tourist rest house at Dhanbad was taken up.

The objective would continue to be promotion of tourism in the state by developing infrastructure suited to the needs of various types of tourists. Inadequacy of resources had been a limiting factor in the proper development of tourism in the state. To overcome the limitation by attracting institutional finance, it had been decided in principle to set up the Bihar Tourism Development Corporation. The objective of the Corporation would be creation of suitable infrastructure for all-round development of tourism in the state. Accordingly, a major chunk of the proposed fund had allocated to the Corporation as assistances. The remaining funds would be utilised for construction of buildings already in hand, like, Paryatan Bhawan at Patna. Tourist rest house at Dhanbad. Tourist cottage and rest-house at Netarhat. The following, in brief, were the programmes for 1980-85.

1980-81 Programmes: With the setting up of the Bihar Tourism Development Corporation, all the programmes hitherto being implemented by the development excepting construction of building in hand, would be taken over by the Corporation. Therefore, no provision beyond 1980-81 was proposed for transport services, information and publicity, tourist centres, beautification of places, renovation and expansion of tourist bungalows and youth hostels. The amount approved for 1980-81 in respect of above-mentioned programmes was Rs. 9.70 lakhs.

(a) Assistance to the Bihar Tourism Development Corporation

The main objective of the Corporation would be promotion of the tourist image of the state and development of infrastructure suited to the needs of various types of tourists. Accordingly, the Corporation would have to take care of almost all the programmes of the Department. Moreover, it was expected to attract institutional finance to accelerate efforts. As such, assistance to the Corporation in shape of share contribution and loan would be necessary. A sum of Rs. 70.00 lakhs including Rs. 12.00 lakhs for 1981-82 was approved in Table 7.3.

(b) Completion of Buildings in Hand

The state P.W.D. has taken up construction of Paryatan Bhawan at Patna, a tourist rest house at Dhanbad and a Tourist Cottage and rest house at Netarhat completion of which would require Rs. 24.30 lakh, including Rs. 7.00 lakh for 1981-82, was approved in Table 7.3.[22]

Table 7.3

Sl. No.	*Programme*	*Outlay*			
		State Plan		*Sub-Plan*	
		1980-85	*1981-82*	*1980-85*	*1981-82*
1.	1980-81 Programmes	9.70	—	3.10	—
2.	Assistance to the Bihar Tourism Development Corporation	70.00	12.00	17.90	3.10
3.	Completion of building in hand	24.30	7.00	5.00	1.40
	Total	104.00	19.00	26.00	4.50

Rajgir, Bodh Gaya, Vaishali and Deoghar have rich historical background and large potential for development as pilgrim centres. Development work like provision of accommodation, drinking water supply, street lighting and floodlighting, sanitation, sewerage, public latrines and urinals, metalling and widening of approach roads leading to the temples situated at different places, vehicle sheds and transport facilities, construction of market and beautification of these centres was taken up in Sixth Five Year Plan in order to utilize these potentialities. The amount earmarked for the task during the plan period was Rs. 61.00 lakhs, inclusive of Rs. 11.00 lakhs for 1981-82 given as in Table 7.4.

Table 7.4

Outlay on Pilgrim Development During Sixth Five Year Plan

(Rs. in lakhs)

Sl.	*Programme*	*Outlay*	
No.		*1980-85*	*1981-82*
1.	Development of facilities at Rajgir	26.00	4.00
2.	Development of facilities at Bodh Gaya	21.00	3.00
3.	Development of facilities at Vaishali	9.00	2.00
4.	Development of facilities at Deoghar	5.00	2.00
	Total	61.00	11.00

Source : Sixth Five Year Plan (1980-85), Bihar, pp. 112-13.

Altogether, Rs. 165.00 lakhs inclusive of Rs. 37.00 lakhs for 1981-82 were earmarked for tourism and pilgrim development during Sixth Five Year Plan (Table 7.5).

Table 7.5

Outlay on Tourism and Pilgrim Development During Sixth Five Year Plan

(Rs. in lakhs)

Sl.	*Programme*	*Outlay*			
		State Plan		*Sub-Plan*	
No.		*1980-85*	*1981-82*	*1980-85*	*1981-82*
1.	Tourism	104.00	26.00	19.00	4.50
2.	Pilgrim development	61.00	11.00	—	—
	Total	165.00	37.00	19.00	4.50

Source: Sixth Five Year Plan (1980-85), Bihar, p. 113.

An outlay of Rs. 150.00 lakhs had been earmarked for the Sixth Plan (1980-85) period. Out of this amount Rs. 38.00 lakhs, Rs. 28.00 lakhs and Rs. 34.00 lakhs were spent during 1980-81, 1981-82 and 1982-83 respectively. An outlay of Rs. 34.00 lakhs had been approved for the year 1983-84 which was fully utilized. The outlay proposed for 1984-85 was Rs. 40.00 lakhs.

Construction work of Paryatan Bhawan at Patna was completed in 1981-82 and 4 deluxe tourist coaches purchased in 1982-83. Tourist bungalows at Rajgir, Bodh Gaya and Netarhat are maintained by Bihar State Tourism Development Corporation. An Aerial Ropeway was prepared by B.S.T.D.C. at a cost of Rs. 4.50 lakhs provided out of Plan funds in 1980-81. Construction of Tourism Bhawan of Sitamarhi, Deoghar and Basukinath under progress and necessary funds were transferred to Bihar State Tourism Development Corporation for the work in 1982-83. The building of Paryatan Bhawan at Dhanbad was completed under P.W.D. and was handed over to the department. Sethia Compound at Ranchi had been purchased for construction a Paryatan Bhawan-*cum*-Shopping Complex. A building Prasant Bhawan at Hazaribagh, was purchased for the Paryatan Bhawan. Necessary funds have been allotted to District Magistrate, Vaishali and Gaya for the Development of Vaishali and Bodh Gaya.

Tourism

Bihar State Tourism Development Corporation was registered on the 28th November, 1980. Presently 5 Tourist Bungalows, the Aerial Ropeway Project at Rajgir and the Tourist Transport Service and Paryatan Bhawan at Patna are being operated by the Bihar State Tourism Development Corporation on a commercial basis. Hotel Ranchi Ashok was constructed under the joint venture of Bihar State Tourism Development Corporation and India Tourism Development Corporation. The authorised share capital of Bihar State Tourism Development Corporation was Rs. one crore. A sum of Rs. 57.50 lakhs had already been subscribed by the State Government towards share capital up to 1982-83 and Rs. 14.00 lakhs was approved for 1983-84. A sum of Rs. 10.75 lakhs was given to the Corporation during 1984-85 as share capital.

(c) Direction and Administration

Strengthening of administrative set up is essential for the

proposed functioning of Tourist Information Centres and the Development Tourist Facilities. The present administrative set up of the Department of Tourism is too inadequate to bear even the load of work. It is, therefore, absolutely necessary to have substantial expansion of the administrative set-up right from the headquarters to the Divisional level. At present most of the divisional headquarters have no administrative office. It is necessary to open regional tourist offices at divisional headquarters. In view of this fact Regional Tourist offices at Muzaffarpur, Darbhanga, Hazaribagh and Patna more sections at headquarters to cope with the load of work had created. For this a sum of Rs. 0.50 lakh was proposed during 1984-85.

(d) Development of Tourist Places

Development of Tourist places is an important aspect for attracting the tourist. The dirty and uninviting surroundings of the places of tourist attraction prove to be a deterrent factor in the development of tourism. It was, therefore, proposed to beautify tourist places by means of landscaping improvement of tanks, dharamshalas, etc., for this a sum of Rs. 2.00 lakhs was proposed during 1984-85.

(e) Tourist Transport Services

Two mini buses provided by the Government of India are plying from Ranchi to Batla for the use of tourists for site seeing of wildlife in the Batla National Park. A sum of Rs. 0.50 lakh was approved for the year 1983-84 for the maintenance of these two vehicles during 1984-85. For excursion trips of tourists in the Buddhist Travel Circuit, it was proposed to purchase a deluxe bus the cost of which would be approximately Rs. 3.25 lakhs. Thus a sum of Rs. 4.50 lakhs was proposed for the year 1984-85.

(f) Tourist Information and Publicity

Publicity and propaganda are essential to the development of tourism for intensifying tourist publicity programme by various means, such as, publication of tourist literature, installation of tourist pavilion in *melas* and exhibitions, publication of tourist maps etc. A sum of Rs. 0.50 lakh had been approved for the year 1983-84. A sum of Rs. 1.25 lakhs was proposed for the year 1984-85.

(g) Building Project

The following three travel circuits have been identified by the Government of India.

1. Patna—Nalanda—Rajgir, Bhimbandh—Gaya—Bodhgaya—Sasaram—Buxar—Jagdishpur—Maner—Patna (Buddhist Travel Circuit).

2. Patna—Hajipur—Vaishali—Muzaffarpur—Motihari—Barharwa—Bettiah—Lauria Nandangarh—Valmikinagar—Raxaul—Sitamarhi (Vaishali Travel Circuit).

3. Patna—Pawapur—Tilayadam—Parasnath—Hazaribagh—Ranchi—Netarhat—Betia (Chotanagpur Valley Travel Circuit).

In the above three travel circuits Patna, Nalanda, Rajgir, Bodh Gaya, Buxar, Hajipur, Vaishali, Sitamarhi, Hazaribagh, Ranchi, Betla and Netarhat have some basic infrastructure facilities. Muzaffarpur is an important place in the Vaishali Travel Circuit. So, a Tourist Bhawan is essential at Muzaffarpur—Vikramshila near Bhagalpur is an important tourist place. Therefore, a tourist Bhawan at Bhagalpur is also necessary. It was proposed to construct Tourist Bhawans at Muzaffarpur and Bhagalpur. Tourist Bhawan, Dhanbad is nearing completion. Thus, a sum of Rs. 11.00 lakhs was proposed during 1984-85, as detailed below[23]:

	(Rs. in lakhs)
(A) Completion of Paryatan Bhawan, Dhanbad	1.50
(B) Proposed Paryatan Bhawan at Muaffarpur	2.00
(C) Proposed Paryatan Bhawan at Bhagalpur	2.00
(D) Construction of Paryatan Bhawan, Ranchi	5.50
Total	11.00

(h) Development of Places of Pilgrims

Bihar has many pilgrim centres which attract millions of pilgrims. They do not have sufficient accommodation and other basic amenities for the tourists. It is necessary to develop these places. Paryatan Bhawans with rest houses are going to be constructed at Deoghar and Basukinath for the accommodation of pilgrims. A Shanti Stupa and Venu Van Mahavihar is going to be constructed at Vaishali through Rajgir Buddha Vihar Society. A sum of Rs. 10.00 lakhs had been earmarked for the year 1983-84 which was expected to be spent. A sum of Rs. 10.00 lakhs was proposed for the development of pilgrim centres during 1984-85.

The following programmes were proposed to be taken up during 1984-85.[24]

	(Rs. in lakhs)
1. Construction of Paryatan Bhawan at Deoghar	3.00
2. Construction of Paryatan Bhawan at Basukinath	1.00
3. Development of Shivaganga tank at Deoghar	1.00
4. Construction of Paryatan Bhawan at Gaya	2.00
5. Development of Vaishali	2.00
6. Development of other Pilgrim centres	1.00
Total	10.00

Thus a sum of Rs. 40.00 lakhs was approved for Tourism and Pilgrim Development for 1984-85. Out of which Rs. 7.00 lakhs earmarked for sub-plan. Rs. 29.75 lakhs out of this amount would in flow to District Plan.

An outlay of Rs. 150 lakhs was approved for the Sixth Plan period for the sector, out of which a sum of Rs. 128 lakhs was utilized during the first four years of the Sixth Plan. An outlay of Rs. 40 lakhs have been approved for the year 1984-85.

The following infrastructure for tourism have been built up in the State during the Sixth Five Year Plan period:

(a) Two Paryatan Bhawans, one at Patna and another at Dhanbad have been constructed.

(b) A suitable plot of land in the heart of Ranchi town on the main road has been purchased for the Paryatan Bhawan-*cum*-Shopping Complex and the project is underway.

(c) A building named 'Prasant Bhawan' at Hazaribagh was purchased for a Paryatan Bhawan.

(d) The construction of Paryatan Bhawans at Sitamarhi, Deoghar and Basukinath are nearing completion.

(e) About 10 acres of land have been acquired at Vaishali transferred to Rajgir Buddha Vihar Society for—

The construction of Viswa Shanti Stupa by Rev. Fuji Guruji of Japan. A dormitory-*cum*-cafeteria is under construction at Vaishali.

The Bihar State Tourism Development Corporation (BSTDC) has been set up for the development of tourism in Bihar.

Six deluxe buses have been purchased and they are being run by BSTDC.

A pilgrim shed at Mahendranath (Siwan) is under construction.

Table 7.6

Sl. No.	*Items*	*State Plan*	*Sub-Plan*	*Total*
1.	Share Capital to Bihar State Tourism Development Corporation	9.75	1.00	10.75
2.	Direction and Administration	0.50	—	0.50
3.	Tourist Transport Service	4.50	—	4.50
4.	Tourist Information and Publicity	1.25	—	1.25
5.	Development of Tourist Places	1.50	1.50	2.00
6.	Building Projects	5.50	5.50	11.00
7.	Pilgrim Centres	10.00	—	10.00
	Total	33.00	7.00	40.00

Hotel Ashok at Ranchi as a joint venture of ITDC and BSTDC

A forest lodge at Betla (Palamau)

This scheme was jointly taken up by the Central and State Governments.

About 200 cases of hostels/motels has been proceeded and forwarded to financial institutions for grant of loan and about 40,000 foreign and 12 lakhs domestic tourists visited the State during the Sixth Plan period.

Objectives of the Seventh Five Year Plan 1985-90

The main objective of the development of tourism in Bihar during the Seventh Plan (1985-90) is to improve the places of historical and tourist interest, to create way side facilities and to enlarge the availability of lodging, boarding and travelling facilities for the domestic as well as foreign tourists; promotion of wildlife tourism, water, sports, entertainment including holding of annual fairs and festivals training of personnel and tourism publicity including FAM programme will also get high priority.

For the development of tourist infrastructure, three travel circuits have already been identified, i.e.:

Patna—Nalanda—Rajgir—Bhimbandh—Gaya—Bodh Gaya—Sasarama—Buxar—Jagdishpur—Maner—Patna.

Patna—Hajipur—Vaishali—Muzaffarpur—Motihari—Basharwa—Bettiah—Lauria-Nandangarh—Valmikinagar—Raxaul—Sitamarhi.

Patna—Pawapuri—Tilaiyadam—Parasnath—Hazaribagh—Ranchi —Netarhat—Betla.

For purpose of development Vikramshila (Bhagalpur) is being associated with Travel circuit no. 1.

The above travel circuits will get the maximum focus under different schemes which will be taken up for implementation during the Seventh Five Year Plan.

The following targets are proposed to be achieved by the end of the Seventh Plan period, i.e., 1985-90:

(i) Foreign tourists	1,20,000
(ii) Domestic tourists	30,20,000

At the end of Sixth Five Year Plan, the department including the Tourist Development Corporation will have 500 beds. It is proposed to raise the total number of beds to 1,500 by the end of the Seventh Five Year Plan.

The following are the programmes for the Seventh Five Year Plan:

(a) Direction and Administration

The present administrative set up of the department which consists of only two Deputy Directors, and one Assistant Director is quite inadequate. There are 48 Tourists Information Centres and two regional offices at Ranchi and Gaya within the State. In order to achieve the tourist arrival targets as also other objectives stated above, it is necessary to strengthen the present organisational pattern both at the headquarters and at field levels. It is, therefore, proposed to create one post each of Deputy Director (Administration), Assistant Director, and Planning-*cum*-Budget Officer along with one section and supporting staff. It is also proposed to purchase one staff car for the headquarters and two jeeps one each for Bhagalpur and Muzaffarpur. For all these items a sum of Rs. 25 lakhs is proposed for the Seventh Plan, including Rs. 4 lakhs for 1985-86.

Tourist Accommodation: Accommodation is the basic requirement of tourists. Hence construction and establishment of Paryatan Bhawan, Rest House, Cottages, Cafeterias deserve high priority. It is proposed to construct Paryatan Bhawans, Rest Houses, Lodges, Youth Hostels and Cafeterias at the following places during the Seventh Five Year Plan:

Construction of Paryatan Bhawans at Bhagalpur, Madhuban (Parasnath), Raxaul, Muzaffarpur, Patna, Jamshedpur and Sasaram.

Renovation of existing tourist bungalows at Deoghar, Vaishali, Dhanbad and Hazaribagh.

Completion and furnishing of Paryatan Bungalows at Sitamarhi and Ranchi.

Extension of existing Paryatan Bungalows at Daltonganj.

Renovation of existing Youth Hostels at Haveli, Kharagpur, Hundrufalls (Ranchi), Bokaro, Parasnath, Bodh Gaya, Nalanda, Barabur, Netarhat, Hazaribagh, National Park and Louria-Nandangarh.

Construction of new Youth Hostels at Ranchi, Motihari, Vikramshila, Madhuban (Parasnath), Dassam fall (Ranchi). Grant to BSTDC for providing wayside facilities, like cafeteria, restaurant, rest room, toilet at the following places—Bihar-sharif (near Agricultural Marketing yard on bye-pass road), Hisua (Nawada), Sikandra (Monghyr), Boduadam Bundu Barauni (Zeromile), Masanjore, Ghagra (Gumla), Anga (Ranchi), Gola (Hazaribagh), Barhi (Hazaribagh) and other places.

(b) Maintenance of Youth Hostel at Patna and Staff Quarters for Forest Lodge at Betla

For all these a sum of Rs. 270 lakhs is proposed during Seventh Five Years Plan including Rs. 42 lakhs for 1985-86.

(c) Survey and Statistics Including Project Formulation and Consultancy

The existing statistical cell which consists of one statistical officer, two statistical supervisors, and two assistant statistical supervisors needs strengthening to undertake survey and project formulation works. A sum of Rs. 10 lakhs is proposed for the Seventh Plan including Rs. 2 lakhs for 1985-86.[25]

(d) Tourist Information and Publicity

Tourist publicity has its own place in the development of tourist traffic. It was proposed to intensify the tourists publicity programme during the Seventh Five Year Plan through the following media:

Publication of tourist literature, brochures etc.

Publication of advertisement organising cultural programmes and tourist day week.

Hoarding and window display.

Joint advertisement through Government of India/ITDC etc. specially for foreign market.

International publicity through FAM tours of international agents, tour operators, who visit India at the invitation on Government of India.

A sum of Rs. 30 lakhs is proposed in the Seventh Five Year Plan for this programme out of which a sum of Rs. 2 lakhs was proposed for 1985-86.

(e) Tourist Information Centre

The present Tourist Information Centres at Calcutta, Puri, Varanasi and New Delhi are in a bad shape, there is a proposal to have a Tourist Information Centre at Bombay also. Within the state a few more Tourist Information Centres are needed at places, like, Ranchi Railway Station, Tamui etc. The existing Tourist Information Centres need renovation. A sum of Rs. 15 lakhs is proposed for the purpose during the Seventh Five Year Plan period including Rs. 2 lakhs for 1985-86.

(f) Tourist Transport Service

There are three travel circuits in the state. Bihar State Tourism Development Corporation is running buses only on Ranchi, Patna, Ranchi—Netarhat—Betla, Patna—Pawapuri—Nalanda—Rajgir, Monghyr—Kharagpur—Bhimbandh, Sikandra—Jamaui—Bhimbandh and Patna city routes. A large number of Tourist places have remained uncovered. To begin with, it is proposed to run at least two bus services in each tourist circuit. It is also necessary to have a few cars for the tourists. A sum of Rs. 25 lakhs was proposed to be sanctioned as grant to the BSTDC for the purchase of deluxe buses/cars etc. during the Seventh Plan. The amount proposed for 1985-86 was Rs. 3 lakhs.

(g) Share Capital to BSTDC

The authorized share capital of BSTDC is Rs. 2 crores, out of which a sum of Rs. ·23 crore has already been subscribed by State Government up to 1983-84. A sum of Rs. 10.75 lakhs is proposed for 1984-85. The BSTDC has already taken steps to increase authorized share capital during the Seventh Five Year Plan.[26]

To create, develop, improve and expand the tourism infrastructure particularly accommodation and transport a sum of Rs. 175 lakhs is proposed to be subscribed to 92 plans.

(h) BSTDC during the Seventh Plan Period Including Rs. 10 lakhs for 1985-86

Development of historical and other Tourist places including Maintenance of Sound and Light Project of Buxar: Development and beautification of historical and other places are important aspects for attracting tourists. Almost all tourist places need some sort of improvement. It is proposed to take up the following schemes of tourist attraction.

Construction of a stage for sound and light show at Kumhrar (Patna) based on ancient history of Patliputra.

(i) Development of Mahendrughat for Water Sports Centre and Tourism and Renovation of Stairs of Golghar at Patna

Floodlight arrangement at Patna Sachivalaya building, Museum Golghar and Other buildings in other parts of the state.

Development of Kanke Dam (Ranchi) including provision of pedal boats, tea stalls, etc.

Providing pedal boats, tea stalls, rose gardens, fishing angles, platforms, benches etc. for Netarhat lake.

Tea stall and park at sun set point at Netarhat.

Establishment of deer parks at Rajgir and Buxar.

Swimming pool at Bodh Gaya behind tourist bungalow no. 2.

Grant to BSTDC for the maintenance of sound and light show at Buxar.

A sum of Rs. 30 lakhs was proposed during the Seventh Five Year Plan for the above programme out of which a sum of Rs. 2 lakhs was proposed to be earmarked for 1985-86.

Tourism Training : The prevailing standard of guides in places of tourist interest leaves much to be desired. The other function areas also need training. It is, therefore, proposed to organise training programmes at the state level and also to take advantage of existing training facilities both within the state and outside the state. A scheme of giving stipends to the trainees will be introduced. A sum of Rs. 5 lakhs is proposed during the Seventh Five Year Plan for tourism training including Rs. 1 lakh for 1985-86.

(j) Development of Pilgrim Centres

Bihar has many pilgrim centres which attract millions of pilgrims and tourists. These centres have to be provided with necessary infrastructural facilities for the comfort of the pilgrims. Accordingly, its proposed to provide Dharamshala cafeteria/ approach road, etc. at Pretshila (Gaya)/Sultanganj (Bhagalpur), Singeshwar Asthan (Saharsa), Areraj (Champaran), Punura (Sitamarhi), Ram Rekha (Simdega), Lachhaura (Monghyr), Rajrappa (Hazaribagh), Rerekha Ghat (Buxar), Jaganathpur Temple (Ranchi), Madhuban (East Champaran) and other selected places. The contribution and furnishing of Deoghar and Busukinath Bungalows will also be completed. A sum of Rs. 70 lakhs is proposed for all these during the Seventh Five Year Plan, including Rs. 8 lakhs for 1985-86.

(k) Fairs, Festivals and Exhibitions

A sum of Rs. 15 lakhs was proposed for the Seventh Plan period for:

Organizing fairs and festivals including annual festivals,

Creating static and mobile exhibition units,

Producing films on tourism,

Installing tourism publicity stalls at different *melas*/exhibitions within State and outside State, and

Preparation of blow ups and other exhibits. The outlay proposed for 1985-86 is Rs. 2 lakhs.

(l) Development of Sports and Water Tourism

The sector has not received adequate attention so far. The Department has two motor launches, one barge and 18 motor boats. The Gangas in Patna and some beautiful lakes, Topchanchi, Tilaiya, Ranchi, etc. Provide ample scope for developing water tourism including floating cafeteria at Patna. Mahendrughat, Railway station building at Patna is now vacant and could be purchased for developing water tourism. The building and the campus will itself cost not less than Rs. 20 lakhs. Netarhat hill (Ranchi), Dalmia hill (Tatanagar) and Patna Golf Club could be selected for developing trekking facilities and a game of golf. A sum of Rs. 30 lakhs is, therefore, proposed under this programme for the Seventh Five Year Plan period including Rs. 22 lakhs for 1985-86.

Thus an outlay of Rs. 700 lakh is proposed for the Seventh Plan for the development of tourism and pilgrim centres, as summarised in Table 7.7.[27]

Table 7.7

Sl. No.	*Item*	*Seventh Plan 1985-90*		*Annual Plan 1985-86*	
		State Plan	*Sub-plan*	*State plan*	*Sub-plan*
1	*2*	*3*	*4*	*5*	*6*
1.	Direction and Administration	25.00	—	4.00	—
2.	Tourism accommodation (including supplementary accommodation, Youth Hostels, Maintainance of Youth Hostels; Forest Lodge, Betla wayside amenities like cafeteria etc.	270.00	90.00	42.00	12.00
3.	Survey and statistics including Projects formation and consultancy	10.00	—	2.00	—
4.	Tourism Information and publicity including FAM programme	30.00	3.00	2.00	—
5.	Tourist Information Centres	15.00	3.00	2.00	—
6.	Tourist Transport Service	25.00	6.00	3.00	3.00
7.	Share Capital to BSTDC	175.00	25.00	10.00	3.00
8.	Development of historical and other tourist places including SEL at Buxar	30.00	5.00	2.00	1.00
9.	Tourism Training	5.00	1.00	1.00	0.25
10.	Development of Pilgrim Centres	70.00	—	8.00	—
11.	Fairs, Festivals and Exhibitions	15.00	2.00	2.00	—
12.	Development of Sport and water Tourism	30.00	—	22.00	—
	Total	700.00	135.00	100.00	20.00

Present Position of Tourism in Bihar

Bihar offers to the tourists a variegated wealth of Indian civilisation and culture coupled with exquisite scenic beauty. The magnificent ruins of the ancient royal cities of Rajgir, Vaishali and Patliputra as well as the International Universities at Nalanda and Vikramshila are places of attraction of tourists from different parts of the world.

The ancient temple of Gaya, Bodh Gaya, Deoghar, Pawapuri and Parasnath, besides the Sikh Gurudwara at Patna, attract millions of pilgrims professing Hinduism, Buddhism, Jainism and Sikhism.

The fascinating forests of Chotanagpur, interspersed with verdant hillocks and attractive waterfalls have made south Bihar a veritable paradise of tourists. It is said that forest provides various aspects to human life to make it complete. It is in the forest, Aryans wrote first mantra of Veda, human being found music of life, ray of civilization for the first time beamed, human life found mobility from waterfalls, and it is the forest on which existence, a well-being and happiness of human beings depend. According to Lord Buddha forests provide security to all including those who try to destroy it. Jawaharlal Nehru has generously expressed his fascination about the forest. The attractive forests of Bihar attract tourists from all over the world. Forest area in Bihar is spread over 29,232 sq kms. Out of the total forest area 4,427 sq. kms. has been developed as wild-life sanctuaries.

The tourist department of Bihar has made appropriate arrangements in order to enable tourists to visit this attractive and pleasing sanctuaries. Betla sanctuary is of special information. Betla is situated at about one thousand feet above the sea-level, 16 kms. away from Daltonganj and consists of deep attractive forests and scarce animals. Betla Tiger Project is open for tourists all through the year. However, period between February to April is most appropriate. There are heart forts in the Park to see animals. There is comfortable rest house for tourists within the Park. The tourist department at Ranchi has two small buses for getting tourists visit Betla. Tourists can get necessary informations, guidelines, and accommodational facilities from tourist information centre and rest house of the tourist department at Daltonganj. In the north-eastern direction from Betla there is ruins of places and forts of Cherokings by the side of Auranga river.

The National Park at Hazaribagh, 22 kms. away from Hazaribagh town, spread in 186 kms. and situated at 1,800 feet from the sea-level provides alluring attraction to the tourists. Deep forests on hills of different heights, pillars, dams, and tiger trap are chief attraction of the Park. The forest department has made special arrangement for tourists to visit the Park. The necessary services, information etc. can be had from tourist information centre and rest house, Hazaribagh. It is most appropriate to visit the Park between October to March.

Besides, the Government of Bihar has developed other ten forest areas into wildlife sanctuaries. These include Lavalong Park, Hazaribagh in 207 sq. kms of area, Mahuandar sanctuary Palamau, which spread in 63.25 sq. kms of area. Bhimbandh sanctuary 60 kms. from Monghyr is spread in 682 sq. kms. Dalma Zoological garden in Singhbhum district, 10 kms. from Jamshedpur spread in 193 sq. kms. Topchanchi in Dhanbad, Udaipur and Valmikinagar in West Champaran, Kamour in Rohtas and Gautam Buddha Park in Gaya.

According to 1984 census there are 138 tigers and 113 cheetas in the forests of Bihar. Black deers can be seen in herds in Buxar. Deers with four horns are rare. They can be seen in the forests of Palamau and Hazaribagh. One can see both he and she deers of a particular specie with horns in Kamour Park in Rohtas district. The Ganda an animal is of special attraction for tourists coming from within the country and abroad in Kanha National Park, Madhya Pradesh. This animal can easily be seen in sanctuaries of Palamau and Hazaribagh. The forest in Bihar has immense potential for attracting tourists from all over the world.

The tourist department of Bihar has taken a number of measures to utilize the tourist potentials and to develop tourism in the state, with the development of tourist centres and tourist facility. This is continuous increase in the number of tourist coming to the state from other states and abroad. The social, cultural and religious life style has not only influenced Indians but also influenced and attracted foreigners. Two of the great religions of the world have found the birth on the very soil of Bihar. Bodh Gaya, where Lord Buddha get enlightened still give messages of truth, non-violence, love and affection to the world. There are attractive temples at Bodh Gaya made by Japan, Burma, Sri Lanka, Thailand, China. The propounder of Jainism Mahavira's birth place Vaishali and Nirvansthal Pawapuri attract tourists from all corners of the world.

The eye-catching hills of Parasnath and Jain temple at Parasnath mountains are one of important attractions of the state.

The Tenth and last Guru of Sikh Panth Guru Gobind Singh got birth to Patna. The Gurudwara Takht Shri Hari Mandir at Patna Sahib is the religious tourist place for tourists all over the world.

Darghas at Maner Sharif and Biharsharif are important religious places for Muslims.

Bihar offers a wide range of natural beauties. The natural beauties sun-rise and sun-set are unique in eastern India. The industrial complex at Jamshedpur and lakes, waterfalls and hills of Ranchi are famous for their beauties. The beauties of Hindu Jouha, Dasan waterfalls in Ranchi and Kakolet waterfall in Gaya instantly catch eyes of the tourists. The lakes of Ranchi, Hazaribagh, Tilaiya and Masanjor are also famous for their beauties.

The climatic conditions of Deoghar, Ranchi, Hazaribagh and Ghatshilla are convalescing and conducive to health. These places are good holiday resorts for tourists.

Among historical reserves, Ashoka Pillars of Nandangadh (Bettiah) and Areraj (East Champaran), ruins of ancient universities at Nalanda and Vikramshila, Tomb of Shershah at Sasaram, ruins of the Maurya Empire at Kumrar near Patna tell the pride story of the royal and powerful kings and cultural heritage.

The tourist department of Bihar has made planned effort to develop tourism in Bihar. The emphasis has been on proving quick, better and easily available facilities to the tourists in order to attract more and more tourists. There are 43 Tourist Information Centres in all the important tourist centres of the State. There are also Tourist Information Centres of Bihar at Delhi, Calcutta, Varanasi and Puri. There are well-furnished tourist Bungalows and rest houses at Bodh Gaya, Rajgir, Netarhat, Patna, Deoghar, Vaishali, Hazaribagh, Chapra and Daltonganj. In order to provide transport facilities to tourists, there are a large number of deluxe and mini bus services. Among these services, important services are Patna—Ranchi, Patna—Rajgir—Nalanda, Pawapuri, Sikandra —Jamui—Bhimbandh, Munghr, Bariarpur, Kharagpur—Bhimbandh, Betla—Ranchi—Netarhat, Ranchi—Betla / Daltonganj and Patna city and airport services. Elephants are available for tourists at Betla for viewing the wildlife. The tourist department also conducts special tours by deluxe / mini buses.

There is good tourist hotel at Patna. Bihar tourism is constructing another hotel namely Hotel Ranchi Ashok at Ranchi in joint venture with ITDC. The construction of Tourist Bhawan at Dhanbad is complete. Tourist Bhawan is to be completed at Deoghar, Basukinath, Sitamarhi and Ranchi.

Attractive Tourism literature and Bihar tourist map have been made available to tourists to facilitate their travelling.

The tourist department has also other achievements. These include acquisition of 10 acres of land for erecting Vishwa Shanti Stupa at Vaishali, development of Pipar-Pahari, Biharsharif and construction of pilgrim shed at Dodhsthan, Saran.

The Government of Bihar with the help of tourist development and Bihar State Tourism Corporation has set a number of physical targets for the development and expansion of tourism in the State. They include expansion of Tourist Bhawan at Patna, construction of Hotel Ranchi Ashok, construction of hotel and tourist complex at Hazipur near Ganga Setu, construction of Tourist Bhawan at Muzaffarpur and Bhagalpur and construction of cafeteria at Vaishali etc. There is also scheme to open regional tourist offices in different parts of the state.

The Government of India has also chalked out certain programmes to boost up and develop tourism in the state. Among the important programmes of the Government of India are light and sound scheme at Buxar for entertaining tourists and construction of forest lodge at Betla for providing accommodational facilities.

Role of Road Transport in Development of Tourism

Transport is the basic requirement for development of tourism industry in an economy. It cannot be said that tourism and pilgrimage do not take place in absence of transport facilities. The religious bound and the intense attraction of natural beauties and scenario make people reach places which have no transport link. Adventure is very much inherent in human behaviour. There are so many instances in the history when people took pain to travel a long-long distance on foot through odd places, odd seasons and odd times to quest their thirst for acquainting themselves with the nature, for understanding new world, for overwhelming with the pleasure of the nature, for discovering new facts, for strengthening their religious faith and bonds, and the like. Even today there are number of tourist places which are far away from transport access. However, transport definitely boosts the tourism industry. It makes travelling convenient, quicker, safer and wider in scope and thereby increases the volume of tourists visiting a place. Transport multiplies the movement of people to tourist places manifold. Transport is rightly the life blood of tourism industry.

Of the various means of transport rail transport and road

transport are common, easily available and within the reach of common men. Rail transport is convenient, comfortable and only way for long distance.

It connects important places coming on the rail path. The smaller places which in many cases have tourist attraction usually remain away from rail-link. Road transport alone provides accessibility to such places. Road transport is comparatively quicker, more convenient, more economical and after all more flexible in case of short distance travel. So far the question of approaching tourist and pilgrim centres is concerned road transport is almost all cases only way. At the best, railway can bring tourists to the places of attraction but rest of the task of visiting different nearby places lies with the road transport. Road transport certainly plays a vital role in the development of tourism. Its role is especially important in Bihar where rail network is not in a satisfactory state.

Most of the tourist places of Bihar are without rail link and road transport is the only way to reach these places. The important tourist places of Bihar are Vaishali, the seat of ancient Lichhvis and the first republic of the world and also the birth place of Lord Mahavira, Bodh Gaya, the enlightenment place of Lord Buddha, Hazaribagh (National Park), Betla (Wildlife sanctuary), Kaimur, Kodarma etc. These places attract tourists from other states as well as from abroad. They have, however, no rail-link. One has to resort to road transport in order to reach these places.

Usually, most of the tourist places such as hill stations, national parks, sanctuaries, temples are found in hilly areas. Where rail-link is difficult to construct, expensive and time-taking. Road link is comparatively easier to construct in such places. The case is not different in Bihar. South Bihar especially two districts of Chotanagpur and Santhal Parganas divisions is thickly wooded and consists of a succession of hills making construction of rail-link difficult. North Bihar and northern places of South Bihar are hit by recurring floods. As such, road transport is to be preferred to railway in Bihar. It becomes more important in case of tourist places.

Rail-link in India can make tourists reach near the tourist places at its best but road-transport is to be resorted to reach the actual place of attraction. This is the case of most of the important places of tourist attraction in India. The temple of Vaishno Devi is about 200 kms far from its nearest railway station Jammu-Tawi. Khajuraho which is famous for its beautiful temple and attracts more tourists from abroad than from within the country is about 150 kms away from the nearest railway station, Satna. The Hill stations, wildlife sanctuaries and National Parks of U.P., M.P., Maharashtra, Karnataka etc. are connected only with road. Not only these sites, which are naturally situated in woody and hilly tracts where rail-links are difficult and expensive to construct but also the sites which are a coastal places like Sun Temple, Konark, Jagannath Temple, Puri etc. have only road-link. Bihar is not an exception, Bodh Gaya in Bihar is some 15 kms. away from the Gaya station whereas Vaishali is 32 kms. away from its nearest railway station, Muzaffarpur for instance. Even important places and cities, so strategic from economic, social and political points of view, are not connected by rail. Besides the poor rail network, rail schedule is not adequate and well maintained, there is usually lack of link trains posing various inconveniences to the tourists. The problem gets aggragated in cases of tourist and pilgrim centres which by their very nature lack easy accessibility. All the tourists places in Bihar like Bodh Gaya, Vaishali, Betla wildlife sanctuaries, National Park, Hazaribagh etc. have no rail-link.

Road transport is the most convenient and quicker link which connects Patna, the capital of Bihar which has tourist attraction for its historical reserves and for its being the birth place of Guru Gobind Singh with North Bihar which is main agricultural base of the state. Sitamarhi, the birth place of Goddess Sita, the spouse of Lord Rama is also poorly situated on rail-link. It is connected to the major portion of the state with road-link only. It is Sitamarhi—Muzaffarpur—Patna road which provides vital to and from Sitamarhi. The situation becomes panic and there remains no link with Sitamarhi when this road is disturbed in rainy season due to flood.

Whereas, there is tremendous improvement in the comforts and other facilities provided by the road transport even though roads are in a sordid state, it is becoming hard everyday to travel by rail. The difference is sharp and sufficiently marked on roads connecting important places including tourist places, pilgrim centres and tourist resorts. With the easy schedule, high frequency of vehicle movement on roads and sufficient link service the travel on roads becomes easy and it increases interactions between different areas and between people of different places. The force of integration and unification is thus strengthened. The heritage and culture are better known and brotherhood is furthered.

Road transport provides door to door service and it is, therefore, convenient to travel by road transport. This consideration is especially of vital importance for tourists. It helps them avail the maximum amount of pleasures and happiness which tourist places provide. It is really difficult to involve in the pleasure of nature and centres of attraction if one is conscious of ones travelling. Road transport providing services even in odd hours relieves the tourists of such anxieties.

Whereas rail, air and even water transport have no in-way association with the natural and human habitats. Road transport, however, helps closer look on the nature, village life and human settlements. This helps learn while travelling. Travelling becomes more pleasant. Road transport thus adds attraction to the tourism.

By unifying different regions and different sectors, road transport augments economic activities and the process of economic prosperity is encouraged with increase in economic prosperity movement of people increases giving boost to tourism.

Thus, road transport has various roles to play in developing tourism in India in general and in Bihar in particular.

Road Transport and Tourism in Bihar

It has been made clear in the previous section that road transport is an essential ingredient of any tourist development strategy in any economy. It is particularly essential in Bihar which like in other respects, lags behind in respect of rail network. Even if rail network is sufficient, road transport is still a *sine qua non* for the development of tourism from the analysis made in previous sections of this chapter it can be derived that there has been a number of measures for developing tourism and there is also an increasing trend in the number of tourism coming to the state. But it is still a hard fact that the large proportion of tourist potentials that Bihar have is still to be utilized. The number of tourists to the state is far away from the optimum size. There are certain tourist centres, viz., Vaishali which are losing tourist attraction. The tourism in Bihar cannot be sad in a satisfactory state although it has shown well promises.

There may be various reasons as to why tourism has not prospered to the level it should be like, lack of adequate accommodation facilities at the tourist centres, lack of publicity, absence of literature, absence of publicity, ill-maintenance of tourist centres, and the like. Among these factors transport especially road transport occupies utmost importance. Inadequacy of road transport makes travelling difficult, disgusting, time-consuming and thus hampers the progress of tourism industry as a whole even when other facilities are available. Tourists would like to bear with other inconveniences if their movement is simpler, quick and comfortable. They can find accommodation far away the tourist centres if easy and fast transportation facilities are available.

It has been brought to that road network of the state is poor. There are lack of good roads with sufficient link-roads. Instead, road lengths are inadequate, roads are ill-maintained, they lack link-roads, they are usually broken surface, long patches, making driving uncomfortable, risky and time consuming, they are unbridged in number of cases and they are inaccessible due to floods for a good part of the year. In absence of adequate and well-maintained roads there is huge rush on roads and every passenger vehicles are overcrowded demanding for a heroic courage and boldness on the part of passengers wishing to travel.

The main reason as to why tourism in Bihar has not developed to its optimum level is the road transport bottleneck in the state. So far tourist development programmes in the state centre road the tourist centre and this is no doubt essential. No serious attention is paid to develop road-link and provide adequate transport facilities to visit tourist places. There is very small number of buses for Vaishali. The road-link to Sitamarhi from southern direction is severed every rainy season for a good number of days. Development of sufficient road transport facilities is essential for development of tourism in Bihar.

From the above analysis it may be derived that tourism industry in Bihar is in infant stage of development. The state of tourism in Bihar is quite unsatisfactory in comparison to that in India as a whole. However, tourism industry in Bihar is progressing promising not. The Government of Bihar and the tourist department are well concerned with the development of tourism in the state. A number of measures have been taken up to boost-up the tourism industry in the state. These measures include beautification of tourist places, construction of tourist centres, provision of accommodational facilities, drinking water, guiding materials and literatures, opening up of information centres within and outside the state, provision of bus services, publicity etc. However, adequate attention could not be paid to the provision of road transport facilities to make tourists journey comfortable, easier, quicker and safer and thereby to attract tourists in an increasing number. Taking inadequacy of roads, absence of link-roads, ill-maintenance of roads and consequent overcrowding on transport vehicles in view one has to blame lack of adequate road transport facilities for poor development of tourism in Bihar.

There is need, thus, to connect all the tourist and pilgrim places of the state with well metalled roads and there should be sufficient number of transport vehicles on roads so that travelling is simple and easy. It would attract tourists in large number even if other facilities are lacking.

The tourist department should run sufficient number of luxury buses at cheap rate to the benefit of tourists. It has definitely its own limitation. It may not be possible for it to run as much buses as required at different tourist centres in view of financial constraints. Attempt should be made to encourage private buses to tourist centres by increasing the attraction of the tourist centres from aesthetic, commercial and other points of view. Commercialisation ruins natural beauties of a place. Thus, there needs a balance between the two. A commercial centre near the tourist centre may bring such a balance.

There must be provision of basic amenities at tourist centres. A good progress has been done in this direction. However, much is still to be done, construction of hotels, resort and motels would be steps in the direction.

The cultural and historical heritage of the state is not well-known to the people especially to young people who constitute major portion of tourist population. Attempt should be made to provide detailed literature about different tourist centres, pilgrim places and natural scenarios. There should also be wide publicity. The efforts made so far by the tourist department in this regard are not adequate.

Whereas development, expansion and beautification of tourist places are needed maintenance of tourist centres also requires top priority. Some tourist centres are beautified and added with various facilities, while other centres are ignored. This tendency should be stopped. Development of tourism would depend on the wholesome view of tourism industry in the State.

There is an urgent need for an integrated tourism planning. Tourism is a multicomposite activity and serves its purpose best when planning is done in a multidisciplinary fashion. Planning for tourism involves an integration of knowledge at the different levels of policy-making and the enmeshing of tourism with other sectors of economic and social policy including health, housing, education etc. a task which is not only monument in scope but challenging as well.

Notes and References

1. Sixth Five Year Plan, New Delhi, 1980-85, p. 309.
2. Draft of Annual Report of 1984-85, Bihar (Chapter 36), p. 461.
3. *The Economic Times,* April 20, 1983, p. 12.
4. Sixth Five Year Plan, Planning Commission, New Delhi, May 1984, pp. 309-10.
5. Sixth Five Year Plan (1980-85), New Delhi, 1985, pp. 309-10.
6. *Ibid.*
7. India, 1980, pp. 369-70.
8. *Ibid.*
9. *Ibid.*
10. *Yojana,* 26 January 1981, p. 45.
11. India, 1984, pp. 417-18.
12. *Ibid.*
13. Fourth Five Year Plan, Bihar (1969-74), Chapter VIII, p. 8.7.
14. *Ibid.*
15. Statistical Handbook, Bihar, 1979, p. 330.
16. Sixth Five Year Plan (1980-85), Bihar, pp. 112-13.
17. Sixth Five Year Plan (1978-83), Bihar, pp. 119-20.
18. *Ibid.*
19. *Ibid.*, p. 120.
20. *Ibid.*, p. 121.
21. Sixth Five Year Plan (1980-85), Bihar, pp. 111-14.
22. *Ibid.*
23. Draft of Annual Report of 1984-85 (Bihar), pp. 461-62.
24. *Ibid.*, pp. 462-63.
25. Draft Seventh Five Year Plan (1985-90), Bihar, pp. 192-99.
26. *Ibid.*
27. *Ibid.*, pp. 194-201.

Appendix I

DEPARTMENT OF HOTEL AND CATERING ADMINISTRATION

University of Surrey
B.Sc. in Hotel Catering and Administration
COURSE STRUCTURE

	Common Core Studies (Whole Stage)	*Long Options*° (3 or 4 terms)	*Short Options* (1 term)
	(a) rank for credits (b) examined (c) continuously assessed	(a) rank for credits (b) examined (c) cont. assessed	rank for credits
Stage 1 Term 1-2	Accounting I Economics I Law I Foods and Beverages Food preparation Food Sciences I General Studies I		
Stage 2	Accounting II	General Studies II	Advanced Food Preparation
	Economics II	Languages	Business Statistics
	Law II		Industrial

	Administration Catering Operation Food Operation Food Science II		Orientation Manpower Mechanised Accounting Technical French Work Study
IInd Stage (12 months)	Industrial Training		
Stage 3	Human Resource Management Catering Administration	Language and Accounting Bill Food Technology	Stage 2 Short Options and Business Promotion Electronic Data Processing
	Environmental Studies	Hotel Administration Nutrition Tourism	Ergonomics Market Research Operational Research Organisation & Method Personnel Adminis-s tration

Each student is required to take no less than one and no more than two. Long Option in Stage, 2, no less than two and no more than three in Stage 3.

Appendix II

INDIA TO FUEL TOURISM BOOM IN SOUTH ASIA

A World Tourism Organisation study says India will fuel a 4.5 times growth (base year 1995) in international tourist arrivals in South Asia with 19 million tourists visiting in the year 2020.

The 'Tourism Vision 2020' study released at the 12th General Assembly of the organisation here, however, warns that the region needs "to concentrate on image improvement, and to establish fuller air links." India will attract more than half of the total arrivals in South Asia.

The study is a part of the commitment of the organisation, the only inter-governmental tourism body, to assist members in developing authentic tourism forecasting capabilities. The study says the year 2020 will see 1.6 billion international tourist arrivals world-wide with a spending power of $2 trillion. These figures represent a sustained annual growth rate of 4.3 per cent and 6.7 per cent respectively—much above the maximum probable expansion of 3 per cent per annum in the world's wealth.

The massive growth in tourist arrivals, the study says, will have extensive economic, socio-cultural and environmental consequences. This will necessitate strategic planning approach for the development of their tourism.

"The unstoppable growth in tourism will be accompanied by intensified competition ... To be a winner, there are a number of imperatives: (1) development focussed on quality and sustainability; (2) offering value-for-money destinations; and (3) complete utilisation of information technology to identify and communicate effectively with market segments and niches." People will be travelling further afield on their holidays in future as the share of by the year 2020. China will make a dramatic entry on the international tourism front emerging as the number one destination with 137.1 million arrivals by the year 2020.

Hong Kong (taken as a separate entity) and the Russian federation will also graduate to take their place amongst the top 10 tourist destinations in the world over the next two decades, says the study.

In 1996, China ranked sixth with 2,27,65,000 tourist arrivals, the Russian Federation 14th with 1,45,87,000 arrivals and Hong Kong 15th with 1,17,03,000 arrivals. France with 6,24,06,000 tourist arrivals, the US with 4,63,25,000 arrivals and Spain with 4,12,95,000 arrivals occupying the first three positions.

China and Russia will also become the major outbound tourist generating countries by the year 2020, the study forecasts.

International tourist arrivals in South Asia grew at an above average global annual rate of 6.3 per cent between 1990 and 1995, with 4.3 million arrivals recorded in 1995 representing a 0.8 per cent share of worldwide arrivals.

The study forecasts a continued higher-than-world average rate of expansion in inbound tourism to South Asia. An annual growth rate of 6.1 per cent between 1995 and 2020 is predicted generating 19 million arrivals in 2020, almost 4.5 times the 1995 level.

World's Top Generating Markets-2020

	Total arrivals generated worldwide (million)	*Market share (%)*
1. Germany	163.5	10.2
2. Japan	141.5	8.8
3. United States	123.3	7.7
4. China	100.0	6.2
5. United Kingdom	96.1	6.0
6. France	37.6	2.3
7. Netherlands	35.4	2.2
8. Canada	31.3	2.0
9. Russian Federation	30.5	1.9
10. Italy	29.7	1.9

Appendix III

AIRPORT MANAGEMENT IN INDIA—THE CHALLENGES AHEAD

R.V. Ranadive, former Deputy DGCA

The seventies witnessed dramatic events which had far-reaching effects on civil aviation all over the world. The introduction of wide-bodied aircraft made the concept of mass transportation a reality. The fuel crisis led to unprecedented inflationary trends and resulted in high costs of operations. Airports and airlines in large numbers became the targets of terrorist attacks. And the reactions of the environmentalists, particularly to aircraft noise around the airports, tended to thwart their growth. The impact of all these events was to put tremendous pressures on airlines and airport operators as the then existing terminals and ancillary facilities had not been designed to cater to these new challenges. In order to meet these challenges, new dimensions had to be added to airport planning and management.

The essence of airport management is speed—time taken to clear the aircraft for landing and take-off, time taken to handle the aircraft on the ground and to transport the passengers, baggage and cargo between the aircraft and the terminals, time taken to facilitate the passengers, baggage and cargo and last but not the least, time taken from the airport to the city. That airport is considered well-managed where the time taken for all these procedures is the least.

I believe that airport planning and management are two sides of the same coin. It should however be emphasised that the 'airport' is not just the terminals which cater to the needs of the passengers or the shippers who use them the most. It not only includes the air and the land side of the airport but even the airspace over and around the airport which is an integral part of it.

The art of good airport planning resolves around making the right predictions, not only about the number of passengers that will use the airport but also the manner in which they arrive and depart. The traffic forecast—passengers, cargo and aircraft—is the lynchpin of airport development policies. But the forecasts have to be made as accurately as possible for there can be no other basis for airport planning.

The advent of the wide bodied aircraft took the airport operator by surprise. The aircraft came in the market even before the life span of the conventional commercial air transport jet aircraft was over. The aircraft provided two to three times the capacity of the conventional jet, thus requiring vast changes in airport planning and management.

The new aircraft, due to its huge capacity, compelled governments to change their air transport policies *vis-a-vis* the foreign airlines. These aircraft required revised techniques and new equipments to control and handle them in the air as well as on the ground. The runways, taxiways and aprons has to be upgraded to suit them. Terminals required expansion to handle their traffic. The security measures also impinge upon the available space in the terminals. And above all, the airport operator/ governments required huge funds to meet the costs of these facilities.

In the past fifteen years, to what extent have we succeeded in meeting these challenges?

The International Airports Authority of India (IAAI) was established in 1972 to manage the airports of Bombay, Delhi, Calcutta and Madras. Until then these airports, along with several other civil airports, were controlled and managed by the Civil Aviation Department (DGCA) of the Government of India. However, the provision of route navigation facilities and air traffic control services at the four international airports in Bombay, Delhi, Calcutta and Madras continued with the DGCA.

That the government-owned airports should be managed by an autonomous body was not a new idea. What was new was that the Government of India had accepted this concept. It was a step, though delayed, in keeping with the Industrial Policy Resolution, that aviation should be in the public sector. But more and more countries are handing over airports to local communities, municipalities etc. and there is a move to privatise the British Airports Authority.

To what extent has the IAAI fulfilled the expectations of the government and the travelling public? I think there should be no two opinions about the view that until recently it had not. Of course, the blame does not entirely lie with the IAAI. It also lies at the doors of the bureaucracies which control policies, purse strings and part of the personnel at the IAAI-managed airports. The management of international airports is a complex business what with the presence of several agencies, each one acting according to its own policies.

I, however, think that the blame for lack of proper planning and failure to execute the required work should lie with the authority. I believe that any comparison, particularly with the developed countries, is not the right way to gauge our performance. Yet I would like to mention that while Bombay Airport, the number one international airport in the country, which handled, according to the traffic statistics published by ICAO, 33 million international passengers (embarked and disembarked) it does not find place amongst the first twenty-five airports. Only our Asian airports viz. Hong Kong (9.8 million), Tokyo (9.2 million), Singapore (8.7 million) and Bangkok (5.4 million) find a place. In respect of cargo, Bombay is placed twenty-third in the list, but Tokyo (7,25,000 tonnes), Hong Kong (4,20,000 tonnes), Singapore (2,99,999 tonnes), Taipei (22,300 tonnes) and Bangkok (1,71,000 tonnes) are placed above Bombay.

Since 1981, IAAI has constructed separate terminals at Bombay and Delhi for international traffic and separate terminals for domestic traffic at Madras. It has also constructed separate cargo terminals at Bombay and Delhi airports. According to IAAI, the two modules of the international terminal will handle five million passengers. In 1985-86, Bombay airport handled over four million international passengers, which means that the two modules are likely to be over-crowded before the third module is completed. Similarly, the new Domestic Terminal at Madras, which has a capacity to handle 1.2 million passengers annually, was commissioned in April 1985. But the domestic traffic at Madras was 1.25 million in 1985-86.

Although the international passenger traffic at Calcutta and Madras was about 4,00,000 in 1985-86, the authority has prepared plans for new international terminals at both these airports. The domestic traffic at Calcutta and Madras is four and three times the international traffic. The need for new international terminals does not seem to be justified at this juncture.

As regards the new cargo terminal at Delhi airport, the industry has already expressed its unhappiness about its inadequacy, lack of facilities, etc.

The idea of a National Airports Authority is good but it is to be seen how it is put in practice. It was established only in June 1986 and I understand that it is already facing financial constraints. It has inherited 84 airports, most of which lack proper facilities for handling of aircraft and passenger and cargo traffic. The upgrading of these airports, to handle the new generation aircraft and future traffic will require enormous funds and a large number of trained personnel. Besides, the NAA is also responsible for providing route navigational facilities and air traffic control services at all airports, including the four international airports. The main sources of revenue are the route navigational charges. The other major source of revenue is the landing charges.

Out of the 86 airports NAA controls, Indian Airlines operates to 37 airports and Vayudoot 41. But these are all low return airports due to the small number of flights and the type of aircraft used (except Trivandrum, Hyderabad and Guwahati). There are three airports which handle more than 5 lakh passengers a year, three aircrafts which handle between 2 and 5 lakh passengers annually and nine airports which handle over 1 lakh passengers annually. Another nine airports will reach the 1 lakh mark soon. Among its airports, there are five which also handle international traffic viz. Trivandrum (2 lakhs), Varanasi (50,000), Trichy (44,000), Patna (24,000) and Amritsar (85,000) passengers. Thus, the NAA has a mixed kettle—domestic and international traffic, minor, intermediate and major airports as classified by the authority and aircraft from Dornier to Airbus. It is clear then the NAA's revenue earnings will be a small percentage of its capital outlay. This means that NAA will have to employ methods which will minimise the costs and maximize the services.

All over the world, air traffic in terms of aircraft, passenger and cargo movement is bound to grow, even if the growth may not take place at the same pace as in the past. In India, air traffic which has not reached anywhere near the total of international traffic handled at some of the major airports in the world, has tremendous growth potential. To handle that volume of traffic, we will need huge capital outlays for the airports. It will be necessary to expand the existing terminal buildings or construct new terminals, improve the runways, taxiways, aprons, instal new equipment to handle the aircraft and passenger and cargo traffic. The requirements at the domestic and international airports will be different.

To meet these challenges, the following steps will have to be taken:

Airport Plans: Prepare integrated national, regional and individual airport plans.

Equipment: NAA should, as far as possible, use indigenous equipment;

Terminals: We seem to build fortresses and not airport terminal buildings. They should be modern in style and in the functional sense. The NAA should, however, avoid wastage of funds on style. Maximum use should be made of the available space as it is expensive and gets more and more expensive. Use of space by agencies such as customs, immigration, health and security should be minimised;

Procedures: At airports handling international traffic, the facilitation procedures need to be revised.

Trained Personnel: NAA will have to provide good training facilities for its personnel.

Traffic Forecasts: NAA will have to start its own statistical unit to make reasonable accurate traffic forecasts or will have to use outside professional agencies.

Finance: Make use of borrowing powers and invent new methods of raising revenues.

Appendix IV

AIR FRANCE'S CONTRIBUTION

P.J. Le Borgne, General Manager Air France

Air France has been commercially operating to India on her South-East Asian routes since 1933. It was one of the very first airlines to introduce, in 1971, wide-bodied planes on this route. India has been, for a long time, one of the principal tourist destinations of our company. Figures in their reality do not always reflect a good appreciation, but you might be interested to know that in 1985, 44,000 French tourists and in 1986 an estimated 52,000 visited India.

But the number does not necessarily represents QUALITY. It is indeed relatively easy to transport a plane-load of tourists to an hotel, and re-transport them back to their homes, a week later, suntanned, without them neither having locally spent a cent more than the price of their travel coupons, nor even having participated in the intrinsic life of the country. In fact, more than the number, it is the foreign exchange generated by the tourist that is important for the recipient country. Of course, and for the same reason, the duration of the stay in the country is equally significant.

It is generally admitted, the world over, that the French tourist, travelling individually or in small groups, spends besides the cost of his travel package, a large amount of money locally, attracted as he is not only by the culture of the country, but also by the local shopping, local food, etc.

It is apparent, that in spite of attractive offers from other countries, the French have always shown a particular interest for

India. It is this reason that has made Air France a keen promoter of India since her commercial operations here.

As you must be aware, the success of the Festival of India in France, with which Air France was actively involved, both in Paris and in the French provinces, has only reinforced the reciprocal interests upheld by India and France. As a result, the tourist traffic between the two countries has increased, and will continue to increase. In her responsibilities as the Official French Government Tourist Office in India, Air France favours contacts between Indians and the French, which in time will generate a wider interest in France for India.

Within the framework of its promotional action, Air France has recently brought in two special charters of the Concorde and the Boeing 747. The 400 passengers would have returned home, knowing India better, and carrying with them the message of the potential and quality of her hospitality. You may already know that our subsidiary SOTAIR, which only handles exclusive quality oriented tourists, actively participates in promoting India. India occupies a privileged position in the 1.2 million catalogues published annually, in which 10 pages are devoted to India. 3,000 passengers have thus been able to discover, in 1986, in a special manner, the richness of the subcontinent, which was presented by Air France in the promotional travel marts organised for the French market—in December 1986, 400 French travel professionals were invited to Paris for a one-day seminar on India.

Of minor importance perhaps, but not neglible in its totality, is ATLAS. Our inflight magazine, distributed monthly to one million passengers, published in three of their issues in 1986, exclusive articles on the Indian subcontinent. Similarly, two of the 12 images depicted on our 1987 pictorial calendar, largely distributed (3,50,000 copies in the world) represent India.

A special mention should be made of the modest but continued contribution of Air France Cargo towards the economic progress of India. You know that Air France has been the first and the only airline to operate, since 1975, an all cargo 747 service. With the rapid development of exports, we have since 1978, put at the disposal of our clients, a weekly 747 cargo service with a 100 ton capacity. Thus Air France has transported from India to other parts of the world, about 12,000 tons of cargo in 1985, and 11,000 tons in 1986. This has been made possible through 37 supplementary lights, besides our weekly cargo flights. This goes to show evidence of the choice made by Air France in favour of India, in view of the strong export cargo demands from South-East Asia, especially Hong Kong.

In order to provide as efficient a service possible to our exporters, we are proud to be the only airline to have introduced computerized methods such as suivi Automatique du fret par ordinateur (Automatic Tracking of Cargo through Computers)—SAFO, which permits us, at any given moment, to track with precision, the despatched cargo. We hope to do better soon with the Pelican, an improved and more detailed system which gives information to clients as soon as the cargo has been handed over to Air France.

AIR FRANCE in its capacity as national carrier intends to participate, along with her commercial activities, in all aspects of Indian life, be it scientific, cultural, etc. And it is in this spirit that, when we have obtained the necessary approvals, we will be organising by end 1988, workshops on general medicine between internationally renowned French professors attached to Air France and their Indian counterparts. In the same context, we hope to organise a similar event on Aviation Medicine, which will herald the beginning of exchanges between experts.

What has been said before goes to show that Air France will do its best to cement the existing bonds between India and France.

Air France in India will continue to be A VOTRE SERVICE!

Appendix V

SINGAPORE AIRLINES CONTRIBUTION

Choo Por Leong, General Manager, Singapore Airlines

Distinguished guests, ladies and gentlemen. It is indeed an honour for Singapore Airlines to be invited and given an opportunity to speak at this seminar on Civil Aviation in India. Airlines do play an important role in the development of tourism and in the context of India, which lies at the crossroads between the East and the West, they serve to provide an important means of transport for people to experience the tourist delights of the country. To appreciate the important role played by airlines, I would like, during the course of my presentation, to touch on the potential of tourism as a GNP contributor, the importance of the Asia-Pacific region, including India, as a tourist destination and our views on how airlines can contribute towards promoting tourism and economic progress.

The international travel and tourism industry has grown from almost nothing a century ago to what today can only be described as a megamarket. Total world spending on tourism now exceeds US$1.5 trillion. Tourism spending in 1985 was estimated at 12 per cent of the world's gross national product and, according to the World Tourism Organisation, international tourism ranks third in world trade, after energy products and motor vehicles. It accounts for 5 per cent to 6 per cent of total world trade.

The industry's average annual growth rate since 1975 has been 6 per cent which far exceeds economic growth in most Western economies. This was achieved despite the fuel crisis in 1979 and the world economic recession of the early 80s.

Tourism development is highly dependent on an integrated network of air links. Few tourist arrivals will be by sea or land. By far the majority will come by air, and the airlines, therefore, will have a fundamental and crucial role if the tourism potential is to be fulfilled.

It is hardly surprising that Asian airlines like SIA, Thai, Air India, Cathay Pacific and Japan Airlines have made such an impact on the world aviation scene when one considers the tremendous aviation growth that is already occurring in this part of the world. The Asia-Pacific region remains the fastest growing in world aviation, currently accounting for 26.5 per cent of the world air traffic market. The major forecasting agencies all predict this trend will continue, particularly as a result of the burgeoning economies and increasing affluence of nations within the region.

Some of our European and American competitors have also not been slow to realise this potential. Lufthansa and British Airways have said that their major growth prospects lie mainly in the Far East. Others are expected to make forays into the region this year. The American giant, United, has announced its intentions to double the size of its Pacific operations it purchased from Pan Am within five years.

Similarly, aircraft manufacturers have also recognised the growth potential of this region and are planning accordingly. Boeing has changed its design emphasis from one of concentrating solely on the range requirement of US and European carriers to one which heeds the requirements of the Asia-Pacific operators.

The region is essentially one of long sectors. Of 20 city pairs that were fundamental to Boeing's decision to develop the B747-400 series, 18 involved a capital city in the Asia-Pacific region. In the longer term Boeing believes that Asia-Pacific will stimulate a demand for yet larger aircraft. Of about 250-747 aircraft operating to and from the Asia-Pacific countries, 70 per cent were on routes with a frequency of at least seven flights a week, and an average of 14.

From 1975 until the year 2004, Airbus Industries expects traffic in the Asia-Pacific region to increase by an average of 5.5 per cent against a global 4.5 per cent. McDonnell Douglas sees the region beating its forecast of a compounded 7.4 per cent average world growth in revenue passenger kilometres between 1975 and 1985.

Aircraft manufacturers and foreign carriers agree, therefore, on the growth potential of this part of the world. We want to develop our air links within this region. And given the right aviation environment, our contribution—both in tourism and trade—can be very significant.

This is the essential message I wish to impart in may address today. Growth and the immense benefits it can bring will only be achieved in a liberal aviation environment. Artificial barriers, restrictions on market access, will only hamper the development of this country and this region's true potential in tourism and trade.

Given adequate access, foreign carriers will make it their business to promote India and other Asian countries as an attractive tourist destination.

Singapore and India have been making considerable efforts to promote both countries, tourism and trade potential. Trade and tourism missions have been especially active in recent years in an attempt to realize the vast commercial opportunities that exit in both nations.

Singapore Airlines has played an integral part in this process. Passenger growth during the 1980s ranks among the highest of our entire world-wide operations. In just four years—from 1981-82 to 1985-86, SIA passenger growth between Singapore and India rose by a compounded annual rate of 11.2 per cent, from 75,242 to 1,15,215. Over the same period total passenger traffic by all carriers between both countries increased even more spectacularly, by a compounded annual rate of 20.5 per cent from 1,77,585 to 3,73,861.

These growth rates look pretty healthy on paper. But our market research indicates they could be greatly improved given increased capacity on existing routes and the development of new air links. Air India would appear to share our view. It was reported recently that Air India's perception was that South-East Asia and Japan were the biggest markets for the future in terms of both tourist and business traffic and the airline hoped to provide more capacity accordingly. We at SIA can only echo those sentiments.

It is clear that if the air bridges are provided, people will use them. But equally important is that the right facilities and infrastructure be developed to cater for this growth. It is conservatively estimated that some US $20 billion is being spent on airports in the Far East, which is US $5 billion more than in the United States and Europe. Hong Kong is now looking at establishing a second airport and in Indonesia, the government is actively investigating the possibility of developing air links to new tourist resorts.

Our one home base at Changi is also undergoing major expansion. With Changi's 12 million capacity likely to be reached in the near future, a second terminal is under way, due for completion by early 1989 and with capacity to handle a further 12 million passengers. If traffic growth runs anywhere near current predictions there will be a need for a third terminal at Changi around the turn of the century and a third runway.

India, too, is now moving rapidly to exploit its tourist potential. I note that the emphasis in the current five year plan is to vigorously promote domestic tourism and move towards diversification of overseas tourism to India, away from the traditional sight-seeing tours centred primarily on places of cultural interest and towards the more rapidly growing holiday tourism market.

I note the diversification programme includes development of beach resort tourism, conventions and conferences, trekking and mountaineering, winter sports, wild life tourism and incentive holiday tourism. But I also note that some local tourist bodies are fearful that India won't have the necessary support infrastructure to accommodate its ambitious target of 2.5 million tourists annually within the next few years. Co-ordinated, planned development of the appropriate infrastructure is, therefore, clearly going to be crucial.

Much activity is under way throughout southern Asia and the Far-East region to ensure that we can cater for the expected growth in tourists in the near future. But to ensure that we do capitalize on it, apart from the right infrastructure we also need a good network of transportation and minimum barriers to travel within the region.

The fragmented nature of the Asia-Pacific region makes it imperative that we develop far more extensive air links than those currently existing. With more air links the opportunity to combine tour packages to take in more than one country will improve considerably. With joint co-operation there is no reason why we cannot encourage the growing influx of tourists to the Far East to explore more of central and southern Asia, including India. The reverse also applies to tourists coming to India. They can be encouraged to travel further afield to the Far East.

We must capitalize on the diverse attractions within the whole region, selling Asia and the Pacific as a whole to longhaul tourists from Europe and the United States.

I would like to end this address, however, with a note of caution. Certainly there is every reason to be optimistic about the future of tourism in this part of the world. The growth potential is enormous. But that growth will not be realised if we adopt narrow, restrictive aviation policies. By far the bulk of tourists will come by air, so it is up to the aviation policy makers and the airline operators of the region to ensure greater access and increased capacity.

With advanced aircraft technology, lower fuel prices and more efficient airlines, there will be improved operating economies, resulting in lower air fares. More competition will also encourage a lower fare structure.

And that really is the key if the Asia-Pacific region is to really challenge Europe and America for a much greater slice of the growing tourist cake. The distances involved dictate that we must prune fares to the minimum to encourage Europeans and Americans to travel further abroad.

India and Singapore have something in common in their geographical locations. We both straddle the major crossroads between East and West. India, with its vast riches in population, culture and scenery, can certainly take advantage of its strategic location. Given the right aviation environment, we at Singapore Airlines are certainly prepared to make a strong contribution towards the promotion of tourism in India.

Appendix VI

LUFTHANSA'S CONTRIBUTION TOWARDS TOURISM IN INDIA

E.W. Daubenfeld, General Manager Lufthansa Airlines

Lufthansa's Contribution as a Carrier

Flight Schedules: Lufthansa has continuously improved its flight schedules between Germany and India for the convenience of air travellers:

— Introduction of non-stop flights Frankfurt-Delhi and Frankfurt-Bombay.

— Convenient departure times from/to Frankfurt in order to provide excellent connections from all airports in Germany and major cities in Europe via Frankfurt to India. Lufthansa currently offers 4 non-stop flights Frankfurt-Bombay (B747) and 4 non-stop flights Frankfurt-Delhi (DC 10).

Capacity Increases: The steady increases in demand for air travel from Germany and other parts of Europe to India led to a shortage of seats. Lufthansa has put more capacity on its services to India to meet the demand. India plays today a major role in Lufthansa's Far-Eastern network and it will become even more important in the future:

— 1986: 30 per cent more seat capacity with the introduction of services operating only between Delhi and Frankfurt.

— 1987: 8 per cent capacity increase by changing schedules to Bombay from transit flights to terminators. Two out of four flights to Bombay will thus become independent services.

— Further increase of seat capacity is planned for the next few years within the framework of the existing bilateral agreement. We feel that the actual demand by the end of this decade may however exceed the capacity we would be able to offer.

Promotion of Tour Programmes into India: Lufthansa is maintaining a very close relationship with all leading tour operators in Germany and many other parts of Europe. As a carrier, Lufthansa relies solely on the professional and entrepreneur spirit of the tour operators and refrains from running its own package tours. Many efforts were made—directly and indirectly—to promote India as a tour destination :

— Implementation of attractive, special IT-fares (GIT and FIT) as well as APEX/Holiday fares from Germany to India.

— Providing opportunities for Indian incoming-tour operators to meet business contracts in Germany.

— Joint promotions with the leading tour operators in Germany and other places in Europe targeted to new potential travellers to India.

— Invitations to selected travel agents, travel writers and opinion leaders to come to India.

Operating Charter Flights into Goa: As an alternative to existing packages, German tour operators were looking for new opportunities in 1985. The destination of Goa, which already enjoyed a very high awareness, was chosen for point-to-point charter operations from Munich to Goa. The appointed carrier was Condor Flugdienst—the charter subsidiary of Lufthansa.

During the first six months of operations (November 1985 to April 1986), nearly 3,800 passengers were carried. The success of this package in Germany led to a continuation of the Condor charter operations in 1986/1987. The growth of this traffic is, however, limited to availability of hotel space.

This charter project is not considered as competition for the scheduled air services because both charter and IT/GIT have their clearly distinguished markets and functions. The charter is a point-to-point traffic carrying large numbers of passengers which require very specific infrastructure in the respective tourist areas. The scheduled air services provide all kinds of combinations with regard to destinations and routings and of course more flexibility.

India as a Destination

India has today become an important destination for longhaul tourism from Germany. The increased demand for travel to India is also reflected in Lufthansa's passenger statistics. 1985/1986 was considered as a record year with the growth rate exceeding 35 per cent in the tourist segment.

Uptil now the majority of travellers from Germany prefers circular trips in India, involving places of historical and cultural interest in addition to the metropolitan cities like Delhi and Bombay. Some of the package tours are also extended to other countries beyond India.

The introduction of charter flights has shown a visible trend of staying at only one or two destinations (e.g, Goa).

The main reasons for the growing demand of travel to India are as follows:

— India received a very wide and positive coverage in the German media during the past few years. TV series, movies and editorial features in magazines created a considerable awareness for India within the general public in Germany and adjacent countries. As a result, more and more Germans took an interest in the Indian cultural heritage, the scenic beauty of the country and the hospitality of the Indian people.

— The ratio of the costs of the package tour to India and the services included has become more favourable to India. This trend started in autumn 1985 with the strengthening of the Deutsche Mark and other major European currencies and the lowering of air fares from Germany.

Problems and Risks Affecting Tourism to India

The trend of travel to India is booming and is undoubtedly expected to grow continually in the coming years. However, some undermining factors become apparent, particularly during peak periods, which might have a negative effect and thus restrict further development of this trend:

Transportation: The network of domestic air services is often not sufficient to accommodate the demand on the most frequented tourist routes. The actual frequency of flights to some important destinations, the seat capacity offered and the operational standards have not always kept pace with the growth rate of air traffic. There is a shortage of airconditioned limousines and buses. The equipment being used at present often does not meet international standards.

Accommodation: The acute shortage of hotel space in metropolitan cities and important tourist places is probably the most severe problem. Overbooking procedures, cancellation of group rates and other restricting factors could have a negative influence of further growth rate in the tourist sector.

Service Standards: There are already complaints from overseas tour operators about the deteriorating standards of service. During the travel boom in 1986, it was felt that there is a certain lack of qualified staff in India.

Seasonalities: It is still generally understood in Germany that because of climate conditions, travel to India should be restricted to the period from October till March. Such a tendency with foreign tour operators and many potential travellers to India affect the economical operations of most of the service-related companies, including airlines like Lufthansa.

Entry and Visa Formalities: According to feedback received from tour operators abroad, visas which are applied for in Germany seem to take several weeks in processing and entry formalities at Indian airports are also time-consuming.

Suggestions

There is still a strong potential for further growth rates in tourism to India. In our opinion, however, increases in the future would much depend on the successful handling of the following areas :

— Improvement of service standards by educating and providing more qualified staff for the tourist sector.

— Solution to infrastructural problems with an emphasis on hotel space and transportation.

— Efforts to be made to attract more visitors in the lean season by comfortably accommodating their needs when climatic conditions in most parts of India are less favourable.

— Enforced promotions in order to attract people to India all the year round (Congresses and incentive tourism etc.).

— Only moderate rate increases in future in view of the possible reverse trends in currency development and international competition.

— Development of new tourist areas (e.g. South India/Kashmir) to widen the range of opportunities particularly for point-to-point traffic (charters).

— Facilitation in travel formalities.

Lufthansa has already expressed its vital interest in the market to and from India. With the launching of non-stop services to India, we are providing most convenient schedules. The implementation of independent Lufthansa schedules between Frankfurt and Delhi/Bombay, instead of transit flights through India, provided more seat capacity. Our long-term planning upto 1991 takes into consideration the further growth rate in tourism to India.

Opportunities are there and we are prepared.

Index